LMS ENGINES

Names, Numbers, Types & Classes

J. W. P. Rowledge C.ENG, M.I.MECH.E

DAVID & CHARLES
Newton Abbot London

British Library Cataloguing in Publication Data

Rowledge, J. W. P. (John Westbury Peter)
LMS engines: names, numbers, types & classes.
1. Great Britain. Railway services: London, Midland
and Scottish Railway. Locomotives, history
I. Title
625.2'6 0941

ISBN 0–7153–9381–2

Printed in Great Britain by
Redwood Burn Limited, Trowbridge Wiltshire
for David & Charles Publishers plc
Brunel House   Newton Abbot   Devon

CONTENTS

ACKNOWLEDGMENTS

Apart from published sources in many magazines and railway society journals much of the information contained within this volume has been made available by the kindness of John Edgington, both in his time at Euston House, London Midland Region and at the National Railway Museum where he has answered many queries, and Ray Ellis and Brian Radford, both of Derby. Of others who have helped in the many years since the author began to compile a list of LMS engines (it was started in 1952!) A.St.G.Walsh and George Toms deserve special mention. The records formerly held by British Transport Historical Records and now at the Public Record Office, Kew have also been invaluable. The drawings were prepared by Ray Ellis.

Naturally space limitations have been a problem but it is hoped that all the essentials have been incorporated; it has not been possible to quote all the many variations in dimensions, particularly boiler tube arrangements and superheater modifications in the early Stanier years and so only representative details are given.

Finally the inspiration for this book came from Mr. David St.John Thomas and the author has enjoyed labouring through masses of data in order to produce a short history of London Midland & Scottish motive power even though forty years have elapsed since the company ceased to exist - it lives on in published works and railway preservation.

J.W.P.Rowledge
Newton Abbot

July 1988

One of the bestselling books in my youth was *GWR Engines Names and Numbers*. My own copy became much worn, and now nearly twenty years ago my publishing house reprinted it for another generation of enthusiasts . . . It is still in print selling merrily.

Even before nationalisation many of us were regretting there was not a comparable work on any of the other Big Four. While it was of course possible to discover quite a lot about the locomotives of the other railways, there was not within a single book of reasonable size that useful combination of historical introduction, mechanical detail, illustrations and lists of numbers and names.

Even today as a working railway historian, I consult the GWR's volume as the easiest source of reference on its locomotives. Now all these years later it will be possible so far as LMS-built engines are concerned. Apologies for the delay, but the book will be useful as well as appealing to many of us, hopefully into the next century, much though we would have liked to have had it for our enjoyment of the scene at Rugby or Crewe when most of the locomotives were at work.

The LMS of course did not benefit from the great continuity of the GWR. The number of classes it inherited in 1923 was simply enormous – many 'classes' consisting of only a handful of locomotives. Sensibly, J. W. P. Rowledge has concentrated on LMS-built locomotives and sensibly, again, has pragmatically included these even when they were built after nationalisation – in some cases quite a few years later.

What emerges is just how much building – and of brand new designs for the most part – the LMS achieved during its turbulent years of the Depression and World War II. And what machines many of them were! How big and sometimes new-fangled they seemed to the eyes of young travellers coming up from Great Western territory. And how they became part of the very scene and way of life of much of the largest quarter of Britain.

Thank you Mr Rowledge. I just wish I could have taken this book with me when I first went LMS engine spotting in 1938!

David St John Thomas

NAMING OF LOCOMOTIVES

The naming of a locomotive gives an individual identity more evocative than just a number and some early railways used names exclusively until engines became so numerous that not enough names could be thought of. At the Grouping the LMS inherited a large number of named engines from both the LNWR and HR, each having a rich variety of persons, places, events, etc. commemorated, some of which became class names. Engines of the Knott End and the Cleator & Workington Junction Railways had names of local association; both the narrow gauge engines inheritied by the LMS on the Leek & Manifold Valley Light Railway were named. Of the remaining railways only the CR and G&SWR had named engines, one each at the Grouping.

As early as the end of May 1923 the LMS decided that engines were not to be named in future but allowed existing names to remain. In fact just a few former LNWR locomotives were named in the first few months of that year. Some which had names painted on instead of nameplates lost their names over the years.

An early exception to not naming was the locomotive specially built for the 1924-5 British Empire Exhibition at Wembley. It was exhibited as Prince of Wales.

When the first of the company's newest passenger class was delivered in July 1927 the directors relented to the extent that they agreed to act on Sir Henry Fowler's suggestion that No 6100 be named The Royal Scot, but ordered that no others be named. However at the end of October approval was given to a list of 50 names. In the event the names were not applied as listed, alternatives being chosen for many. Half the 50 were named after army regiments with a strong Scottish flavour and the rest revived names of early locomotives, mostly those of Liverpool and Manchester Railway origin.

An unofficial naming took place in 1928 when 2-6-4T No 2313 bore the name The Prince following a visit to Derby Locomotive Works by the Prince of Wales.

The special experimental high pressure compound of 1929, No 6399, was given the name Fury; this began a process by which the company found it necessary to change names from time to time, as Fury had already been used on No 6138.

The next class to carry names actually conformed to the 1923 decision not to name locomotives! Being regarded as conversions of the LNWR Claughton Class 4-6-0 engines only those named before continued to carry names, but later many more of this class were named or renamed, to the extent that a particular name was moved from one to another. When the LNWR War Memorial locomotive was scrapped the name was later revived by renaming No 5500 Patriot, which in turn became the class title. Several of this class were named after resorts served by the company.

A total change of policy over naming took place in 1933 with the introduction of the company's first Pacific express locomotives. It was expected that the Scottish services would influence the choice, the public taking a considerable interest by expressing a desire for a Scottish theme – national newspapers had devoted space to the fact that No 6200 appeared un-named. The company's public relations department also thought up a selection of names, but unknown because it took place at the highest levels was an approach to the Monarch for permission, eventually granted, to name the first locomotive after the Sovereign's (King George V) daughter The Princess Royal. This also became the class name and the theme for naming after Royal ladies all but one of the class (and even that one was so named years later by British Railways after a major reconstruction). Thus it became policy to name express passenger locomotives and many regimental names displaced early steam locomotive names on the Royal Scot class, interesting exceptions being The Girl Guide and the Boy Scout on Nos 6168 and 6169. The reconstructed Fury became British Legion (No 6170).

When new Pacifics were under construction in 1935 thought was given to the Dominions and from this came the long series of names of the British Empire applied to the new 5XP locomotives, the majority of which were nameless at first. Actually the first was named to commemorate the Silver Jubilee of King George V in 1935 and so they became the Jubilee class; the next to be named was a special choice Lord Rutherford of Nelson (No 5665) and then the Empire names followed on no less than 86 locomotives, 39 admirals, eight sea battles, 44 ships of the line, eight early steam locomotive names and finally the four provinces of Ireland completing the selection. It was not until March 1938 that all of the class were named; all but one of the final 63 had been named from new.

In 1936-7 four of the Stanier 5P5F locomotives in Scotland were named after Scottish army regiments.

The impending coronation of King Edward VIII in 1936 gave an oportunity to approach Buckingham Palace with the suggestion to continue the royal naming theme for further Pacifics, especially as the former LNWR locomotive Coronation was due for scrapping. Within a year there was a new monarch, King George VI and it was his coronation that was honoured when the new streamlined Pacific No 6220 was completed in the summer of 1937. The names continued with Queens, Princesses, Duchesses and then cities served by the company.

During the war years, apart from further Pacifics, one more engine was named, No 5543 Home Guard; it remains something of a mystery whether or not another, No 5155, was in fact named, although listed! Official sources indicate that it was named in 1942 and that the name was removed in 1944, yet alone of named LMS engines its history cards do not record the fact.

The last engine to be named by the company honoured at a special ceremony at Euston station just before Christmas 1947 the former Chief Mechanical Engineer, Sir William A. Stanier, F.R.S. (No 6256).

British Railways named just a few more, and altered some others, but a series that had been drawn up for rebuilt 5XP engines was hardly used.

POWER CLASSIFICATION

The LMS little used class names, con-
ceeding only a few specials such as Royal
Scot, Patriot, Princess Royal and Coronation, more for publicity, but reluctantly
for operating. Thus the correct designation
for the Royal Scot class was 6P (it there-
fore became necessary for descriptive pur-
poses to distinguish classes of the same
power class and wheel arrangement by such
means as 'Standard 7F 0-8-0' or 'LNWR G2
0-8-0' (thus retaining pre-Grouping means
of identity).

The first power classification system
was issued in February 1923. It was based
on the existing MR system, using tractive
effort, at 50 mph for passenger classes and
at 25 mph for goods (boiler power was con-
sidered but discarded as of questionable
utility). The original groupings were:-

	Passenger classes t.e. (lbs)		Goods classes t.e. (lbs)	
1	3,360	- 4,480	6,384	- 8,064
2	4,480	- 5,600	8,064	- 9,744
3	5,600	- 6,720	9,744	- 11,424
4	6,720	- 7,840	11,424	- 13,104
5	7,840	- 8,960	13,104	- 14,784
6	-		14,784	- 16,464

It became necessary to add groups 6 and 7
for passenger and 7 for goods:-

6	8,960	- 10,080	-	
7	10,080	- 11,200	16,464	- 18,144

Tank engines on the Midland Division were
listed with P or G added, but all other
classes were given only the number.

In 1928 the system was modified by adding P or F to the numbers and the smallest

unclassified locomotives now became OP or OF. Dual classification also came into use so that a combination such as 5P4F was needed. To suit operating needs 5XP was introduced to distinguish an enhanced rating for the reboilered LNWR Claughton Class as an intermediate between 5P and 6P, but it was later used for two new classes. A slight extension was made in 1937 when the most powerful goods class was altered from 7F to 8F.

The dual classification was abolished for wartime repaints, uprating certain classes, but the 5P5F mixed traffic locomotives became just '5'.

Certain classes remained unclassified, notably the Garratts, the others being the Sentinel shunting engines.

POWER CLASS OF LMS BUILT LOCOMOTIVES

1923	1928	Locomotive class		
2	2P	0-4-4T	(CR design)	
3	3F	0-6-2T	(NSR design)	
3	3F	0-6-0T		
3P	3P	4-4-2T	(LTSR design)	
4	4P	4-4-0	(Compound)	
4	5P4F	2-6-0	- 5F from 1946	*
4	4F	0-6-0		
4	4P	4-6-0	(LNWR design)	
4	4P	4-6-0	(CR design)	*
5	7F	0-8-4T	(LNWR design)	
5	7F	2-8-0	(Great Central design)	
5	5P	4-6-0	(LYR design)	
5	5P	4-6-4T	(LYR design)	
6	6P	4-6-0	Royal Scot	**

The classification for subsequent classes was:-

OF	0-4-0ST	OF
2P	4-4-0	

11

```
2P  *     2-6-2T
2F  *     2-6-0
2P        0-4-4T
2F        0-6-0T
3P  *     2-6-2T   (parallel and taper boiler)
4P  *     2-6-4T   (parallel and taper boiler)
4F        2-6-0
5P5F      4-6-0    - 5 from 1946
5XP **    4-6-0    (parallel and taper boiler)
7P  **    4-6-2    (Princess Royal and
                    Coronation classes)
7F        0-8-0
8F        2-8-0    (initially 7F)
```

*   P or F discarded by British Railways in 1951 when regraded as mixed traffic.

** 5XP became 6P, 6P became 7P and 7P became 8P in 1951.

All diesel shunting locomotives were classified OF.

RAILWAY COMPANY ABBREVIATIONS USED IN THIS BOOK

CR	Caledonian Railway
C&WJR	Cleator & Workington Junction Railway
FR	Furness Railway
G&SWR	Glasgow & South Western Railway
G&PJtR	Glasgow & Paisley Joint Railway
HR	Highland Railway
LNWR	London & North Western Railway
LYR	Lancashire & Yorkshire Railway
L&MVR	Leek & Manifold Valley Railway
MR	Midland Railway
MCR	Maryport & Carlisle Railway
NSR	North Staffordshire Railway
SMJR	Stratford-upon-Avon & Midland Junction Railway

The normal abbreviations for the 'Big Four' are used (LMS, LNER, GWR and SR) and WD is used for the War Department.

The numbering systems of LMS constituents varied from the orderly MR grouping in classes to the apparently hap-hazardness of the LNWR on which engines of classes, with few exceptions, were scattered throughout a capital list and a separate duplicate list. It was decided immediately that a complete renumbering based the MR method was necessary; in doing this the pre-Grouping number identity of all but most Midland locomotives was destroyed. The method adopted was briefly:-

MR (including former LTSR stock) engines retained their existing numbers, only a few being specially altered to make blocks available for NSR and SMJR locomotives in a range of numbers from 1 to 4999.

LNWR (including former NLR stock) engines utilised the series 5000 to 9999; the handful of Wirral Railway locomotives were numbered into this range.

LYR, FR, MCR, C&WJR and Knott End Railway locomotives used the series 10000 to 12999.

CR, G&SWR, HR and G&PJtR locomotives were renumbered in the range 14000 to 17999.

Within each group passenger tender took the lowest numbers, followed by passenger tank, freight (as the Midland called goods locomotives) tank and then freight tender; the least powerful classes took the lowest numbers in each series.

The blocks of numbers allotted to the constituent and absorbed companies' stock are listed in subsequent pages. The total number of steam locomotives and steam rail cars at the beginning of 1923 was:-

Railway	Locomotives	Railcars	Miscellaneous
MR	3,019	1	1
SMJR	13	-	-
NSR	192	1	5
L&MVR	2	-	-
LNWR	3,469	8	51
Wirral	17	-	-
LYR	1,651	18	18
FR	136	-	1
MCR	33	-	-
C&WJR	5	-	-
Knott End	4	-	-
CR	1,077	-	-
G&SWR	528	-	-
HR	171	-	-
G&PJtR	2	-	-
	10,319	28	76

The miscellaneous totals consist of locomotives in departmental use, 23 of which were narrow gauge, three battery electric, three petrol engined, one petrol engined railcar and one petrol engined inspection car. The LNWR had by far the most non-revenue stock, comprising 38 steam locomotives, 12 narrow gauge steam and the petrol railcar. With the exception of the six LYR locomotives the miscellaneous stock was not included in the renumbering of stock.

There is a legal complication as the CR, NSR, Wirral and Knott End Railways were not part of the LMS until 1st July 1923; thus 1,291 of the locomotives listed above (which includes one of the G&PJtR locomotives) were not LMS stock during those six months. During this period there were 26 new LMS engines and 45 withdrawn, with four new NSR locomotives, two NSR steam cars reinstated and five CR engines withdrawn, thus making a total of 10,299 locomotives and 30 railcars at the half year.

LMS NUMBERS OF CONSTITUENT COMPANIES' LOCOMOTIVES

The following number blocks were allotted in 1923 (blocks marked * had blanks, due either to withdrawals before 1923 in the MR list or unallotted numbers in the remainder).

LMS Numbers	Type	Power Classes	LMS Numbers	Type	Power Classes
(A) MR (including LTSR):					
1– 281*	2-4-0	1	2000– 2039	0-6-4T	3P
300– 327*	4-4-0	1	2100– 2107	4-6-4T	3P
328– 562	4-4-0	2	2120– 2179	4-4-2T	1P/2P
600– 683*	4-2-2	1	2200– 2209	4-4-2T	1P
700– 779	4-4-0	3	2220– 2233	0-6-2T	3G
1000– 1044	4-4-0	4	2290	0-1-0-0	–
1200– 1430*	0-4-4T	1P	2369– 2867*	0-6-0	1, 2
1500– 1537*	0-4-0T	–	2900– 3834	0-6-0	2, 3
1605– 1899*	0-6-0T	1G	3835– 4026	0-6-0	4
1900– 1959	0-6-0T	3G			
(B) NSR:					
595– 599	4-4-0	3	1600– 1603	0-6-0T	1G
1431– 1439	0-4-4T	3P	2040– 2055	0-6-4T	4P/5P
1440– 1451	2-4-0T	1P	2180– 2186	4-4-2T	3P
1454– 1459	2-4-2T	1P	2234– 2269	0-6-2T	2G/3G
1550– 1598	0-6-0T	2G	2320– 2367	0-6-0	1, 2, 3
(C) SMJR:					
290	2-4-0	1	2300– 2311	0-6-0	1, 2
(D) LNWR (including NLR):					
5000– 5109	2-4-0	1	6950– 6996	4-6-2T	4
5110– 5186	4-4-0	2	7200– 7216	0-4-0T	–
5187– 5409*	4-4-0	3	7217	0-4-2CT	–
5450– 5554	4-6-0	3	7220– 7532	0-6-0T	2
5600– 5844	4-6-0	4	7550– 7841	0-6-2T	2
5900– 6029	4-6-0	5	7850– 7869	0-4-2T	–
6420– 6434	2-4-0T	1	7870– 7899	0-8-2T	5
6435– 6512	4-4-0T	1	8000– 8624*	0-6-0	1, 2
6515– 6657	2-4-2T	1	8700– 8869	4-6-0	4
6780– 6829	4-4-2T	3	8900– 9454	0-8-0	3, 4, 5
6860– 6936	0-6-2T	2	9600– 9645	2-8-0	3, 5

(0-4-2T were initially allotted numbers 6400-19, being mistakenly included in the passenger tank classes).

LMS Numbers	Type	Power Classes	LMS Numbers	Type	Power Classes
(E) Wirral:					
6758– 6762	2-4-2T	1, 2	6850– 6851	4-4-4T	1
6770– 6776	0-4-4T	1, 2	6948– 6949	0-6-4T	3
6830	4-4-2T	1			
(F) LYR:					
10000	2-4-0	1	11303–11546	0-6-0T	2, 3
10100–10130	4-4-0	2	11600–11621	0-6-2T	1
10150–10183	4-4-0	2	11700–11716	2-6-2T	3
10190–10193	4-4-0	3	11800–11804	0-8-2T	6
10300–10339	4-4-2	2	12015–12064	0-6-0	2
10400–10433	4-6-0	5	12083–12467	0-6-0	3
10600–10617	Rail motors		12515–12619	0-6-0	4
10621–10954*	2-4-2T	2, 3, 4	12700–12994	0-8-0	5, 6
11200–11257	0-4-0T	–			

LMS Numbers	Type	Power Classes	LMS Numbers	Type	Power Classes
(G) FR:					
10002	2-4-0	-	11547-11562	0-6-0T	1, 2
10131-10146	4-4-0	1	11622-11644	0-6-2T	2, 3
10185-10188	4-4-0	2	12000-12014	0-6-0	-
10619-10620	2-4-2T	-	12065-12076	0-6-0	1
11080-11085	4-4-2T	1	12468-12483	0-6-0	2
11100-11104	4-6-4T	4	12494-12512	0-6-0	3
11258	0-4-0T	-			
(H) MCR:					
10005-10007	2-4-0	1	11563	0-6-0T	1
10010-10013	0-4-2	1	12077-12082	0-6-0	1
10618	0-4-4T	-	12484-12493	0-6-0	2
11259-11260	0-4-0T	-	12513-12514	0-6-0	3
(I) Knott End:					
11300-11302	0-6-0T	-	11680	2-6-0T	1
(J) C&WJR:					
11564-11568	0-6-0T	1, 2			
(K) CR:					
14010	4-2-2	1	16000-16039	0-4-0T	-
14100-14115	4-4-0	2	16100-16102	0-6-0T	-
14290-14365	4-4-0	2, 3	16150-16173	0-6-0T	2
14430-14508	4-4-0	3, 4	16200-16376	0-6-0T	3
14600-14626	4-6-0	4	16500-16505	0-8-0T	4
14650-14655	4-6-0	4	17000-17020	0-4-2	1
14750-14761	4-6-0	4	17101-17102	0-6-0	1
14800-14803	4-6-0	5	17230-17473	0-6-0	2
15000-15001	0-4-2T	-	17550-17692	0-6-0	3
15020-15031	4-4-0T	1	17800-17804	2-6-0	3
15100-15240	0-4-4T	1, 2, 3	17900-17915	4-6-0	3
15350-15361	4-6-2T	4	17990-17997	0-8-0	5
(L) G&SWR:					
14000-14002	2-4-0	1	16103-16117	0-6-0T	-
14116-14270	4-4-0	1, 2	16377-16379	0-6-0T	2
14366-14378	4-4-0	2	16400-16427	0-6-2T	3
14509-14521	4-4-0	3	17021-17075	0-4-2	1
14656-14674	4-6-0	3	17100	0-6-0	1
15241-15254	0-4-4T	1	17103-17212	0-6-0	2
15400-15405	4-6-4T	5	17474-17524	0-6-0	2, 3
16040-16049	0-4-0T	-	17750-17764	0-6-0	4
16080-16085	0-4-4T	-	17820-17830	2-6-0	4
(M) Glasgow & Paisley Joint:					
16050-16051	0-4-0T	-			

(Jointly owned by CR and G&SWR - nominally one each).

LMS Numbers	Type	Power Classes	LMS Numbers	Type	Power Classes
(N) HR:					
14271-14285	4-4-0	1	15300-15307	0-6-4T	4
14379-14422	4-4-0	2	16118-16119	0-6-0T	-
14522-14523	4-4-0	3	16380-16383	0-6-0T	2
14675-14693	4-6-0	3	17693-17704	0-6-0	3
14762-14769	4-6-0	4	17916-17930	4-6-0	4
15010-15017	4-4-0T	-	17950-17957	4-6-0	5
15050-15054	0-4-4T	-			

Outstanding orders completed by the LMS and a few subsequent orders for locomotives of pre-Grouping design resulted in the following being placed in service in 1923-30:-

4-6-0	LYR	Nos 10434-74	1923-5
4-6-0	LNWR	No 5845	1924
4-6-0	CR	Nos 14630-49	1925-6
4-6-4T	LYR	Nos 11110-9	1924
0-8-4T	LNWR	Nos 7930-59	1923-4
4-4-2T	LTSR	Nos 2110-34/51-60	1923-30
0-4-4T	CR	Nos 15260-9	1925
0-6-2T	NSR	Nos 1, 2, 10, 48	1923
		(LMS Nos 2270-3)	

All of these locomotives are included in the stock totals given in tabular form on pages 27 and 28.

The building of the LTSR pattern 4-4-2T locomotives was the cause of renumbering many of the older LTSR engines in 1923 to 1930 so that all the Class 3 became 2110 to 2179, the other changes being:-

4-4-2T Nos 2110-34 to 2200-14 and 2190-9 in 1923-7 and then 2077-91 and 2067-76 in 1929,

4-4-2T Nos 2135-45 to 2056-66 in 1929,
4-4-2T Nos 2146-57 to 2135-46 in 1929,
4-4-2T Nos 2158-75 to 2092-2109 in 1929,
4-4-2T Nos 2176-9 to 2147-50 in 1929.

These changes made it necessary to alter the surviving LTSR 4-6-4T as well, becoming Nos 2195-8. These LTSR locomotives were involved in more renumberings twenty years later.

Before mentioning the standard classes the purchase of no less than 75 surplus locomotives built to government orders in 1917-20 has to be described. These were of a Great Central Railway design and were actually taken in 1927 for their tenders, but it was decided that 20 should be put to work. They were numbered 9646-65, following 30 of the same type which had been purchased by the LNWR. Of the unused engines 30 were sold to Armstrong, Whitworth (after reconditioning 22 went to China) and the rest were scrapped; eventually 69 of the tenders were used on various LNWR classes.

For the standard classes no specific scheme of numbering was ever drawn up, new classes being fitted into appropriate series, which in a number of instances made renumbering of existing locomotives necessary. Up to 1932 new classes were numbered as follows:-

4-4-0	2P	(1928-32)	563- 700	
4-4-0	4P	(1924-32)	1045- 1199	and
			900- 939	
0-6-0	4F	(1924-28)	4027- 4556	
0-6-0T	3F	(1924-31)	7100- 7149	and
			16400-16764	
2-6-0	5P4F	(1926-32)	13000-13244	
Garratt		(1927-30)	4967- 4999	
4-6-0	6P	(1927-30)	6100- 6169	
2-6-4T	4P	(1927-32)	2300- 2384	
2-6-2T	3P	(1930-32)	15500-15569	
0-8-0	7F	(1929-32)	9500- 9674	
0-6-0T	2F	(1928-29)	11270-11279	
0-4-0ST	0F	(1932)	1540- 1544	
0-4-4T	2P	(1932)	6400- 6409	

The two Midland type 4-4-0 classes were placed among former MR passenger engines; only numbers between 600 and 683 had been used before for LMS engines, but when the 4P compounds overflowed into the 900-39 series Nos 800-9 were allotted to the Cl. 3 999 Class 4-4-0 locomotives. The Midland type 0-6-0 continued the existing series onwards from 4027, following similar locomotives numbered 3835-4026. The Garratts, being intended for Midland Division work, sensibly took numbers at the end of the 4XXX series. Also placed in the Midland Division number range were the new 2-6-4T engines, although displacing old goods engines.

The Royal Scot Class was numbered into the series used for Western Division passenger tender classes and the 0-4-4T took numbers vacant in the range allotted to former LNWR passenger tank classes. Also numbered within the LNWR series the new standard 7F 0-8-0 locomotives followed 0-8-0 Nos 8900-9454. The outside cylinder 0-6-0T, although built at Derby, found numbers following the Central Division 0-4-0ST as Nos 11270-9. However the Horwich designed Moguls, widely known as 'Crabs', used the vacant 13000 series after all other Central Division classes.

The placing of 50 0-6-0T in the LNWR number range as 7100-49 among goods tank rather than in the MR series was necessary because there were no suitable blanks in the latter, the apparently natural place. However when the class was greatly expanded the new locomotives were placed after Scottish goods tanks, but starting at 16400 rather than 16600 which caused some renumbering of existing classes. For the same reason the standard 2-6-2T followed Scottish passenger tanks. A few that could hardly be regarded as standard types were fitted into the full number ranges when the Sentinel shunters became Nos 7160-4, the experimental high pressure compound locomotive Fury became No 6399 and five Kitson built 0-4-0ST took numbers 1540-4, following the former MR four-wheeled shunting engines.

A small amount of renumbering was necessary to accommodate the new classes. Thus surviving SMJR and NSR 0-6-0 in the 2300 series were altered to 2397-9 and 8650-89 and other NSR engines affected were the five 4-4-0 which became Nos 5410-4. To make way for the 7F class a few LNWR 0-8-0 (converted from 2-8-0 by then) left in the 9600-15 group became No 8892-9 and the remaining government surplus 2-8-0 (ex-Railway Operating Division) were altered to take numbers between 9455 and 9482. In the Northern Divison list (former Scottish locomotives) it was necessary to alter 0-6-2T Nos 16400-27 and 0-8-0T Nos 16500-7 to Nos 16900-27 and 16950-7; in fact for a few days in 1926 it was possible to see both 0-6-2T and new 0-6-0T together with the same numbers!

In 1930 the 80 locomotives of the Somerset and Dorset Joint Committee were renumbered into LMS stock and most took appropriate Midland Division numbers:-

4-4-0	2P	300-3/20-6, 633-5 (which had been LMS Nos 575/6/80 when built)
0-4-4T	1P	1200-7/30/1, 1305
0-6-0ST	2F	1500-7
0-6-0	2F	2880-90
0-6-0	3F	3194/8, 3201/4/11/6/8/28/48/60
0-6-0	4F	4557-61
0-6-0T	3F	7150-6
0-4-0T	-	7190/1
2-8-0	7F	9670-80

To make way for the 0-4-4T two older MR 0-4-4T were renumbered from 1201/3 to 1212/3. The 3F 0-6-0 locomotives used numbers vacated by withdrawn MR engines. The 2-8-0 class followed Western Division 2-8-0 types and like them had to be renumbered to make way for the new 7F class, becoming 13800-10

in 1932. There was an interesting sequel
to these numbers for a proposed 2-8-0 of
1931 was to take the numbers 13811-5.

Not regarded as a new class, but in
fact new in all but a few parts, the conversion of two 4-cylinder Claughton Class
locomotives into Midland pattern 3-cylin-
der locomotives in 1930 did not start a
new number series as the previous numbers
were retained. When another 40 were so
'converted' (but in LMS records regarded
as new) they also retained the numbers of
the displaced locomotives between 5901 and
6027.

When Stanier arrived in 1932 the system
of numbering continued for two years until
it was decided to renumber all standard
classes numbered above 10000 to four-figure
numbers. Thus the following changes were
made:-
```
    0-6-0T  11270-11279  to  7100-7109
    2-6-0   13000-13244  to  2700-2944
   ·2-6-2T  15500-15569  to     1-  70
    0-6-0T  16400-16764  to  7317-7681
```
The renumbering also included two batches
of 0-6-0T, the former MR locomotives
Nos 1900-59 and standard 3F Nos 7100-56,
the two lots becoming Nos 7200-7316. The
Kitson 0-4-0ST were altered from 1540-4
7000-4.

A special renumbering tidied up the
scattered numbers of the 'rebuilt' 5XP
4-6-0 locomotives which became Nos 5500
to 5541; they were soon followed by ten
further examples which were numbered
5542-51.

The 1934 renumbering, which took until
1938 to complete, included one new class,

for the 1933-4 2-6-0 locomotives appeared as
Nos 13245-84; their new numbers were 2945-84.
However 40 more of the 2-6-4T were built to
the 1927 design in 1933-4 and continued the
numbers from 2385 to 2424. Another pre-1932
design was also multiplied in 1937-41 when
a further 45 of the 4F 0-6-0 class appeared
as Nos 4562-4606.

   From 1933 until the Second War thoroughly changed LMS locomotive construction policy new classes comprised the following:-

2-6-2T	3P	(1935-38)	71- 209	
2-6-4T	4P	(1934-43)	2425-2494,	2537-2672
2-6-4T	4P	(1934)	2500-2536	
4-6-0	5P5F	(1934-43)	5000-5499,	4800-4806
4-6-0	5XP	(1934-36)	5552-5742	
4-6-0	6P	(1935)	6170	
4-6-2	7P	(1933-35)	6200-6212	
4-6-2	7P	(1937-44)	6220-6252	
2-8-0	8F	(1935-39)	8000-8125	
2-6-0	5P4F	(1933-34)	2945-2984 built as	
			Nos 13245-13284	

Thus some gathering together of similar
classes was achieved but it was necessary to
renumber pre-Grouping classes which occupied
the newly allotted number series; this was
done by adding 20000 to their existing numbers, thus forming in effect a duplicate
number system. A few other classes were
specially renumbered as their numbers were
taken by new construction:-

0-6-0T	7100-9	became	7160-9
0-4-0T	7160-4	became	7180-4
Garratt	4967-99	became	7967-99
0-6-2T	2220-33	became	2180-93

The renumbering of the 0-6-2T locomotives
was interesting as they reverted to their
pre-Grouping numbers!

   During this period diesel shunting power
became established and it is worthy of remark

that in 1934 the last steam shunting engine to enter service on the LMS was an experimental compound oil-fired Sentinel No 7192. Diesels are described in a later chapter.

When the 1940 locomotive construction programme was agreed in June 1939 steam locomotive requirements were limited to only five 2-8-0 and 45 2-6-4T. The restocking programme of 1934-9 had provided no less than 1,349 steam locomotives, although the war delayed completion of some of the orders until 1944; in fact the 1940 programme was discarded and the 2-6-4T were not re-ordered until 1944.

Wartime construction was confined to two classes, apart from completion of outstanding work (even so two of the pre-war ordered Pacifics were never built). The 4-6-0 5P5F and 2-8-0 8F classes expanded by the following numbers:-

4-6-0	5P5F	4807-4966
2-8-0	8F	8126-8225,
		8226-8325 (government orders allotted to LMS in 1940),
		8301-8399,
		8400-8479 (8480-9 ordered but not built),
		8500-8559,
		8600-8704

The last three batches of 2-8-0 were ordered under the direction of the wartime Railway Executive Committee and 140 were used by the GWR and LNER before transfer to the LMS after the end of the war. A further 100 of this class ordered from North British Locomotive Co (Glasgow) were cancelled in favour of the Ministry of Supply 2-8-0 design. 'In the National Interest' the London & North Eastern Railway agreed to adopt the LMS 2-8-0 for its own use and

100 were to have been ordered, but no more
than 68 were built. They were transferred
on loan to the LMS/LMR in 1947-8 and became
Nos 8705-72.

This is not the place to describe Military use of the LMS 2-8-0 design beyond
mentioning that after changes of requirements 208 were built and a further 51 taken
by requisitioning from the company. The
numbers were:-
    300-399 (300-37 ran as LMS 8226-63)
    400-449 (400-14 ran as LMS 8286-8300)
    500-524
    540-571 and 623
Nos 572 to 622 were the requisitioned locomotives. When overseas requirements had
been met eight engines were sent back to
the company and 24 new locomotives, WD
Nos 407, 553/5-71, became LMS Nos 8293 and
8264-85.

It will be seen that all these orders
for the 8F locomotives filled most of the
numbers from 8000 to 8704; 43 of those intended for the LNER were at one stage
allotted LMS numbers 8274-85, 8391-9, 8490-
9, 8590-9 and 8705/6.

Post-war LMS steam locomotive orders
continued with two Stanier designs, a modified version and three new classes, which
started new number series. The existing
LMS construction programmes were completed
and further augmented by British Railways,
to the extent of adding to the 1932 batch
of 0-4-0ST, which when delivered in 1953-4
represented the first new steam shunting
power of LMS type since 1934! The numbers
used for the existing classes were:-
    4-6-0   5   44658-44747, 4748-53, 447 54-7,
                4758-99, 4967-99

```
4-6-2    7P  6253-6,  46257
0-4-0ST  OF  47005-9
```
The modified class was a continuation of the 2-6-4T and numbers used were 2673-99, 42050-42186, 2187-2299.

The three new classes were:-
```
2-6-2T   2P  (1946-52)  1200-9  41210-41329
2-6-0    2F  (1946-53)  6400-19,  46420-46503
2-6-0    4F  (1947-52)  3000-10,  43011-43161
```
Their numbering followed established patterns for two of the classes, the tank locomotives succeeding older passenger classes and the 4F 2-6-0 being numbered among goods types, but the 2F 2-6-0 started a new series by taking numbers formerly used by passenger classes.

Apart from adding 20000 to several locomotives number blocks were cleared for the new construction by more renumberings:-
```
4-4-2T  2092-2109  to  1910-1927
4-4-2T  2110-2160  to  1928-1978
0-6-2T  2180-2193  to  1980-1993
0-4-4T  6400-6409  to  1900-1909
```
0-4-0ST Nos 7000-4 were to have become Nos 250-4 and 0-6-0T Nos 7160-9 were allotted 7900-9 but none were so altered.

Under British Railways ownership the numbers of LMS engines were altered by the addition of 40000 with the exception of those numbered above 20000 for which the series starting at 58000 was allotted. No LMS standard locomotives required the special renumbering. However to make way for the expanding 4F 2-6-0 class it was necessary in 1952 to alter MR 3F 0-6-0 from 3137 to 43750.

In 1948 no less than 39 8F engines were repatriated from Egypt and ten reverted to their former LMS numbers. For the rest new numbers 48246-63/86-92/4-7 were allotted. The final addition to LMS numbers took place in 1957 when three more of the class were obtained from the War Department and they became Nos 48773-5 - the fact that one of them had been LMS No 8025 was ignored.

So far only slight mention has been made of LMS diesel traction. Apart from the experiment with an old steam locomotive which retained its number 1831, the early orders were allotted Nos 7400-8, but during delivery the numbers were altered to 7050-8. New construction followed from 7059 onwards but under British Railways ownership a new series starting at 12000 came into use and reached 12138. For the main line locomotives of 1947-8 the numbers 10000 and 10001 were used and retained by British Railways. Another smaller locomotive on order was to have been LMS No 800 but when completed in 1950 it emerged as No 10800.

Year end total	Tender Engines							Garr- att	Tank Engines					Non Std (d)	LMS built	Total LMS (e)
	2-8-0 (a)	0-8-0	4-6-2	4-6-0	2-6-0	0-6-0	4-4-0 (b)		2-6-4	2-6-2	0-6-0	0-4-4	0-4-0 (c)			
1923	–	–	–	–	–	–	–	–	–	–	–	–	–	64	64	10291
1924	–	–	–	–	–	11	40	–	–	–	42	–	–	92	185	10246
1925	–	–	–	–	–	172	136	–	–	–	50	–	–	113	471	10203
1926	–	–	–	–	13	305	140	–	–	–	178	–	–	131	767	10157
1927	–	–	–	50	100	441	190	3	4	–	214	–	–	149	1191	10125
1928	–	–	–	50	108	530	237	3	25	–	376	–	–	161	1490	9868
1929	–	100	–	50	130	530	256	3	75	–	410	–	–	153	1707	9797
1930	–	103	–	72	225	530	260	33	75	21	410	–	4	160	1893	9319
1931	–	135	–	72	235	530	290	33	75	50	425	–	5	153	2003	9023
1932	–	175	–	87	245	530	330	33	75	70	425	9	10	151	2140	8442
1933	–	175	2	112	260	530	330	33	124	70	425	10	10	151	2232	8225
1934	–	175	2	258	285	530	328	33	162	70	425	10	11	147	2436	7996
1935	12	175	13	478	285	530	328	33	170	144	425	10	11	136	2750	7885
1936	69	175	13	613	285	530	328	33	286	144	425	10	11	120	3042	7660
1937	96	175	18	766	285	545	328	33	313	183	425	10	11	113	3301	7657
1938	98	175	28	786	285	545	328	33	347	209	425	10	11	110	3390	7613
1939	126	175	33	786	285	565	328	33	348	209	425	10	11	108	3442	7508
1940	126	175	38	786	285	573	328	33	349	209	417	10	11	107	3447	7498
1941	140	175	38	786	285	575	328	33	358	209	417	10	11	103	3468	7522
1942	204	175	38	786	285	575	328	33	366	209	417	10	11	102	3539	7589
1943	359	175	42	806	285	575	328	33	368	209	417	10	10	102	3719	7759
1944	486	175	46	875	285	575	328	33	368	209	415	10	10	100	3915	7928
1945	556	175	46	947	285	575	328	33	413	209	415	10	10	97	4099	8049
1946	556	175	49	1005	295	575	328	33	460	218	415	10	10	86	4215	7925
1947	623	175	50	1056	308	575	328	33	498	219	415	10	10	80	4380	7872

NOTES:

(a) Includes 245 locomotives built to wartime Railway Executive Committee orders; the 1947 total includes 67 locomotives transferred on loan from the LNER (the 68th locomotive was still in service on the LNER).

(b) 3 built as LMS Nos 575/6/80 in 1928 and transferred to SDJC in 1928 not included.

(c) Includes Sentinel type locomotives.

(d) Comprises 1 LNWR 4-6-0, 30 LNWR 0-8-0, 41 LYR 4-6-0, 10 LYR 4-6-4T, 35 LTSR 4-4-2T, 4 NSR 0-6-2T, 20 CR 4-6-0, 10 CR 0-4-4T and 20 Great Central Railway type 2-8-0 purchased 1927.

(e) End of 1922 total for constituent and absorbed railways is 10319; also includes 80 SDJC locomotives taken into LMS stock 1930.

BRITISH RAILWAYS (LMS TYPE LOCOMOTIVES) STOCK TOTALS 1948-1968

Year end total	Tender Engines							Garratt	Tank Engines					Non Std LMS	LMS/ BR built	Total LMS types
	2-8-0 (a)	0-8-0	4-6-2	4-6-0	2-6-0 (b)	0-6-0	4-4-0		2-6-4 (b)	2-6-2 (b)	0-6-0	0-4-4	0-4-0			
1948	624	175	51	1096	343	575	328	33	544	239	420	10	10	68	4516	7704
1949	663	114	51	1128	370	575	328	33	574	269	420	10	10	62	4607	7527
1950	663	77	51	1154	447	575	328	33	628	299	420	10	10	57	4752	7474
1951	663	53	51	1156	535	575	328	33	645	309	420	10	10	44	4832	7339
1952	663	47	51	1155	562	575	322	33	645	339	420	10	10	39	4871	7214
1953	663	43	51	1155	575	575	309	33	645	339	420	13	10	37	4868	7055
1954	663	41	50	1155	575	575	285	33	645	339	420	14	10	37	4842	6930
1955	663	38	50	1155	575	575	248	33	645	339	420	12	10	32	4788	6728
1956	663	32	50	1155	575	575	221	26	645	339	420	10	10	24	4732	6513
1957	666	20	50	1155	575	575	186	13	645	339	420	10	10	24	4676	6237
1958	666	20	50	1155	575	531	150	1	645	339	420	10	10	23	4638	6045
1959	666	9	50	1152	575	490	95	-	640	297	394	1	10	13	4436	5473
1960	665	5	50	1152	575	467	81	-	626	287	346	1	10	10	4298	5150
1961	665	1	44	1139	571	393	14	-	577	209	313	1	10	2	4013	4509
1962	661	-	35	1022	498	259	-	-	425	109	238	-	10	-	3394	3564
1963	664	-	22	942	432	108	-	-	350	91	195	-	9	-	2964	3060
1964	638	-	-	780	346	11	-	-	222	65	144	-	4	-	2307	2343
1965	543	-	-	642	224	-	-	-	118	39	81	-	4	-	1662	1674
1966	381	-	-	464	110	-	-	-	57	8	3	-	-	-	1023	1024
1967	150	-	-	151	6	-	-	-	-	-	-	-	-	-	307	307
1968	-	-	-	-	-	-	-	-	-	-	-	-	-	-	-	-

NOTES:

(a) Includes 39 locomotives recovered from overseas wartime service in 1949; 3 locomotives purchased from War Department in 1957 also included.

(b) Includes LMS type engines built by British Railways and allocated to Eastern, North Eastern, Southern and Western Regions in 1950-1953 (206 locomotives - a few new to the Scottish Region were sent intially to former LNER sheds in that region).

This survey details LMS locomotive history year by year, giving introduction dates for each class, annual construction and some general notes.

1923: 1st January - LYR 4-6-0 No 1663 was hailed as the company's first new locomotive when it entered service on this day.
Feb: LNWR 0-8-4T No 380 (LMS 7930) entered traffic.
May: MR(LTSR) 4-4-2T No 2110 started work.
During the year a numbering scheme was prepared, but it took until 1930 before the last locomotive in pre-Grouping livery disappeared.
NEW LOCOMOTIVES

4-6-0	(21)	10434-54
0-8-4T	(29)	7930-58
4-4-2T	(10)	2110-9
0-6-2T	(4)	2270-3

A committee investigating locomotive standardisation reported that it would be ten years before any benefits could become effective.

1924: First LMS standard classes introduced.
Feb: Standard version Midland compound 4-4-0 introduced.
Mar: LYR pattern 4-6-4T appeared. In 1922 no less than 60 of this type were authorised by the LNWR but only ten were completed as tank locomotives, another 20 were finished as 4-6-0 tender locomotives and the remainder were never built.
Mar: For display at the British Empire Exhibition in 1924-5 Wm. Beardmore of Glasgow wished to build a new locomotive and chose the LNWR Prince of Wales 4-6-0 design, having built no

less than 90 for the LNWR. The LMS
sanctioned this and took the locomotive into stock at the end of the
exhibition as No 5845. This engine
was fitted with a modified form of
outside Walschaert's valve gear to
drive inside cylinder valves.
Jul: Standard version 0-6-0T introduced; some had carriage warming
apparatus and Nos 16560-4 had vacuum
control gear for motor trains.
Nov: Standard version 0-6-0 introduced.
NEW LOCOMOTIVES

4-6-0	(19)	10455-73
0-8-4T	(1)	7959
4-6-0	(1)	5845
0-6-0	(11)	4027-34, 4107, 4177/8
0-6-0T	(42)	7100-41
4-6-4T	(10)	11110-9

Left hand drive was adopted as standard
but of the early orders 4-4-0 Nos 1045-
84 and 0-6-0 Nos 4027-4206 were built
as right hand drive; however all of the
0-6-0T were built as right hand drive.

1925: No new standard classes were introduced
but two types copied from CR designs
were adopted for service on the Northern Division.
May: 0-4-4T derived from CR 439 class.
Jul: 4-6-0 based on CR 60 class.
NEW LOCOMOTIVES

4-4-2T	(5)	2120-4
0-6-0	(160)	4035-4105, 4108-58, 4179-4216
0-6-0T	(8)	7142-9
4-4-0	(95)	1085-1129, 1135-84
4-6-0	(2)	14630/1
0-4-4T	(10)	15260-9

1926: The first entirely new LMS design made
its appearance, being a 2-6-0 heavily
influenced by Horwich practice; vari-

ous Derby features were imposed in the name of 'standardisation', particularly the MR pattern tender. The class remained remarkably uniform, but in 1931-2 five were fitted with Lentz rotary cam poppet valves (Nos 13118/22/4/5/9) - the original plan included two 2-6-4T with a reciprocating version but it was decided that the tender engines were more suitable for trials. The first of the 245 locomotives of this class appeared in May.

NEW LOCOMOTIVES

0-6-0	(119)	4106/59-76, 4217-87, 4302-11/32-42/82-99
0-6-0T	(128)	16400-16518, 16535-43
4-4-0	(5)	1130-4
4-6-0	(18)	14632-49
2-6-0	(13)	13000-6/30-5

An important rebuilding was the conversion of 4-6-0 No 10456 to a four-cylinder compound in July for test working in connection with a proposed compound Pacific express passenger class.

1927: New ground was broken by the purchase of three Beyer-Garratt locomotives for Midland Division coal trains to London. The Anglo-Scottish main line express motive power crisis was at last solved by the introduction of the Royal Scot class, following a successful demonstration of the type of locomotive needed when the Great Western Railway 4-6-0 Castle Class No 5000 Launceston Castle ran between Euston and Carlisle in late 1926. Feb: 75 redundant wartime 2-8-0 locomotives were purchased and it was ordered that 20 be put to work. The need for a large eight-coupled goods type had been recognised since 1923

and the locomotive construction programme agreed in November 1923 included 100 such machines; in 1924 after it
proved 'impossible' to design a 2-8-0
acceptable for all divisions it was
decided to order 100 of then standard
0-6-0 class. The suggestion to obtain
100 of the surplus locomotives was
first made in June 1924 but it was not
until February 1927 that authority was
given. Their working life on the LMS
was short, the last being withdrawn in
1932.
Apr: Three Garratts, 2-6-6-2 wheel
arrangement, of Beyer Peacock design
with Derby features arrived.
Jul: 4-6-0 Royal Scot class three-
cylinder express locomotives first
delivered.
Dec: An entirely new design of passenger tank, 2-6-4T, appeared. Following
public concern over the Sevenoaks
disaster on the Southern Railway earlier in the year, which involved an
express 2-6-4T, the Ministry of Transport was assured that the new design
would not be used for high speed work.
The final 30 of this class built in
1933-4 appeared with enclosed foot-
plates but after a while the doors
were removed.
NEW LOCOMOTIVES

4-4-2T	(10)	2125-34
0-6-0	(134)	4288-4301, 4312-7, 4343-79, 4400-46, 4477-4506
0-6-0T	(36)	16519-34, 16544-9, 16555-60, 16625-32
4-4-0	(50)	1185-99, 900-34
2-6-0	(87)	13007-29/36-99
Garratt	(3)	4997-9
4-6-0	(50)	6100-49

```
2-8-0     (8)   9646/7/9/50/2-4/6
2-6-4T    (4)   2300-3
```

1928: A new standard class and a special
outside cylinder short wheelbase tank
class for docks were introduced.
Mar: Inside cylinder 4-4-0 based on
MR Cl. 2; of these locomotives No 601
was fitted experimentally with Owen's
double beat regulator (in the dome)
and it was oddly numbered out of place
as the order of entering service was
563-71, 601, 573-600, 572, 602-12.
Three after completion as Nos 575/6/80
were altered to become Somerset & Dorset Nos 44-6 (later LMS Nos 633-5).
In 1933-4 Nos 633/53 were fitted
experimentally with Dabeg feedwater
heaters and pumps.

NEW LOCOMOTIVES

```
0-6-0     (96)  4318-31/80/1, 4447-76,
                4507-56
0-6-0T   (155)  16550-4, 16561-16624,
                16633-69, 16675-16723
2-6-0     (8)  13100-7
2-8-0    (12)  9648/51/5/7-65
2-6-4T   (21)  2304-24
4-4-0    (50)   563-612
0-6-0T    (7)  11270-6
```

1929: In March a heavy goods type was at
last introduced, but it failed to live
up to expectations, being heavy on
boiler and frame maintenance. After
tests the cylinder diameter was
increased from 19in to 19½in for new
construction from No 9620. The last
three built, Nos 9672-4, were fitted
for about ten years with ACFI feed-
water heaters. The frames of No 9617
were adapted as a bridge test unit
in 1957.
At the end of the year in December an
experimental high pressure compound

based on the Royal Scot class was completed by North British. It was soon in trouble on trials, leading to a fatality. Numbered 6399 and named Fury it was not taken into stock in this form.

NEW LOCOMOTIVES

0-6-0T	(51)	16670-4, 16724-69
2-6-0	(22)	13108-29
4-6-0	(1)	6399
2-6-4T	(50)	2325-74
4-4-0	(19)	575/6/80, 613-28
0-6-0T	(3)	11277-9
0-8-0	(100)	9500-99

1930: Additional Garratt locomotives were obtained; these had only steam brakes and one had a rotating bunker (No 4986), others being so fitted in 1931-2 (only No 4997 of the first batch was altered to a rotating bunker).

Twenty more of the Royal Scot class were built by the company.

Two new standard classes appeared, one by rebuilding, and the last locomotives of pre-Grouping design were completed (4-4-2T).

Mar: 2-6-2T developed from a design for a 0-6-2T authorised in 1928 but discarded because of weight distribution; this class proved to be of doubtful value, especially compared with the highly successful 2-6-4T. Twenty were built with condensing gear, Nos 15520-39, for services to Moorgate, London. Nine were modified with vacuum control for motor trains in 1935-9 (Nos 10, 20, 43, 56-61 – No 58 was replaced by No 12 in 1947) and two more were altered in 1954 (Nos 17 and 45).

Jun: Four-wheeled chain drive Sentinel light shunting locomotives were purchased after some trials in 1927.

Nov: The first conversion of the LNWR
four-cylinder Claughton to a three-
cylinder locomotive was No 5971, soon
followed No 5902. Both were regarded
as rebuilt, having used a few parts,
and not new. The Belpaire boiler had
been first used in 1928 to reboiler
20 of the Claughton class. A further
40 'conversions' took place in 1932-3
but they were really new; a final ten
of 1934 were treated as new construction.
NEW LOCOMOTIVES
4-4-2T	(10)	2151-60
2-6-0	(95)	13130-13224
Garratt	(30)	4967-96
4-6-0	(20)	6150-69
4-4-0	(4)	629-32
0-8-0	(3)	9600-2
2-6-2T	(21)	15500-20
Sentinel	(4)	7160-3
4-6-0	(2)	5971, 5902

1931: Further standard locomotives were
built.
NEW LOCOMOTIVES
0-6-0T	(15)	16750-64
2-6-0	(10)	13225-44
4-4-0	(30)	636-65
0-8-0	(32)	9603-32/4/5
2-6-2T	(39)	15521-59

1932: 1st January; W.A.Stanier became Chief
Mechanical Engineer and a new era of
LMS motive power was destined to begin.
Two new classes appeared, both ordered
on the 1931 locomotive construction
programme.
Jan: Sentinel No 7164, of the maker's
industrial type, was obtained specially for the Clee Hill branch.
Nov: 0-4-0ST supplied by Kitson to
their design, modified to company requirements (in place of LMS design

originally to have been built at
Crewe Works).
Dec: 0-4-4T of obsolete Derby design;
eventually all ten were fitted with
vacuum control gear for motor trains.

NEW LOCOMOTIVES

4-4-0	(5)	935-9
2-6-0	(10)	13235-44
2-6-4T	(10)	2375-84
4-4-0	(35)	666-700
0-8-0	(40)	9633/6-74
2-6-2T	(10)	15560-9
4-6-0	(15)	5959/85/87/49/74/36, 6010/05/12, 5942/66/58/ 83/92/82
Sentinel	(1)	7164
0-4-0ST	(5)	1540-4
0-4-4T	(9)	6400-8

The order for the 0-8-0 locomotives
was shortened by five and the authority transferred to five planned 2-8-0
locomotives which had been allotted
numbers 13811-5.

1933: After a survey of the locomotive stock
a scheme of reboilering was proposed,
using a series of new taper superheater Belpaire boilers; some were for new
classes:-

Boiler type	Intended use
1	New Pacifics
2	Royal Scots
3A	4-6-0 Claughton, 4-6-0 LYR and 4-6-4T (LYR)
3B	4-6-0 Prince of Wales rebuild- ing and 2-8-0 - both new class- es
3C	Existing 2-6-0 and a new 2-6-0
4A	0-8-0 LNWR and standard 7F
4B	4-4-0 compound
4C	2-6-4T, including new versions
4D	4-6-0 HR Clan and Castle.

4E	4-4-0 standard, 0-6-0 standard (including MR and SDJC locomotives), 0-6-0 MR 3F
5, 5A	CR 4-6-0 Nos 14600-8/19-26, HR Jones Goods and Superheater Goods
6	2-6-2T, including new version, 0-6-0 MR 2F, standard 0-4-4T, standard 0-6-0T (including MR built locomotives)

All were shown on the chart to be dome-less, having smokebox regulators. Only boilers of 1, 2, 3A, 3B (as 3B and 3C), 3C (as 3D), 4C and 6 (as 6, 6A and 6B) were manufactured and were used on new classes. It was soon established that the cost of adapting older locomotives could not be justified (in June 1941 it was proposed to use the 2-8-0 boiler on one of the 7F 0-8-0 but the idea was dropped). Of particular interest is the anticipation of the reboilering of the Royal Scot class a decade before it came about.

The principal event of 1933 was the appearance of Stanier's first design, a Pacific for the Anglo-Scottish trains. Apr: The Royal Scot tour of the United States commenced. The fully overhauled locomotive had a new design of bogie and a replacement tender of larger capacity; officially the locomotive was No 6100 but due to exchange of components in shops much of it was No 6152. Jun: Pacific No 6200 was the first of the Princess Royal class; three were initially authorised but one was completed in 1935 as an experimental turbine drive machine (No 6202). No 6201 ran a few trials with a double exhaust and chimney in late 1934. Oct: Stanier version with a taper boil-

er of the standard 2-6-0 and clearly
influenced by GWR practice, even having horizontal cylinders in sharp
contrast to the steeply inclined cylinders of the Horwich design. An
early but little used appellation of
'Camels' arose from the boiler shape.
NEW LOCOMOTIVES
2-6-4T   (39)   2385-2423
4-6-0   (25)   5952, 6006/08, 5954/33/
                73, 6026, 5907/16/63/44/
                96/26, 6022/27/11, 5905/
                35/97, 6018/15/00, 5925/
                01/03
0-4-4T   (1)   6409
4-6-2   (2)   6200/1
2-6-0   (15)   13245-57/60/3
1934: Three new standard classes were intro-
      duced.
      Apr: 2-6-4T - three-cylinder version
      with taper boiler of the 1927 design
      (the first five were authorised as
      part of the final batch of the latter).
      These locomotives were noted for their
      use on Fenchurch Street and Southend
      line trains but they were used at many
      other depots during the war years.
      Nos 2500-24 were built with cab doors,
      later removed.
      May: Taper boiler version of the 1930
      5XP three-cylinder locomotives, the
      initial five being constructed again-
      st the authority for the last batch
      of the parallel boiler design. In
      minutes the new type was referred to
      'Improved Claughtons'. Nameless at
      first the class later became known as
      the 'Silver Jubilees', but also often
      called 'Red Staniers'. Five had
      double chimneys at various dates, Nos
      5553, 45596, 5684, 5722 (for tests)
      and 5742.

Sep: The all purpose two-cylinder
4-6-0 known firstly as 'Black Staniers' and then 'Black Fives' first
appeared, being built over no less
than 17 years and eventually total-
ing 842. They were used almost
everywhere on the LMS and they developed a particularly strong
association with the Highland part
of the company. From 1938 they
could reach Bournemouth. Important
variations later appeared which will
be described under 1947-51. The
design originated from two proposed
types which had been authorised for
construction, an Improved Prince of
Wales 4-6-0 and a light 4-6-0 for
Scotland, but civil engineering
work enabled the single design to
cover routes that had required the
smaller design.
Nov: A Sentinel-Doble oil fired 200
hp compound started trials but was
not successful (the order placed on
Sentinel called for two such locomotives and three similarly powered
steam railcars but only No 7192 was
built).
NEW LOCOMOTIVES
2-6-4T   (1)   2424
2-6-4T   (37)   2500-36 (3-cylinder)
2-6-0   (25)   13258/9/61/2/4-84
4-6-0   (46)   5020-65
4-6-0   (90)   5552-93, 5607-46/55-64
Sentinel (1)   7192
1935: More Princess Royal Pacifics appear
ed, along with the experimental turbine locomotive. A taper boiler
version of the 1930 2-6-2T came out
and the experimental locomotive Fury
was rebuilt. Further 2-6-4T were
built, reverting to two cylinders,

and the only entirely new type, a heavy goods and mineral 2-8-0 was introduced.

Feb: The first of the taper boiler 2-6-2T was completed.

Jun: The 2-8-0 rated 7F (later 8F) was introduced, two having been initially ordered somewhat cautiously on an experimental basis, then a further ten added. Until 1940 relatively small numbers were authorised but all that changed when firstly the design was adopted for overseas military use in December 1939 and then for quantity production by the wartime Railway Executive Committee, being put to work on the LNER and GWR as well as the LMS. In all 852 were built (but cancelled and amended orders, if built in full, would have resulted in no less than 1,208 all told).

Jun: The 'Turbomotive' as No 6202 was frequently called, began its experimental service and despite some serious failures this Pacific proved to be one of the most successful experiments ever undertaken in Britain.

Jul: The first of the ten additional Pacifics Nos 6203-12 was ready. The major modification to the design was the boiler which had a larger firebox and twice as large superheater.

Nov: The experimental locomotive Fury re-entered service as a normal three-cylinder engine, but differed from the Royal Scot class in having a taper boiler (a few trial trips had been made in 1934 before it was decided in July 1934 to convert the locomotive).

Dec: Construction of 2-6-4T locomo-

tives reverted to the two-cylinder
type, the use of three cylinders having proved no advantage; in fact the
eight completed in 1935 had been ordered as three-cylinder machines.
NEW LOCOMOTIVES
2-6-2T   (74)   71-144
2-6-4T   (8) 2537-44
4-6-0   (179) 5000-19, 5066-5224
4-6-0   (40) 5594-5606, 5647-54/63-81
4-6-0   (1) 6170 (rebuilt Fury)
4-6-2   (1) 6202 (Turbomotive)
4-6-2   (10) 6203-12
2-8-0   (12) 8000-11
The redesign of the new taper boilers
was undertaken after many trials with
differing tube arrangements. Apart
from enlarging the fireboxes and using bigger superheaters the obvious
change was to use domes housing the
regulator. The two versions were not
readily interchangeable and as no
spare domeless boilers were built it
was necessary to alter the frames of
sufficient locomotives of each class
to release some for spares. Only
Nos 5665-81 and 6170 of the 1935
locomotives had domed boilers, but
interestingly 108 out 113 domeless
boilers of the Jubilee 4-6-0 class
were altered to domed. To provide
the spares the following were altered:-
Nos 5002/20/2/3/6/7/40/7/54/7-9/97,
5108/42/65 by the LMS and Nos 45007/
8/11/45/9/66/82/7, 45109/51/63/97 by
British Railways.
Nos 5567/90, 5607/8/10/6/21/2/39/40/
57.
Of the 225 domeless boilers for the
'Black Staniers' 57 were altered to
have domes and for the rest of their

41

days Nos 5000-5224 and 5552-5664, other than those with altered frames could have either a domed or domeless boiler. Nos. 5552 and 5664 exchanged numbers permanently in April 1935.

The LMS altered two of the three boilers that fitted Nos 6200/1 to have a dome, but the two 1936 spares for the rest of the class, one of which spent much of its life on No 6202 did have domes; it was left to British Railways to alter the rest of the boilers for the Princess Royal class.

For the 2-8-0 Nos 8000-11 a spare was provided by altering No 8003 to take a domed boiler.

Post 1935 tank engine boilers (types 4C and 6A/6B) had longer fireboxes which prevented interchange. To provide the spares the following were modified:-

Nos 83/7, 114/39
Nos 2505/13/23/38

To complete these boiler notes, although anticipating a little in this chronology, a slightly larger boiler was produced for the 2-6-2T class and was fitted to Nos 148/63/9, 203 by the LMS and Nos 40142/67 by British Railways.

1936: No new types appeared but advantage was taken of the Government Loans Guarantee Scheme to place large orders for 227 4-6-0, 69 2-8-0 and 73 2-6-4T locomotives.

NEW LOCOMOTIVES

2-6-4T	(116)	2425-75, 2545-2609
4-6-0	(74)	5225-98
4-6-0	(61)	5682-5742
2-8-0	(57)	8012-4, 8027-80

1937: The Coronation year of King George VI gave the oportunity to name the new 'high-speed' Anglo-Scottish service to compete with the LNER the 'Coronation Scot' and build a new streamlined Pacific class. The class became the high-water mark of LMS steam motive power. The operating department being satisfied with its performance, and showing no interest in an improved type, encouraged the construction of more of the standard 0-6-0 locomotives.

Jul: First of the new streamlined Pacifics completed as No 6220 and named Coronation. An important change from the Princess Royal Class was the use of outside valve gear only, the inside valves being driven by rocker arms. The boiler was enlarged to the maximum permitted within the loading gauge despite which there was an enlargement of 3in of the driving wheel diameter. To assist the fireman the large 10 tons tender was fitted with a a coal pusher.

NEW LOCOMOTIVES

2-6-2T	(39)	145-72/85-95
2-6-4T	(27)	2476-94, 2610-7
0-6-0	(15)	4562-76
4-6-0	(153)	5299-5451
4-6-2	(5)	6220-4
2-8-0	(27)	8015-26/81-95

1938: Construction of standard classes continued. Five of the Pacifics, Nos 6230-4, were not streamlined.

NEW LOCOMOTIVES

2-6-2T	(27)	173-84, 195-209
2-6-4T	(34)	2618-51
4-6-0	(20)	5452-71
4-6-2	(10)	6225-34
2-8-0	(2)	8096/7

1939: Further orders for standard classes were in hand. Trials with No 6234 in February showed that a double chimney and exhaust was a great improvement and resulted in all of the class being fitted.

In January No 6220 Coronation (actually locomotive No 6229) set out on its tour of the United States and exhibition at the World's Fair in New York. The locomotive did not return to Britain until February 1942.

NEW LOCOMOTIVES

2-6-4T	(1)	2652
0-6-0	(20)	4577-96
4-6-2	(5)	6235-9
2-8-0	(28)	8098-8125

1940: Concentration on munitions requirements made new locomotives a low priority so construction was limited, but the completion of five more Pacifics was allowed as they were almost ready in September 1939.

NEW LOCOMOTIVES

2-6-4T	(1)	2653
0-6-0	(8)	4597-4604
4-6-2	(5)	6240-4

In addition 53 government ordered locomotives ran as Nos 8226-63 and 8286-8300 (but as the GWR was desparately short of engine power 25 were put to work on that railway); later all were recalled for military use. Eight 0-6-0T were requisitioned by the government (a further five which had been prepared were not sent).

1941: The government requisitioned 51 locomotives for use in Egypt and Persia.

NEW LOCOMOTIVES

2-6-4T	(9)	2654-62
0-6-0	(2)	4605/6
2-8-0	(14)	8126-39

1942: Large orders for 2-8-0 locomotives had been placed and many came into

service during the year.
NEW LOCOMOTIVES
2-6-4T   (8) 2663-70
2-8-0   (68) 8140-57, 8176-8225
Two of the 5XP Jubilee class were
fitted with larger boilers (type 2A)
during the year (reclassified 6P in
1943).

1943: By fitting a 2A taper boiler to the
Royal Scot class the 'Converted'
Scot resulted. The work was authorised on the basis of providing enhanced engine power for heavy wartime
traffic, particularly between Leeds
and Carlisle, as well as the need to
overcome wear and tear of the original locomotives. Conversion of the 70
locomotives was completed in March
1955.
NEW LOCOMOTIVES
2-6-4T   (2) 2671/2
4-6-0   (20) 5472-91
4-6-2   (4) 6245-8
2-8-0   (41) 8158-75, 8301-16/31-7
In addition eight 2-8-0 previously
requisitioned by the government were
returned to LMS stock after working
on loan; they resumed their old LMS
numbers. A further 23 built for the
government which had not been sent
overseas were taken into LMS stock
after a period of loan, becoming
Nos 8264-85/93.
The first locomotives built to Railway Executive Committee orders entered traffic:-
2-8-0 Nos 8400-26 (on GWR), 8510 (on
LNER), 8600-60/71/9/80 (on LMS).

1944: The four Coronation class Pacifics
completed this year entered service
without the streamlined casing.
Two 0-6-0T, Nos 7456, 7553, were

transferred to Northern Ireland to
work on the Northern Counties Commi-
tee, the gauge being altered to
5ft 3in.
NEW LOCOMOTIVES
4-6-0   (69) 5492-9, 4800-6
4-6-2   (4) 6249-52
2-8-0   (62) 8317-30/8-81
Further REC ordered locomotives were
completed:-
2-8-0 Nos 8427-62 (GWR), 8500-9/11-
27/40-2 (LNER), 8661-70/2-8/81-99,
8700-4 (LMS).
In addition 25 of the 2-8-0 were completed for the LNER, Nos 7651-75
(later Nos 3100-24 and then 3500-24).

1945: Production of tank engines resumed
with a modified (shorter wheelbase)
version.
NEW LOCOMOTIVES
2-6-4T   (45) 2673-99, 2200-17
4-6-0   (72) 4861-4920, 4932-43
2-8-0   (24) 8382-99, 8490-5
The REC orders were also completed:-
2-8-0 Nos 8463-79 (GWR), 8528-39/43-
59 (LNER).
Further locomotives were completed for
the LNER, Nos 3125-34/48-55 (later
Nos 3525-34/48-55).

1946: A start was made on the removal of
the streamlined casing of the Coronation class Pacifics (completed in
1949).
Two new classes specifically for use
on branch lines and secondary duties
appeared at the end of the year, in
contrast to past practice of downgrad-
ing older classes for such work.
Dec: 2-6-0 and 2-6-2T having as much
in common as possible produced. Both
were designed with regard to tender/
bunker first running and low axle

loadings on minor lines. A new boiler, type 7, was introduced for these locomotives. Many of the tanks were fitted with vacuum control gear for motor trains (Nos 41210-29/70-89, 41320-9)

Approval was given in 1946 to provide by rebuilding additional power for post-war 'high speed services'; thus the conversion of 18 of the parallel boiler 5XP 4-6-0 three-cylinder locomotives commenced and was completed in 1949.

NEW LOCOMOTIVES

2-6-2T	(9)	1200-8
2-6-4T	(47)	2218-64
4-6-0	(58)	4921-31/44-90
4-6-2	(3)	6253-5
2-6-0	(10)	6400-9

The order for 2-8-0 for the LNER was completed by Nos 3135-47/56-67 (later Nos 3535-47/56-67).

At the end of the year the company announced that for the future a series of ten steam locomotive classes (and the diesel electric shunter) would be the standard classes:-

4-6-2	7	(non-streamlined)
4-6-0	6	(converted)
4-6-0	5	(mixed traffic)
2-8-0	8	(freight)
2-6-0	4	(freight)
2-6-0	2	(freight)
2-6-4T	4	(2673 series)
2-6-2T	2	(1200 series)
0-6-0T	3	shunting
0-6-0T	2	dock shunter

The list implied that the 5XP 4-6-0 types would be reboilered to 6P but did not mean that more of the 0-6-0T were to be constructed.

1947: Important variations of two classes

made an appearance and the final new
LMS steam locomotive design entered
traffic just before Nationalisation
took effect.
Sep: Roller bearing axleboxes for the
coupled wheels were introduced on new
4-6-0 Nos 4758-67; three, Nos 4765-7
had double chimneys and the last had
the novelty of outside Stephenson link
motion. This batch, and all subsequently built had a slightly longer
wheelbase.
Dec: A totally new taper boiler (type
4D) 2-6-0 was ready, being an outside
cylinder design intended to replace
the standard 0-6-0 dating from 1911.
The first 50 were built with double
chimney but later were altered to a
conventional single exhaust.
Dec: The final version of the LMS express passenger class appeared as a
modified Coronation Pacific, using
many lessons learnt from the use of
American built 2-8-0 locomotives during the war and the difficulties of
servicing engines in wartime blackout
and staff shortages. This last LMS
express engine was named after the
designer, Sir William A. Stanier at
a special ceremony at Euston station.
NEW LOCOMOTIVES
2-6-2T   (1) 1209
2-6-4T   (38) 2187-9, 2265-99
2-6-0   (3) 3000-2
4-6-0   (51) 4758-99, 4991-9
4-6-2   (1) 6256
2-6-0   (10) 6410-9
1948: 1st January - all LMS locomotives became national property under the
British Transport Commission, the railways being run by the Railway Executive
as British Railways. Instantly the LMS

was divided into the London Midland
Region and Scottish Region (part, the
remainder being former London & North
Eastern Railway). Locomotive numbers
were to be increased by 40000, but
in February and March many appeared
prefixed by M, pending the issue of
the above instruction.
The repatriation of 39 locomotives
(8F 2-8-0) no longer needed by the
military in the Middle East was nego-
tiated.
Feb: A further variation of the mixed
traffic 4-6-0 appeared with 20 fitted
with Caprotti valve gear, Nos 4738-
57, of which Nos 4748-57 had roller
bearing axleboxes and the last three
had double chimneys.
NEW LOCOMOTIVES
2-6-2T (20) 41210-29
2-6-4T (46) 42147-82, 2190-9
2-6-0   (20) 3003-10, 43011-22
4-6-0   (40) 44698-44717, 44738-47,
             4748-53, 44754-7
4-6-2   (1) 46257
2-6-0   (15) 46420-34
In addition five of the standard 3F
0-6-0T locomotives which had been requisitioned in 1940 returned to this
country and were put back into traffic.
1949: British Railways continued to build
locomotives of LMS design. The 2-8-0
recovered from the Middle East were
put back to work.
Mar: Ten locomotives, Nos 44718-27,
had steel instead of copper fireboxes.
Dec: The first of a batch of thirty
more of the 4-6-0 appeared with roller
bearing axleboxes, Nos 44658-87; the
last two, Nos 44686/7, were not completed until April 1951 and were fur-

ther different in having Caprotti
valve gear, their appearance being
being quite removed from the first
of the class in 1934 by having not
only a double chimney but high
platforms over the coupled wheels.
NEW LOCOMOTIVES

2-6-2T	(30)	41230-59
2-6-4T	(30)	42107-32/83-6
2-6-0	(27)	43023-49
4-6-0	(32)	44658-69, 44718-37

1950: Pending the introduction of British
Railways standard steam classes locomotives of LMS design were put to
work on other regions in 1950-3.
NEW LOCOMOTIVES

2-6-2T	(30)	41260-89
2-6-4T	(54)	42050-78, 42096-42106,
		42133-46
2-6-0	(47)	43050-96
4-6-0	(26)	44670-85/8-97
2-6-0	(30)	46435-64

1951: NEW LOCOMOTIVES

2-6-2T	(10)	41290-9
2-6-4T	(17)	42079-95
2-6-0	(58)	43097-43135, 43137-55
4-6-0	(2)	44686/7
2-6-0	(30)	46465-94

The 'hybrid' rebuilding of the former
turbine locomotive No 46202, using the
front end of the Coronation class, in
August was authorised by the British
Transport Commission. In fact the
'new' locomotive was close in some
respects to a 1936 proposal which pre-
ceded the building of the Coronation
Pacifics.

1952: NEW LOCOMOTIVES

2-6-2T	(30)	41300-29
2-6-0	(7)	43136/56-61
2-6-0	(20)	46495-46514

1953: The last batch of LMS designed steam
      locomotives was completed in March
      with the entry of No 46527 into ser-
      vice on the Western Region. However
      the last engines of LMS type to be
      built were five 0-4-0ST, a British
      Railways variation of the Kitson de-
      sign of 1932!
      NEW LOCOMOTIVES
      2-6-0   (13) 46515-27
      0-4-0ST (4) 47005-8
1954: NEW LOCOMOTIVE
      0-4-0ST (1) 47009
1957: British Railways purchased three re-
      dundant 8F 2-8-0 from the government
      and put them to work as Nos 48773-5.

To complete the annual survey of LMS locomotives it is useful to record the demise
of each class:-
1932: Feb: 2-8-0 (ex-Railway Operating
           Division)
1937: Oct: 0-6-2T (NSR design)
1942: Jan: 4-6-4T (LYR design)
1943: Jun: Sentinel-Doble No 7192
1947: Nov: 4-6-0 Prince of Wales 4-6-0
1950: Mar: 4-6-2 No 46202 ceased working
           as a turbine locomotive
1951: Oct: 4-6-0 (LYR design)
      Dec: 0-8-4T (LNWR design)
1953: Dec: 4-6-0 (CR pattern)
1954: May: 4-6-2 No 46202 (after accident
           in 1952)
1955: Dec: Sentinel (industrial type)
           No 7184
1956: Nov: Sentinel shunter
1958: Mar: Garratt
1960: Nov: 4-4-2T (LTSR design)
1961: Jul: 4-4-0 compound
1962: Jan: 0-8-0 7F
      Mar: 0-4-4T 2P

```
1962:  Jun:  2-6-4T (3-cylinder)
       Nov:  4-6-0 Patriot (parallel boiler)
       Nov:  4-6-2 Princess Royal
       Dec:  4-4-0 2P
       Dec:  2-6-2T (parallel boiler)
       Dec:  2-6-2T (taper boiler)
       Dec:  4-6-0 No 46170
       Dec:  0-4-4T (CR pattern)
1964:  Sep:  0-6-0T 2F
       Oct:  4-6-0 Converted Jubilee 7P
       Oct:  4-6-2 Coronation
1965:  Dec:  4-6-0 Patriot (taper boiler)
       Dec:  4-6-0 Royal Scot
1966:  Sep:  2-6-4T (parallel boiler)
       Oct:  0-6-0 4F
       Dec:  0-4-0ST 0F
1967:  Jan:  2-6-0 (parallel boiler)
       Feb:  2-6-0 (taper boiler)
       Jun:  2-6-0 (46400 series)
       Jul:  2-6-2T (41200 series)
       Jul:  2-6-4T (taper boiler)
       Sep:  2-6-4T (42673 series)
       Oct:  0-6-0T 3F
       Nov:  4-6-0 Jubilee
1968:  Jun:  2-6-0 (43000 series)
       Aug:  2-8-0 8F
       Aug:  4-6-0 Class 5
```

In January 1963 several withdrawn locomotives were returned on loan to operating stock in the Scottish Region; these were (date of final working in brackets):-
44198 (5/63); 44283, 44322 (7/63); 44331, 45125 (5/63); 45159 (4/63); 45169/74/9, 45452 (5/63); 48773-5 (6/63 - reinstated in 9/63 as shown on page 152).

LOCOMOTIVE CONSTRUCTION PROGRAMMES

Lot numbers were issued to cover the construction of locomotives (and steam railcars) whether built in the company's own workshops or outside. Some Somerset & Dorset Joint and Northern Counties Committee orders were included. After Nationalisation other regions' order numbers were used for some of the batches built for those regions.

Programme	Lot No	Type	Numbers
1923	1	4-6-0	10434-74
	2	4-6-4T	11110-9
	3	0-8-4T	7930-59
	4	0-6-2T	2270-3
	5	4-4-2T	2110-9
1924	6	4-4-0	1045-84
	7	0-6-0	4027-56
	8	0-6-0	4057-81
	9	0-6-0	4082-4106
	10	0-6-0	4107-76
	11	0-6-0	4177-4206
	12	0-6-0T	7100-19
	13	0-6-0T	7120-34
	14	0-6-0T	7135-49
	15	4-6-0	5845
1925	16	4-4-0	1085-1114
	17	4-4-0	1115-34
	18	4-4-0	1135-59
	19	4-4-0	1160-84
	20	2-6-0	13000-29
	21	2-6-0	13030-99
	22	4-6-0	14630-49
	23	0-4-4T	15260-9
	24	4-4-2T	2120-4
	25	2-8-0	S&D 86-90
	26	4-4-0	NCC 82/3
	27	4-4-0	NCC 79-81
1926	28	0-6-0	4302-11
	29	0-6-0	4207-4301
	30	0-6-0	4312-31
	31	0-6-0	4332-56
	32	0-6-0	4357-81
	33	0-6-0	4382-4406
	34	0-6-0T	16400-59
	35	0-6-0T	16460-16509
	36	0-6-0T	16510-34
	37	0-6-0T	16535-49
	38	4-4-0	1185-99, 900-34
	39	Garratt	4997-9
	40	Sentinel	2233, 4143-54
1927	41	4-6-0	6100-49
	42	0-6-0	4407-36
	43	0-6-0	4437-56
	44	0-6-0	4457-66
	45	0-6-0	4467-76
	46	0-6-0	4477-4506
	47	2-6-4T	2300-24
	48	4-4-2T	2125-34
	49	4-4-0	563-612
	50	0-6-0T	16550-99
	51	0-6-0T	16600-24
	52	0-6-0T	16625-49
1928	53	2-6-4T	2325-74
	54	2-6-0	13100-9
	55	2-6-2T	15500-49
	56	0-6-0	4507-56
	57	0-8-0	9500-99
	58	0-6-0T	16550-74
	59	0-6-0T	16575-84 & S&D 19-25
	60	0-6-0T	16685-16749
	61	0-6-0T	11270-9
	62	Sentinel	S&D 101/2
1929	63	2-6-0	13110-29
	64	Sentinel	4349
	65	Sentinel	7160-3
	66	4-6-0	6399
1930	67	4-4-0	575/6/80, 613-32
	68	2-6-0	13130-49
	69	2-6-0	13150-13224
	70	4-4-2T	2151-60
	71	0-8-0	9600-19
	72	Garratt	4967-96
	73	4-6-0	6150-69
	74	4-6-0	5501/2++
	75	Sentinel	44 (Axholme Jt)
1931	76	4-4-0	636-60
	77	4-4-0	661-85
	78	0-4-4T	6400-9
	79	2-6-2T	15550-9
	80	2-6-0	13225-34
	81	0-8-0	9620-59
	82	0-6-0T	16750-64
	83	Sentinel	7164
1932	84	0-8-0	9660-74
	85	4-4-0	686-700
	86	2-6-0	13235-44
	87	4-6-0	5502-11++
	88	4-6-0	5512-6++
	89	2-6-4T	2375-84
	90	4-4-0	935-9
	91	2-6-2T	15560-9
	92	0-4-0ST	1540-4
	93	2-8-0	13811-5 (cancelled)
	94	0-6-0DH	1831
1933	95	4-6-0	5517-9/23/4/9-32/6-41++
	96	4-6-0	5542-51
	97	4-6-0	5552-6
	98	4-6-0	5520-2/5-8/33-5
	99	4-6-2	6200/1

Programme	Lot No	Type	Numbers
1933 (con')	100	4-6-2	6202
	101	2-6-4T	2385-2424
	102	2-6-4T	2500-4
	103	2-6-0	NCC 90-3
	104	2-6-0	13245-84
	105	4-6-0	∅
	106	0-4-0DM	7400
	107	0-6-0DM	7401-4
	108	0-6-0DM	7405/6
	109	0-6-0DM	7407
	110	0-6-0DE	7408
	111	Sentinel-Doble	7192
1934	112	4-6-0	5607-54
	113	4-6-0	5655-64
	114	4-6-0	5000-19
	115	2-8-0	8000/1
	116	2-6-4T	2505-36
	117	2-6-2T	71-90
	118	4-6-0	5557-5606
	119	4-6-0	5020-69
1935	120	4-6-2	6203-12
	121	4-6-0	5665-94
	122	4-6-0	5070-4
	123	4-6-0	5075-5124
	124	4-6-0	5125-5224
	125	2-8-0	8002-11
	126	2-6-2T	91-144
	127	2-6-4T	2537-44
1936	128	2-6-4T	2425-94
	129	4-6-0	5695-5742
	130	2-8-0	8012-26
	131	4-6-0	5225-5451
	132	2-8-0	8027-95
	133	2-6-4T	2545-2617
1935	134	0-6-0DE	7059-68
	135	0-6-0DE	7069-78
	136	0-6-0DE	7079
1937	137	0-6-0	4562-76
	138	4-6-2	6220-4
	139	2-6-2T	145-84
	140	2-6-2T	185-209
	141	0-6-0DE	7080-99
1938	142	4-6-0	5452-71
	143	2-8-0	8096-8110
	144	2-6-4T	2618-52
	145	4-6-2	6225-34
	146	0-6-0	4577-86
	147	0-6-0	4587-4606
1939	148	2-6-4T	2653-72
	149	2-8-0	8111-25
	150	4-6-2	6235-52
	151	4-6-0	5472-81
	152	4-6-0	5482-91
	153	4-6-0	5492-9, 4800-6
1940	154	2-8-0	8126-75
	155	2-8-0	8176-8225
	156	0-6-0DE	7100-19
WD	157	2-8-0	8226-63
WD	158	2-8-0	8286-8300
1940	159	2-8-0	8301-30
SPL	160	2-8-0	8331-50

Programme	Lot No	Type	Numbers
SPL	161	2-8-0	8400-29
SPL	162	2-8-0	8500-19
SPL	163	2-8-0	8600-19
SPL	164	2-8-0	8430-9
SPL	165	2-8-0	8440-79
SPL	166	2-8-0	8620-59
SPL	167	2-8-0	8520-59
SPL	168	2-8-0	8640-89
SPL	169	2-8-0	8690-8704
SPL	170	4-6-0	4807-71
SPL	171	2-8-0	8351-90
SPL	172	2-8-0 100	Cancelled
SPL	173	0-6-0DE	WD 260-73
1945	174	4-6-0	4872-4966
	175	2-8-0	8391-9, 8490-5
WD	176	2-8-0	8264-85
1945	177	2-6-4T	2673-99, 2200-22
1946	178	2-6-4T	NCC 5-8
1944	179	0-6-0DE	7120-5
	180	0-6-0DE	20 WD cancelled
1946	181	2-6-2T	1200-9
	182	2-6-0	6400-9
	183	4-6-0	4967-96
	184	4-6-2	6253-7
	185	2-6-4T	2223-72
1947	186	2-6-4T	2273-99, 2187-99
	187	4-6-0	4997-9, 4738-99
	188	2-6-0	3000-19
	189	2-6-0	6410-9
	190	2-6-4T	NCC 1-4, 9, 10
	191	0-6-0DE	7126-35
1948	192	4-6-0	4698-4737
	193	2-6-0	3020-39
	194	2-6-0	6420-34
	195	2-6-2T	1210-29
	196	2-6-4T	2147-86
	197	0-6-0DE	7136-45
1947	198	CoCo	10000/1
1949	199	4-6-0	4658-97
	200	2-6-0	3040-9
	201	2-6-0	6435-49
	202	2-6-4T	2107-46
	203	2-6-4T	UTA 50-3
	204	2-6-2T	1230-59
	205	0-6-0DE	7146-55
1950	206	'Fell'	10100
	207	2-6-0	46450-9
	208	2-6-0	46460-4
	209	2-6-2T	41260-89
	210	2-6-4T	42050-65
	211	0-6-0DE	12069-87
	212	2-6-4T	UTA 54-7
1951	223	2-6-0	43112-36
	225	2-6-2T	41290-41329
	226	0-4-0ST	47005-9
	227	0-6-0DE	12088-12102

++ Post 1934 numbers quoted.
∅ Replaced by Lot 114 (10 locos).

(continued on page 122).

The adoption of Midland Railway operating practices, a series of locomotive evaluation trials and the establishment of the Chief Mechanical Engineer's headquarters at Derby in 1925 inevitably lead to former MR designs becoming the earliest standard types and further classes being derived from them. There was however a major deviation from Midland practice with the adoption of outside cylinders for some classes, apart from the obvious need for outside cylinders on three-cylinder designs. The Garratts were also an exception.

The great change came with the advent of Mr. Stanier as Chief Mechanical Engineer in 1932, after which time no further new designs with inside cylinders appeared. In the dimensions which follow inside cylinder classes can be identified from the diagrams.

Two types of tender were used, with variations. What became known as the 'Old Standard' from 1933 was directly derived from MR types, having a water capacity of 3,500 gallons, with coal carrying varying from 4 to 5½ tons. The new standard tenders carried 4,000 gallons of water (apart from 50 built for 3,500 gallons) and 9 tons of coal, increased to 10 tons for the Pacific classes. The tenders attached to the Coronation Class and one Princess Royal had a coal pusher to assist the fireman on a long run. Substituting a welded body for one riveted reduced the weight by one ton. Four special tenders were built with coal weighing bunkers. Entirely different designs of tenders were produced for the two post-war tender locomotive types.

Dimensions quoted are those regarded as

standard at the end of the company's exist-
ence. There were many variations in the
boilers from 1933 onwards, particularly the
number of tubes and the amount of superheating; to record all variations is quite beyond
the scope of a volume of this nature.

To detail liveries the book could become
almost twice as large, so many illustrations
being required if minor variations were to
be illustrated. Suffice it to say that a
form of Midland lake was adopted for passenger classes and quite widely used until in
1928 the number of classes entitled to red
was considerably reduced. Up to then such
types as the 1926 mixed traffic 2-6-0 and
the 1927 2-6-4T passenger classes appeared
in red. For other classes black was always
the standard. Over the years the style of
lettering varied.

A substantial number of LMS locomotives
have been preserved by various bodies and
operating steam railways, but it is outside
the scope of this volume to list them, many
other publications being available which
specialise in their histories and locations
in great detail. However they do give just
some impression of the variety of LMS steam
motive power that remained strongly in evi-
dence until the end of steam traction on
British Railways.

4-4-0 2P and 4P

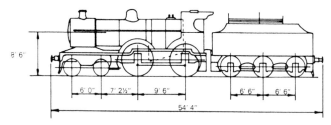

2P Nos 563-700

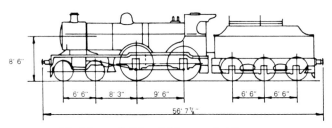

4P Nos 900-939, 1045-1199

Locomotive numbers		563- 700	900- 939, ** 1045-1199
Cylinders (diam X stroke)		19" X 26"	19" X 26" (1) 21" X 26" (2)
Boiler	(length)	10' $4\frac{7}{16}$	11' $9\frac{1}{2}$"
	(diam/s outs)	4' 8"/4' $9\frac{1}{8}$"	4' $7\frac{7}{8}$"/4' $9\frac{1}{8}$"
Firebox	(outside.length)	7' 0"	9' 0"
Tubes	(No/diam)	146/1¾"	146/1¾"
	(No/diam)	21/5$\frac{1}{8}$"	21/5$\frac{1}{8}$"
	(length)	10' 10½"	12' $3\frac{3}{8}$"
Heating surface	(tubes)	1034 sq ft	1170 sq ft
	(firebox)	124 sq ft	147 sq ft
		1158 sq ft	1317 sq ft
Superheating surface		246 sq ft	272 sq ft
Grate area		21·1 sq ft	28·4 sq ft
Boiler pressure.		180 psi	200 psi
Wheels	(bogie)	3' 6½"	3' 6½"
	(coupled)	6' 9"	6' 9"
Loco weight	(light)	50t 7c	57t 9c
	(loaded)	54t 1c	61t 14c
Tractive effort (85% boiler pressure)		17,729 lb	22,649 lb
Coal		4 tons	5½ tons
Water		3,500 gal	3,500 gal
Tender wheels	(diam)	4' 3"	4' 3"
Tender weight	(light)	21t 12c	21t 12c
	(loaded)	41t 4c	42t 14c

** Compound locomotives.

4-6-0 5XP 'PATRIOT' CLASS

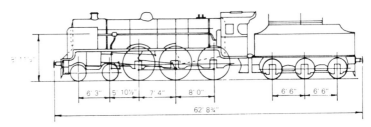

Nos 5500-51 (as built)

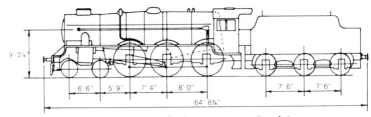

Rebuilt with taper boiler

			Taper boiler*
Locomotive numbers		5500-5551	Taper boiler*
Cylinders (diam X stroke)		18" X 26"(3)	17" X 26"(3)
Boiler	(length)	13' 3¾"	12' 11¹³⁄₁₆"
	(diam/s outs)	5' 3¹¹⁄₁₆"/5' 5⅛"	5' 5"/5' 10½"
Firebox	(outside length)	9' 6"	10' 3"
Tubes	(No/diam)	140/2⅛"	198/1¾"
	(No/diam)	24/5¼"	28/5⅛"
	(length)	14' 0"	13' 0"
Heating surface	(tubes)	1552 sq ft	1667 sq ft
	(firebox)	183 sq ft	195 sq ft
		1735 sq ft	1862 sq ft
Superheating surface		365 sq ft	348 sq ft
Grate area		30·5 sq ft	31·25 sq ft
Boiler pressure		200 psi	250 psi
Wheels (diam)	(bogie)	3' 3"	3' 3"
	(coupled)	6' 9"	6' 9"
Loco weight	(light)	75t 7c	75t 18c
	(loaded)	80t 15c	82t 0c
Tractive effort (85% boiler pressure)		26,520 lb	29,590 lb
Coal		5½ tons	9 tons
Water		3,500 gal	4,000 gal
Tender wheels	(diam)	4' 3"	4' 3"
Tender weight	(light)	21t 12c	26t 16c
	(loaded)	42t 14c	53t 13c

* Nos 5512/4/21/2/3/5-32/4-6/40/5.

"PATRIOT CLASS" 4-6-0
(Introduced 1930)

Serial Numbers:-	Originated by conversion of former LNWR
5500-5551	4-6-0 Claughton Class from 4 cylinders to 3 cylinders and a standard boiler.

Old No	1934 No	Name	Old No	1934 No	Name
5971	5500	Patriot *	5916	5525	Blackpool *
5902	5501	St. Dunstan's *	5963	5526	Morecambe and Heysham
5959	5502	Royal Naval Division	5944	5527	Southport
5985	5503	The Leicestershire	5996	5528	- **
		Regiment **	5926	5529	- * **
5987	5504	Royal Signals	6022	5530	Sir Frank Ree
5949	5505	The Royal Army	6027	5531	Sir Frederick Harrison
		Ordnance Corps	6011	5532	Illustrious
5974	5506	- **	5905	5533	Lord Rathmore
5936	5507	Royal Tank Corps	5935	5534	E. Tootal Broadhurst
6010	5508	-	5997	5535	Sir Herbert Walker,
6005	5509	- **			K.C.B.
6012	5510	-	6018	5536	Private W.Wood, V.C.
5942	5511	Isle of Man	6015	5537	Private E.Sykes, V.C.
5966	5512	Bunsen	6000	5538	Giggleswick
5958	5513	-	5925	5539	E.C.Trench
5983	5514	Holyhead	5901	5540	Sir Robert Turnbull
5992	5515	Caernarvon	5903	5541	Duke of Sutherland
5982	5516	The Bedfordshire and	-	5542	-
		Hertfordshire	-	5543	Home Guard
		Regiment	-	5544	-
5952	5517	-	-	5545	- **
6006	5518	Bradshaw	-	5546	Fleetwood
6008	5519	Lady Godiva	-	5547	-
5954	5520	Llandudno	-	5548	Lytham St. Annes
5933	5521	Rhyl	-	5549	-
5973	5522	Prestatyn	-	5550	-
6026	5523	Bangor	-	5551	-
5907	5524	Blackpool			

* The names given are those allotted at the end of 1947; the
  following had been carried by certain locomotives prior to
  those shown:-
5500 Croxteth	5525 E. Tootal Broadhurst
5501 Sir Frank Ree	5529 Sir Herbert Walker,
5524 Sir Frederick Harrison	K.C.B.

** These locomotives were named/renamed by British Railways:-
5503 The Royal Leicester	5528 REME
Regiment	5529 Stephenson
5506 The Royal Pioneer	5545 Planet
Corps	
5509 Derbyshire Yeomanry	

Names selected but not used were:-
Wemyss Bay (5505); Commando (5509); Sir W.A.Stanier (5513);
Dunoon (5542); R.A.M.C (5549); Sir Henry Fowler (5550); Rothesay
(5551); Vulcan; Goliath; Courier; Velocipede; Champion; Dragon;
Harlequin (the un-numbered names were selected for use on un-
named locomotives when converted with taper boilers).

4-6-0 5XP 'SILVER JUBILEE' CLASS

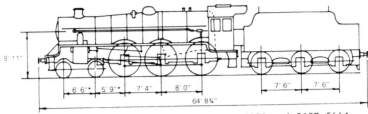

* 6' 3" and 5' 10½" locomotives Nos 5552-5556 and 5607-5664

Nos 5552-5742 (as built)

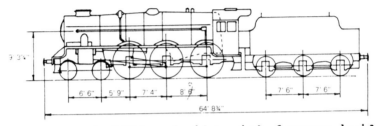

Nos 5735 & 5736 rebuilt with larger boiler

		5552-5742	Larger taper boiler *
Locomotive numbers		5552-5742	
Cylinders (diam X stroke)		17" X 26"(3)	17" X 26"(3)
Boiler	(length)	13' 2$\frac{5}{16}$"	12' 11$\frac{1}{16}$"
	(diam/s outs)	5' 0"/5' 8$\frac{3}{8}$"	5' 5"/5' 10½"
Firebox (outside length)		10' 0"	10' 3"
Tubes	(No/diam)	159/1$\frac{7}{8}$"	198/1$\frac{3}{4}$"
	(No/diam)	24/5$\frac{1}{8}$"	28/5$\frac{1}{8}$"
	(length)	13' 2$\frac{7}{8}$"	13' 0"
Heating surface	(tubes)	1460 sq ft	1667 sq ft
	(firebox)	181 sq ft	195 sq ft
		1641 sq ft	1862 sq ft
Superheating surface		300 sq ft	348 sq ft
Grate area		31 sq ft	31.25 sq ft
Boiler pressure		225 psi	250 psi
Wheels (diam)	(bogie)	3' 3½"	3' 3½"
	(coupled)	6' 9"	6' 9"
Loco weight	(light)	73t 6c	75t 18c
	(loaded)	79t 11c	82t 0c
Tractive effort (85% boiler pressure)		26,610 lb	29,590 lb
Coal		9 tons	9 tons
Water		4,000 gal	4,000 gal
Tender wheels	(diam)	4' 3"	4' 3"
Tender weight	(light)	26t 16c	26t 16c
	(loaded)	53t 13c	53t 13c

* Nos 5735 and 5736 reboilered.

Serial Numbers:-
5552-5741

Taper boiler version of the "Patriot" Class
for express passeneger trains.

No	Name	No	Name
5552	Silver Jubilee	5607	Fiji
5553	Canada	5608	Gibraltar
5554	Ontario	5609	Gilbert and Ellice Islands
5555	Quebec	5610	Gold Coast
5556	Nova Scotia	5611	Hong Kong
5557	New Brunswick	5612	Jamaica
5558	Manitoba	5613	Kenya
5559	British Columbia	5614	Leeward Islands
5560	Prince Edward Island	5615	Malay States
5561	Saskatchewan	5616	Malta, G.C.
5562	Alberta	5617	Mauritius
5563	Australia	5618	New Hebrides
5564	New South Wales	5619	Nigeria
5565	Victoria	5620	North Borneo
5566	Queensland	5621	Northern Rhodesia
5567	South Australia	5622	Nyasaland
5568	Western Australia	5623	Palestine
5569	Tasmania	5624	St. Helena
5570	New Zealand	5625	Sarawak
5571	South Africa	5626	Seychelles
5572	Eire	5627	Sierra Leone
5573	Newfoundland	5628	Somaliland
5574	India	5629	Straits Settlements
5575	Madras	5630	Swaziland
5576	Bombay	5631	Tanganyika
5577	Bengal	5632	Tonga
5578	United Provinces	5633	Aden
5579	Punjab	5634	Trinidad
5580	Burma	5635	Tobago
5581	Bihar and Orissa	5636	Uganda
5582	Central Provinces	5637	Windward Islands
5583	Assam	5638	Zanzibar
5584	North West Frontier	5639	Raleigh
5585	Hyderabad	5640	Frobisher
5586	Mysore	5641	Sandwich
5587	Baroda	5642	Boscawen
5588	Kashmir	5643	Rodney
5589	Gwalior	5644	Howe
5590	Travancore	5645	Collingwood
5591	Udaipur	5646	Napier
5592	Indore	5647	Sturdee
5593	Kolhapur	5648	Wemyss
5594	Bhopal	5649	Hawkins
5595	Southern Rhodesia	5650	Blake
5596	Bahamas	5651	Shovell
5597	Barbados	5652	Hawke
5598	Basutoland	5653	Barham
5599	Bechuanaland	5654	Hood
5600	Bermuda	5655	Keith
5601	British Guiana	5656	Cochrane
5602	British Honduras	5657	Tyrwhitt
5603	Solomon Islands	5658	Keyes
5604	Ceylon	5659	Drake
5605	Cyprus	5660	Rooke
5606	Falkland Islands	5661	Vernon

No	Name	No	Name
5662	Kempenfelt	5703	Thunderer
5663	Jervis	5704	Leviathan
5664	Nelson	5705	Seahorse
5665	Lord Rutherford of Nelson	5706	Express
5666	Cornwallis	5707	Valiant
5667	Jellicoe	5708	Resolution
5668	Madden	5709	Implacable
5669	Fisher	5710	Irresistible
5670	Howard of Effingham	5711	Courageous
5671	Prince Rupert	5712	Victory
5672	Anson	5713	Renown
5673	Keppel	5714	Revenge
5674	Duncan	5715	Invincible
5675	Hardy	5716	Swiftsure
5676	Codrington	5717	Dauntless
5677	Beatty	5718	Dreadnought
5678	De Robeck	5719	Glorious
5679	Armada	5720	Indomitable
5680	Camperdown	5721	Impregnable
5681	Aboukir	5722	Defence
5682	Trafalgar	5723	Fearless
5683	Hogue	5724	Warspite
5684	Jutland	5725	Repulse
5685	Barfleur	5726	Vindictive
5686	St. Vincent	5727	Inflexible
5687	Neptune	5728	Defiance
5688	Polyphemus	5729	Furious
5689	Ajax	5730	Ocean
5690	Leander	5731	Perseverance
5691	Orion	5732	Sanspareil
5692	Cyclops	5733	Novelty
5693	Agamemnon	5734	Meteor
5694	Bellerophon	5735	Comet
5695	Minotaur	5736	Phoenix
5696	Arethusa	5737	Atlas
5697	Achilles	5738	Samson
5698	Mars	5739	Ulster
5699	Galatea	5740	Munster
5700	Britannia	5741	Leinster
5701	Conqueror	5742	Connaught
5702	Colossus		

The names given are those allotted at the end of 1947; the following names had been carried by certain locomotives prior to those shown:-
5572 Irish Free State   5616 Malta   5633 Trans-Jordan

British Railways removed the name Britannia from No 5700 and then bestowed the name Amethyst.

4-6-0 6P 'ROYAL SCOT' CLASS

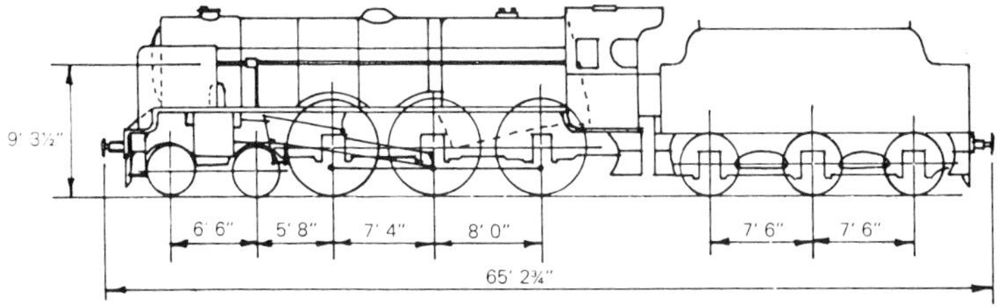

Nos 6100-69 (as built)

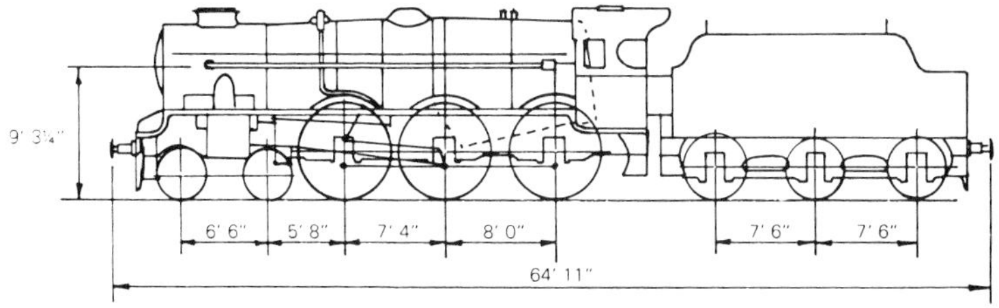

Converted with taper boiler

Locomotive numbers		6100-6169	Taper boiler	6170
Cylinders	(diam X stroke)	18" X 26"(3)	18" X 26"(3)	18" X26"(3)
Boiler	(length)	13' 10⅞"	12' 11 1/16"	14' 2 1/16"
	(diam/s outs)	5' 7⅜"/5' 9"	5' 5"/5' 10½"	5' 4½"/5' 10½"
Firebox	(outside length)	10' 3"	10' 3"	10' 3"
Tubes	(No/diam)	180/2"	198/1¾"	180/1⅞"
	(No/diam)	27/5⅛"	28/5⅛"	28/5⅛"
	(length)	14' 6"	13' 0"	14' 3"
Heating surface	(tubes)	1892 sq ft	1667 sq ft	1793 sq ft
	(firebox)	189 sq ft	195 sq ft	195 sq ft
		2081 sq ft	1862 sq ft	1988 sq ft
Superheating surface		416 sq ft	348 sq ft	348 sq ft
Grate area		31·2 sq ft	31·25 sq ft	31·25 sq ft
Boiler pressure		250 psi	250 psi	250 psi
Wheels (diam)	(bogie)	3' 3½"	3' 3½"	3' 3½"
	(coupled)	6' 9"	6' 9"	6' 9"
Loco weight	(light)	77t 19c	77t 8c	77t 14c
	(loaded)	84t 18c	83t 0c	84t 1c
Tractive effort (85% boiler pressure)		33,150 lb	33,150 lb	33,150 lb
Coal		9 tons	9 tons	9 tons
Water		4,000 gal	4,000 gal	4,000 gal
Tender wheels	(diam)	4' 3"	4' 3"	4' 3"
Tender weight	(light)	27t 16c	27t 16c	27t 16c
	(loaded)	54t 13c	54t 13c	54t 13c

"ROYAL SCOT" CLASS
and
CONVERTED "ROYAL SCOT" CLASS
(Introduced 1927)

<table>
<tr><td>Serial Numbers:-
6100-6170</td><td>Introduced to take over the Anglo-Scottish services in 1927. No 6170 had been built originally as a high-pressure experimental compound.</td></tr>
</table>

No	Name	No	Name
6100	Royal Scot	6112	Sherwood Forester
6101	Royal Scots Grey	6113	Cameronian
6102	Black Watch	6114	Coldstream Guardsman
6103	Royal Scots Fusilier	6115	Scots Guardsman
6104	Scottish Borderer	6116	Irish Guardsman
6105	Cameron Highlander	6117	Welsh Guardsman
6106	Gordon Highlander	6118	Royal Welsh Fusilier
6107	Argyll and Sutherland Highlander	6119	Lancashire Fusilier
		6120	Royal Inniskilling Fusilier
6108	Seaforth Highlander	6121	H.L.I.
6109	Royal Engineer	6122	Royal Ulster Rifleman
6110	Grenadier Guardsman	6123	Royal Irish Fusilier
6111	Royal Fusilier	6124	London Scottish

No	Name
6125	3rd Carabinier
6126	Royal Army Service Corps
6127	Old Contemtibles
6128	The Lovat Scouts
6129	The Scottish Horse
6130	The West Yorkshire Regiment
6131	The Royal Warwickshire Regiment
6132	The King's Regiment, Liverpool
6133	The Green Howards
6134	The Cheshire Regiment
6135	The East Lancashire Regiment
6136	The Border Regiment
6137	The Prince of Wales's Volunteers (South Lancashire)
6138	The London Irish Rifleman
6139	The Welch Regiment
6140	The King's Royal Rifle Corps
6141	The North Staffordshire Regiment
6142	The York & Lancaster Regiment
6143	The South Staffordshire Regiment
6144	Honourable Artillery Company
6145	The Duke of Wellington's Regt. (West Riding)
6146	The Rifle Brigade
6147	The Northamptonshire Regiment
6148	The Manchester Regiment
6149	The Middlesex Regiment

No	Name	No	Name
6150	The Life Guardsman	6161	King's Own
6151	The Royal Horse Guardsman	6162	Queen's Westminster Rifleman
6152	The King's Drogoon Guardsman	6163	Civil Service Rifleman
		6164	The Artists' Rifleman
6153	The Royal Dragoon	6165	The Ranger (12th London
6154	The Hussar		Regiment)
6155	The Lancer	6166	London Rifle Brigade
6156	The South Wales Borderers	6167	The Hertfordshire Regiment
6157	The Royal Artilleryman	6168	The Girl Guide
6158	The Loyal Regiment	6169	The Boy Scout
6159	The Royal Air Force	6170	British Legion
6160	Queen Victoria's Rifleman		

The names given are those allotted at the end of 1947; the following had been carried by certain locomotives prior to those shown:-

6125	Lancashire Witch	6138	Fury
6126	Sanspareil	6139	Ajax
6127	Novelty	6140	Hector
6128	Meteor	6141	Caledonian
6129	Comet	6142	Lion
6130	Liverpool	6143	Mail
6131	Planet	6144	Ostrich
6132	Phoenix	6145	Condor
6133	Vulcan	6146	Jenny Lind
6134	Atlas	6147	Courier
6135	Samson	6148	Velocipede
6136	Goliath	6149	Lady of the Lake
6137	Vesta	6161	The King's Own

No 46121 was renamed Highland Light Infantry, City of Glasgow
Regiment by British Railways.

Following the selection of the name Royal Scot for the first locomotive of the class company minutes recorded the undermentioned 49
names as a prosed list of naming:-

Highland Chief; Royal Scots Grey; Black Watch; Lothian; Royal Scots
Fusilier; Scottish Borderer; Cameronian; Gordon; Argyll; Sutherland;
Seaforth; London Scottish; Lovat's Scouts; Guardsman; Royal Engin-
eer; Grenadier; Royal Fusilier; Sherwood Forester; Royal Welch;
Coldstream; Lancashire Witch; Perseverance; Sanspareil; Novelty;
Meteor; Comet; Liverpool; Planet; Phoenix; Vulcan; Atlas; Liver;
Samson; Goliath; Vesta; Fury; Ajax; Hector; Caledonian; Mail;
Bee; Ostrich; Condor; Jenny Lind; Courier; Velocipede; Lady of the
Lake; Jeannie Deans; Ionic.

The experimental high pressure compound No 6399 was named Fury.

4-6-2 7P 'PRINCESS ROYAL' CLASS

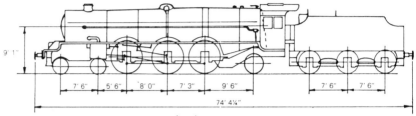

Nos 6200/1/3-12 (as built)

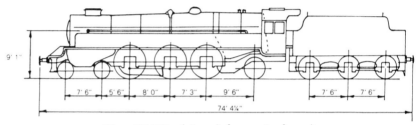

No 6202 (turbine drive)

Locomotive numbers		6200-6201, 6203-6212	6202 (Turbine drive)
Cylinders (diam X stroke)		16¼" X 28"(4)	-
Boiler	(length)	20' 3$\frac{1}{16}$"	20' 3$\frac{1}{16}$"
	(diam/s outs)	5' 8$\frac{5}{8}$"/6' 3"	5' 8$\frac{5}{8}$"/6' 3"
Firebox (outside length)		8' 6"	8' 6"
Tubes	(No/diam)	123/2$\frac{3}{8}$"	81/2$\frac{1}{4}$"
	(No/diam)	32/5$\frac{1}{8}$"	40/5$\frac{1}{8}$"
	(length)	19' 3"	19' 3"
Heating surface	(tubes)	2299 sq ft	1951 sq ft
	(firebox)	217 sq ft	217 sq ft
		2516 sq ft	2168 sq ft
Superheating surface		598 sq ft	540 sq ft
Grate area		45 sq ft	45 sq ft
Boiler pressure		250 psi	250 psi
Wheels (diam)	(bogie)	3' 0"	3' 0"
	(coupled)	6' 6"	6' 6"
	(trailing)	3' 9"	3' 9"
Loco weight	(light)	94t 8c	100t 8c
	(loaded)	104t 10c	110t 11c
Tractive effort (85% boiler pressure)		40,300 lb	-
Coal		10 tons	9 tons
Water		4,000 gal	4,000 gal
Tender wheels	(diam)	4' 3"	4' 3"
Tender weight	(light)	26t 16c	27t 16c
	(loaded)	54t 13c	54t 13c

"PRINCESS ROYAL" CLASS
(Introduced 1933)

Introduced specially for the Anglo-Scottish express passenger services with the capability of working right through from London to Glasgow.

No	Name
6200	The Princess Royal
6201	Princess Elizabeth
6203	Princess Margaret Rose
6204	Princess Lousie
6205	Princess Victoria
6206	Princess Marie Lousie
6207	Princess Arthur of Connaught
6208	Princess Helena Victoria
6209	Princess Beatrice
6210	Lady Patricia
6211	Queen Maud
6212	Duchess of Kent

In addition No 46202 was named Princess Anne by British Railways in 1952.

4-6-2 7P 'CORONATION' CLASS

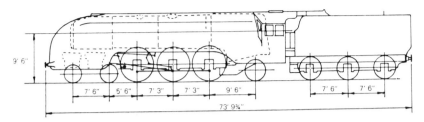

Streamlined locomotives

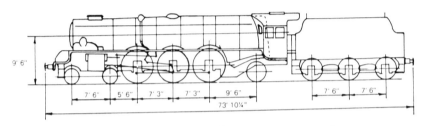

Non-streamlined locomotives

Locomotive numbers		6220-6257
Cylinders (diam X stroke)		$16\frac{1}{2}$" X 28"(4)
Boiler	(length)	20' $3\frac{1}{16}$"
	(diam/s outs)	5' $8\frac{5}{8}$"/6' $5\frac{1}{2}$"
Firebox (outside lenght)		8' 6"
Tubes	(No/diam)	129/$2\frac{3}{8}$"
	(No/diam)	40/5 "
	(length)	19' 3"
Heating surface	(tubes)	2577 sq ft
	(firebox)	230 sq ft
		2807 sq ft
Superheating surface		830 sq ft*
Grate area		50 sq ft
Boiler pressure		250 psi
Wheels (diam)	(bogie)	3' 0"
	(coupled)	6' 9"
	(trailing)	3' 9"
Loco weight	(light)	95t 10c ╪
	(loaded)	105t 5c ╪
Tractive effort (85% boiler pressure)		40,000 lb
Coal		10 tons
Water		4,000 gal
Tender wheels	(diam)	4' 3"
Tender weight	(light)	28t 10c
	(loaded)	56t 7c

╪ Streamlined locomotives 98t 8c and 108t 2c;
  Nos 6256 and 6257 98t 15c and 108t 10c (tender also 3c heavier).

* Nos 6256 and 6257 originally had 979 sq ft of superheating
  surface (special elements).

"CORONATION" CLASS
(Introduced 1937)

Serial Numbers:-
6220-6257

Introduced for the new high speed
Coronation Scot Express between London
and Glasgow and the heaviest of the
company's express trains to Liverpool
and Scotland.

No	Name
6220	Coronation
6221	Queen Elizabeth
6222	Queen Mary
6223	Princess Alice
6224	Princess Alexandra
6225	Duchess of Gloucester
6226	Duchess of Norfolk
6227	Duchess of Devonshire
6228	Duchess of Rutland
6229	Duchess of Hamilton
6230	Duchess of Buccleuch
6231	Duchess of Atholl
6232	Duchess of Montrose
6233	Duchess of Sutherland
6234	Duchess of Abercorn
6235	City of Birmingham
6236	City of Bradford
6237	City of Bristol
6238	City of Carlisle
6239	City of Chester
6240	City of Coventry
6241	City of Edinburgh
6242	City of Glasgow
6243	City of Lancaster
6244	King George VI
6245	City of London
6246	City of Manchester
6247	City of Liverpool
6248	City of Leeds
6249	City of Sheffield
6250	City of Lichfield
6251	City of Nottingham
6252	City of Leicester
6253	City of St. Albans
6254	City of Stoke-on-Trent
6255	City of Hereford
6256	Sir William A. Stanier, F.R.S.

No 6244 was named City of Leeds until renamed in 1941.

The company had allotted names to Nos 6245-54 (construction of the
last two, Nos 6253 and 6254 was cancelled in 1942, the subsequent
locomotives with these numbers being ordered in 1944) as below:-
City of Leicester, Lichfield, Liverpool, London, Manchester,
Nottingham, St. Albans, Salford, Sheffield, Stoke-on-Trent.

No 46257 when completed by British Railways in 1948 was named
City of Salford.

4-6-0 5P5F

Nos 4658-85/8-99, 4700-37/58-67

Nos 4686/7, 4738-57

Nos 4768-5499

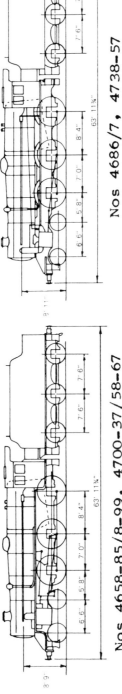

Locomotive numbers	4658-5499
Cylinders (diam X stroke)	18½" X 28"
Boiler (length)	13' 3¼"
(diam/s outs)	4' 11¹¹⁄₁₆"/5' 8½"
Firebox (outside length)	9' 2⅜"
Tubes (No/diam)	151/1⅞"
(No/diam)	28/5¼"
(length)	13' 2⅜"
Heating surface (tubes)	1479 sq ft
(firebox)	171 sq ft
	1650 sq ft
Superheating surface	348 sq ft
Grate area	28·65 sq ft
Boiler pressure	225 psi
Wheels (diam) (bogie)	3' 3½"
(coupled)	6' 0"
Loco weight (light)	65t 13c*
(loaded)	72t 2c*
Tractive effort (85% boiler pressure)	25,455 lb
Coal	9 tons
Water	4,000 gal
Tender wheels (diam)	4' 3"
Tender weight (light)	26t 16c
(loaded)	53t 13c

* Weight variations:-

44658-44667	67t	3c	and	73t 10c
44668-44677	67t	11c	and	73t 18c
44678-44685	68t	19c	and	75t 6c
44686-44687	67t	13c	and	74t 0c
44688-44698	67t	11c	and	73t 18c
44698-44737	67t	3c	and	73t 10c
44738-44747	65t	17c	and	72t 4c
44748-44757	67t	13c	and	74t 0c
44758-44767	68t	19c	and	75t 6c

The following were named:-

5154 Lanarkshire Yeomanry
5156 Ayrshire Yeomanry
5157 The Glasgow Highlander
5158 Glasgow Yeomanry

2-6-0 5P4F (later 5F

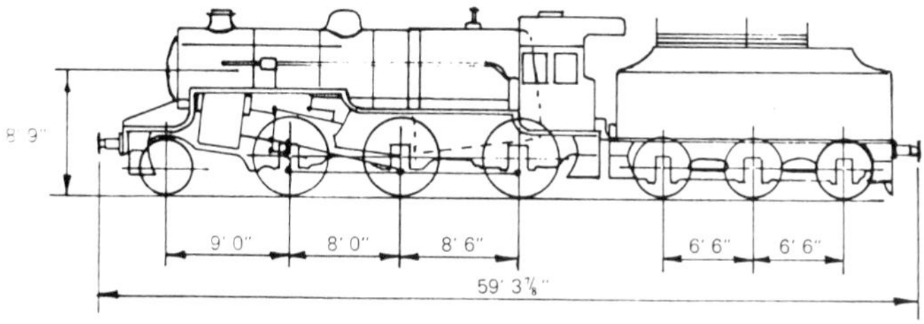

Nos 2700-2944

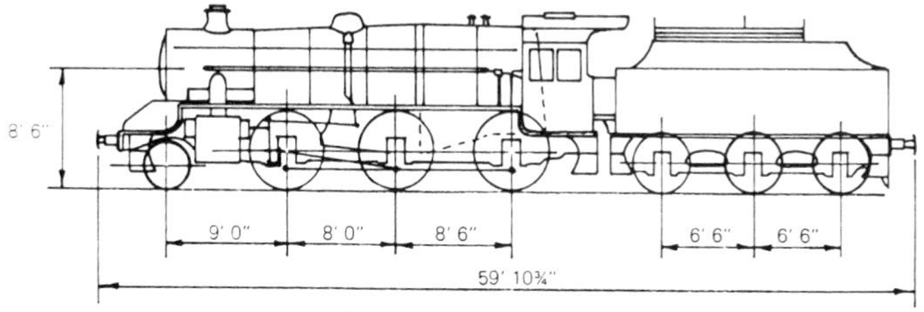

Nos 2945-2984

Locomotive numbers		2700-2944	2945-2984
Cylinders	(diam X stroke)	21" X 26"	18" X 26"
Boiler	(length)	12' 0⅛"	12' 3 9/16"
	(daim/s outs)	5' 3¾"/5' 5"	5' 0"/5' 8⅜"
Firebox	(outside length)	9' 0"	9' 3"
Tubes	(No/diam)	161/1⅞"	202/1¾"
	(No/diam)	24/5⅛"	21/5⅛"
	(length)	12' 2"	12' 2⅞"
Heating surface	(tubes)	1345 sq ft	1479 sq ft
	(firebox)	160 sq ft	155 sq ft
		1505 sq ft	1634 sq ft
Superheating surface		307 sq ft	232 sq ft
Grate area		27·5 sq ft	27·8 sq ft
Boiler pressure		180 psi	225 psi
Wheels (diam)	(leading)	3' 6½"	3' 3½"
	(coupled)	5' 6"	5' 6"
Loco weight	(light)	59t 19c	63t 5c
	(loaded)	66t 0c	69t 2c
Tractive effort (85% boiler pressure		26,580 lb	26,288 lb
Coal		5 tons	5 tons
Water		3,500 gal	3,500 gal
Tender wheels	(diam)	4' 3"	4' 3"
Tender weight	(light)	21t 12c	21t 12c
	(loaded)	42t 4c	42t 4c

2-6-2T 3P

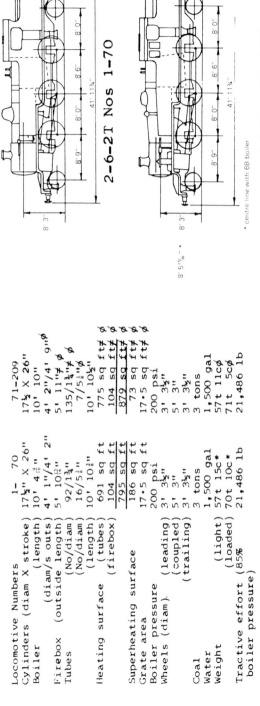

2-6-2T Nos 1-70

2-6-2T Nos 71-209

* centre line with 6B boiler

Locomotive Numbers		1- 70	71-209
Cylinders (diam X stroke)		17½" X 26"	17½" X 26"
Boiler	(length)	10' 4 9/16"	10' 10"
Firebox	(diam/s outs)	4' 1"/4' 2"	4' 2"/4' 9"ø
Tubes	(outside length)	5' 10½"	5' 11"ø
	(No/diam)	92/1¾"	135/1¼"ø
	(No/diam)	16/5 1/8"ø	7/5 1/8"ø
Heating surface	(length)	10' 10 2½"	10' 10½"
	(tubes)	691 sq ft	775 sq ft ø
	(firebox)	104 sq ft	104 sq ft ø
		795 sq ft	879 sq ft ø
Superheating surface		186 sq ft	73 sq ft ø
Grate area		17.5 sq ft	17.5 sq ft ø
Boiler pressure		200 psi	200 psi
Wheels (diam)	(leading)	3' 3½"	3' 3½"
	(coupled)	5' 3"	5' 3"
	(trailing)	3' 3½"	3' 3½"
Coal		3 tons	3 tons
Water		1,500 gal	1,500 gal
Weight	(light)	57t 15c*	57t 11cø
	(loaded)	70t 10c*	71t 5cø
Tractive effort (85% boiler pressure)		21,486 lb	21,486 lb

* Condensing locomotives (Nos 21-40) 59T 5c and 71t 16c.
# Locomotives Nos 121-144 and 145-209:-
ø Locomotives fitted with larger boiler:-

Nos		121-144	145-209	Larger boiler
Firebox	(length)	6' 5"	6' 5"	6' 5"
Tubes	(No/diam)	152/1¾"	181/1 1/8"	171/1 1/8"
	(No/diam)	7/5 1/8"	7/5 1/8"	14/5 1/8"
Heating surface tubes		859 sq ft	939 sq ft	997 sq ft
	(firebox)	107 sq ft	107 sq ft	111 sq ft
		966 sq ft	1046 sq ft	1108 sq ft
Superheating surface		.73 sq ft	78 sq ft	138 sq ft
Grate area		19.2 sq ft	19.2 sq ft	19.2 sq ft
Larger boiler	(diams)	4' 6"/4' 9".		
Weight (with larger boiler)		58t 15c (light)	72t 10c (loaded	

Locomotive numbers		2300-2425	2500-2536	2425-2494, 2537-2672 2673 series
Cylinders	(diam X stroke)	19" X 26"	16" X 26"(3)	19⅝" X 26"
Boiler	(length)	10' 10½"	11' 10¼"	12' 2½"
	(diam/s outs)	4' 8"/4' 9⅛"	4' 9"/5' 3"	4' 9"/5' 3"
Firebox	(outside length)	8' 0"	8' 0"*	8' 6"*
Tubes	(No/diam)	146/1¾"	148/1¾"	157/1¾"
	(No/daim)	21/5⅛"	18/5⅛"	21/5⅛"
	(length)	11' 4⅝"	12' 3"	12' 3"
Heating surface	(tubes)	1082 sq ft	1126 sq ft	1223 sq ft
	(firebox)	138 sq ft	139 sq ft	143 sq ft
		1220 sq ft	1265 sq ft	1366 sq ft
Superheating surface		246 sq ft	198 sq ft	230 sq ft
Grate area		25 sq ft	26·7 sq ft	26·7 sq ft
Boiler pressure		200 psi	200 psi	200 psi
Wheels (diam)	(leading)	3' 3½"	3' 3½"	3' 3½"
	(coupled)	5' 9"	5' 9"	5' 9"
	(bogie)	3' 3½"	3' 3½"	3' 3½"
Coal		3½ tons	3½ tons	3½ tons
Water		2,000 gal	2,000 gal	2,000 gal≠
Weight	(light)	69t 8c	74t 2c	72t 6c≠
	(loaded)	86t 5c	92t 5c	87t 17c≠
Tractive effort (85% boiler pressure)		23,125 lb	24,600 lb	24,670 lb

* Nos 2537-2544 built with shorter 8' 0" firebox; longer firebox later used on four of Nos 2500-2544.

≠ Water capacity reduced on most of Nos 42147-42299, 42673-42699 to 1,875 gal. Weight 2673 series 68t 18c (light) and 85t 5c (loaded - later 84t 14c with reduced water capacity)

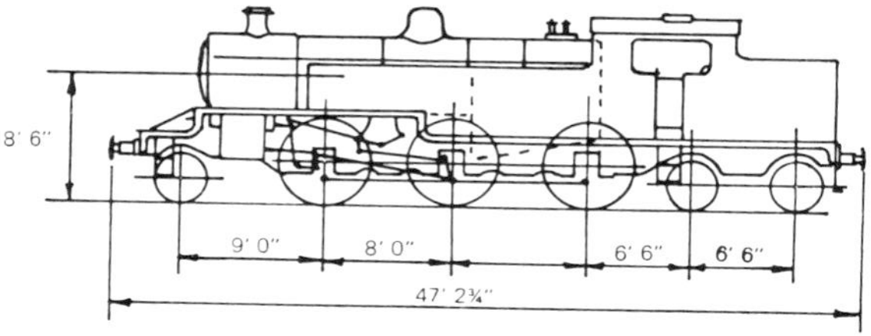

Nos 2300-2424

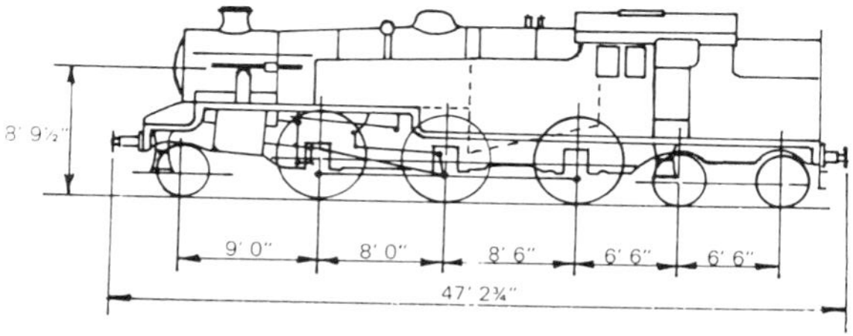

Nos 2500-2536

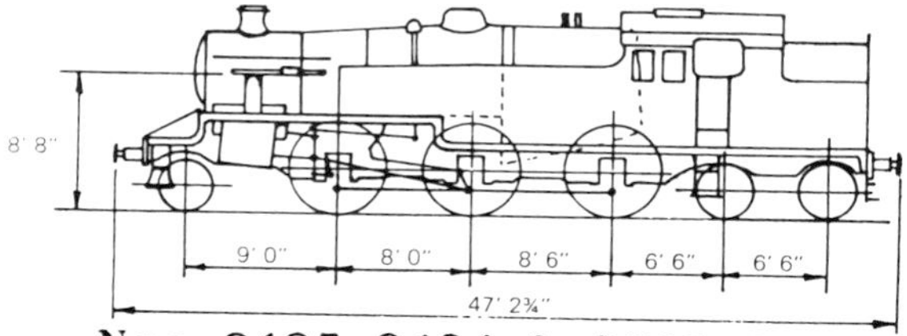

Nos 2425-2494 & 2537-2672

2673 Series

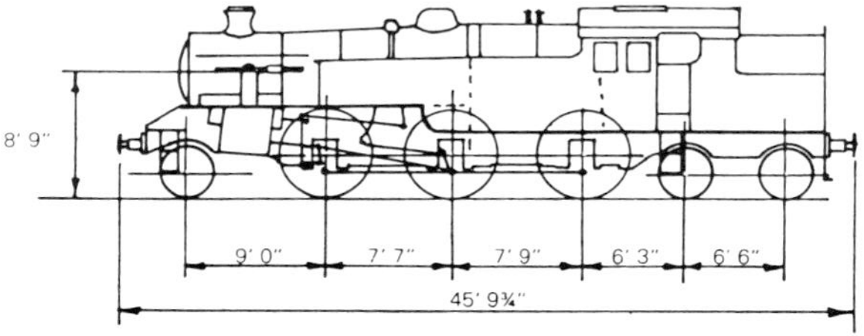

No 2313 was named The Prince when new but was nameless from 1933.

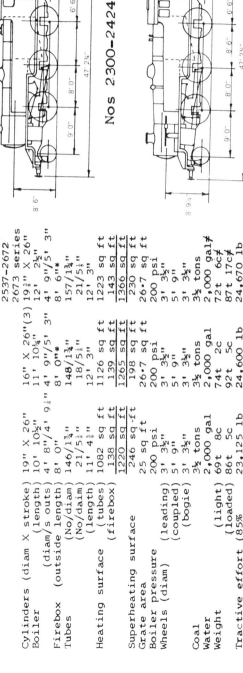

2-6-0 2F 2-6-2T 2P 0-4-4T 2P

	2-6-0	2-6-2T
Locomotive numbers	6400-6527	1200-1329
Cylinders (diam X stroke)	16" X 24"*	16" X 24*
Boiler (length)	10' 9⅞"	10' 9⅞"
(diam/s outs)	4' 3"/4' 8"	4' 3"/4' 8"
Firebox (outside length)	5' 11"	5' 11"
Tubes (No/diam)	162/1⅝"	162/1⅝"
(No/diam)	12/5⅛"	12/5⅛"
(length)	10' 10½"	10' 10½"
Heating surface (tubes)	924·5 sq ft	924·5 sq ft
(firebox)	101 sq ft	101 sq ft
	1025·5 sq ft	1025·5 sq ft
Superheating surface	134 sq ft	134 sq ft
Grate area	17·5 sq ft	17·5 sq ft
Boiler pressure	200 psi	200 psi
Wheels (diam) (leading)	3' 0"	3' 0"
(coupled)	5' 0"	5' 0"
(trailing)	-	3' 0"
Tractive effort (85% boiler pressure)	17,400 lb	17,400 lb
Coal	4 tons	3 tons
Water	3,000 gal	1,350 gal
Tender wheels (diam)	3' 6½"	-
Tender weight (light)	19t 15c	-
(loaded)	37t 3c	-
Loco weight (light)	43t 5c	50t 8c
(loaded)	47t 2c	63t 5c

* Cylinders (diam) 16½" Nos 41290-41329, 46465-46527.

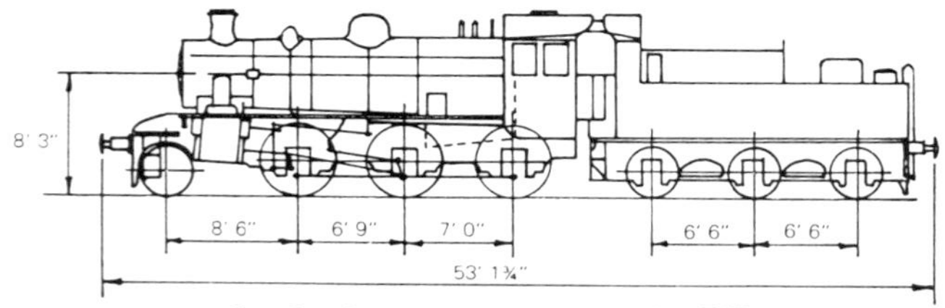

2-6-0 Nos 6400-6527

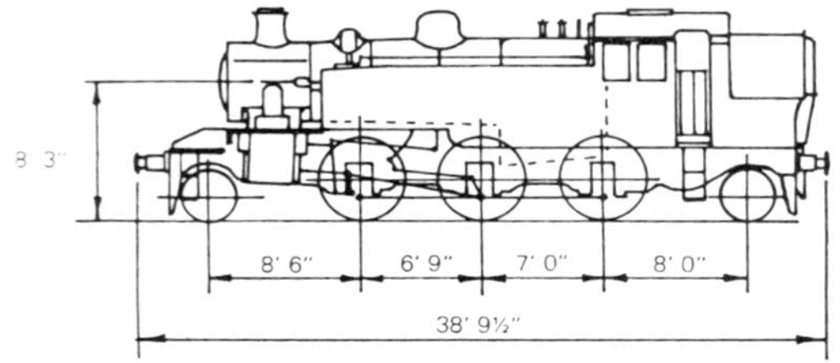

2-6-2T Nos 1200-1329

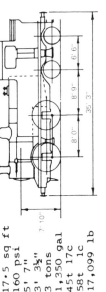

Locomotive numbers	6400-6409 (1900-1909)
Cylinders (diam X stroke)	18" X 26"
Boiler (length)	10' 4 9/16"
(diam/s outs)	4' 1"/4' 2"
Firebox (outside length)	5' 10 15/16"
Tubes (No/daim)	194/1¾"
(length)	10' 10⅝"
Heating surface (tubes)	967 sq ft
(firebox)	104 sq ft
	1071 sq ft

Grate area	17·5 sq ft
Boiler pressure	160 psi
Wheels (diam) (coupled)	5' 7"
(bogie)	3' 3½"
Coal	3 tons
Water	1,350 gal
Weight (light)	45t 17c
(loaded)	58t 1c
Tractive effort (85% boiler pressure)	17,099 lb

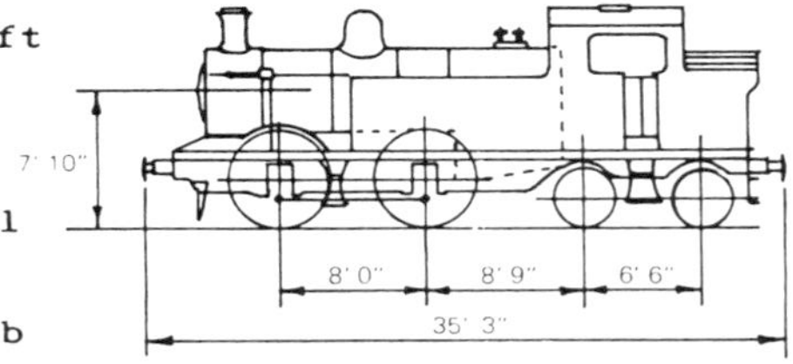

0-4-4T Nos 1900-1909

2-6-0 & 0-6-0 4F

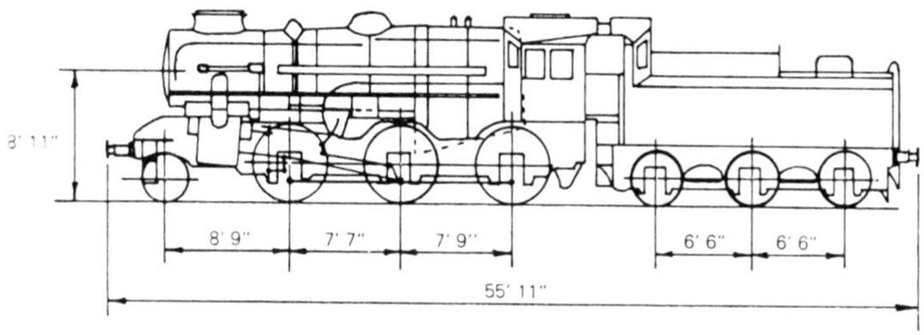

Nos 3000-3161

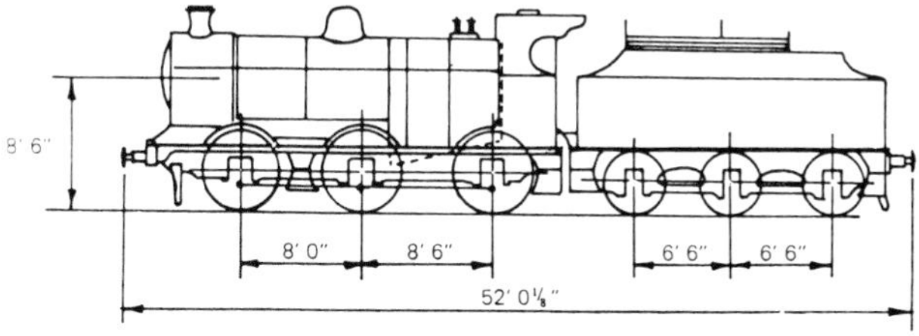

Nos 4027-4556 & 4562-4606

Locomotive numbers		3000-3161	4027-4556, 4562-4606
Cylinders	(diam X stroke)	17½" X 26"	20" X 26"
Boiler	(length)	10' 10⅜"	10' 4 7/16"
	(diam/s outs)	4' 9⅛"/5' 3"	4' 8/4' 9⅛"
Firebox	(outside length)	7' 6"	7' 0"
Tubes	(No/diam)	160/1⅝"	146/1¾"
	(No/diam)	24/5⅛"	21/5⅛"
	(length)	10' 10½"	10' 10½"
Heating surface	(tubes)	1090 sq ft	1034 sq ft
	(firebox)	131 sq ft	124 sq ft
		1221 sq ft	1158 sq ft
Superheating surface		231 sq ft	246 sq ft
Grate area		23 sq ft	21·1 sq ft
Boiler pressure		225 psi	175 psi
Wheels (diam)	(leading)	3' 0"	-
	(coupled)	5' 3"	5' 3"
Loco weight	(light)	55t 6c	45t 0c
	(loaded)	59t 2c	48t 15c
Tractive effort (85% boiler pressure)		24,172 lb	24,555 lb
Coal		4 tons	4 tons
Water		3,500 gal	3,500 gal
Tender wheels	(diam)	3' 6½"	4' 3"
Tender weight	(light)	20t 14c	21t 12c
	(loaded)	40t 6c	41t 4c

2-8-0 8F & 0-8-0 7F

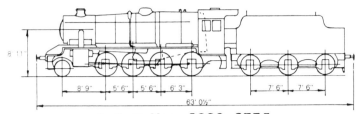

2-8-0 Nos 8000-8775

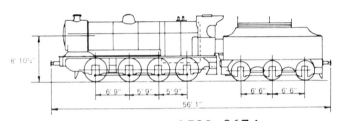

0-8-0 Nos 9500-9674

Locomotive numbers		8000-8775	9500-9674
Cylinders (diam X stroke)		18½" X 28"	19" X 26"*
Boiler	(length)	12' 3 9/16"	14' 3 3/8"
	(diam/s outs)	5' 0"/5' 8 3/8"	4' 11¼"/5' 0¾"
Firebox (outside length)		9' 3"	7' 10"
Tubes	(No/diam)	202/1¾"	120/2"
	(No/diam)	21/5⅛"	24/5"
Heating surface (length)		12' 2 2/8"	14' 10½"
Heating surface (tubes)		1479 sq ft	1402 sq ft
	(firebox)	171 sq ft	150 sq ft
		1650 sq ft	1552 sq ft
Superheating surface		230 sq ft	342 sq ft
Grate area		28·65 sq ft	23·6 sq ft
Boiler pressure		225 psi	200 psi
Wheels (diam) (leading)		3' 3½"	-
	(coupled)	4' 8½"	4' 8½"
Loco weight (light)		65t 18c	55t 10c
	(loaded)	72t 2c	60t 15c
Tractive effort (85% boiler pressure)		32,438 lb	29,747 lb
Coal		9 tons	4 tons
Water		4,000 gal	3,500 gal
Tender wheels (diam)		4' 3"	4' 3"
Tender weight (light)		26t 16c	21t 12c
	(loaded)	53t 13c	41t 4c

* Nos 9620-9674 cylinder diam 19½" when built.

2-6-6-2 GARRATT Nos 7967-7999

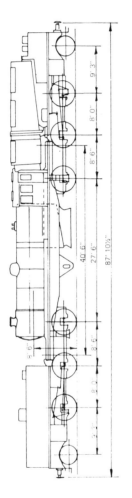

Locomotive numbers   7967-7999
Cylinders (diam X stroke)   18½" X 26"(4)
Boiler   (length)   11' 10"
          (diam/s outs)   6' 1½"/6' 3"
Firebox (outside length)   8' 5"
Tubes   (No/diam)   209/2"
                (No/diam)   36/5⅛"
                (length)   12' 5"
Heating surface   (tubes)   1954 sq ft
                (firebox)   183 sq ft
                            2137 sq ft
Superheating surface   466 sq ft
Grate area   44.5 sq ft
Boiler pressure   190 psi
Wheels (diam)   (leading) 3' 3½"
                 (coupled) 5' 3"
Coal   9 tons
Water   (front engine) 3,030 gal
             (hind engine) 1,470 gal
                            4,500 gal

Weight   Front   Hind   Total
         (light)   58t 7c 62t 0c 120t 7c
         (loaded) 75t 17c 79t 13c 155t 10c

0-4-0ST 0F

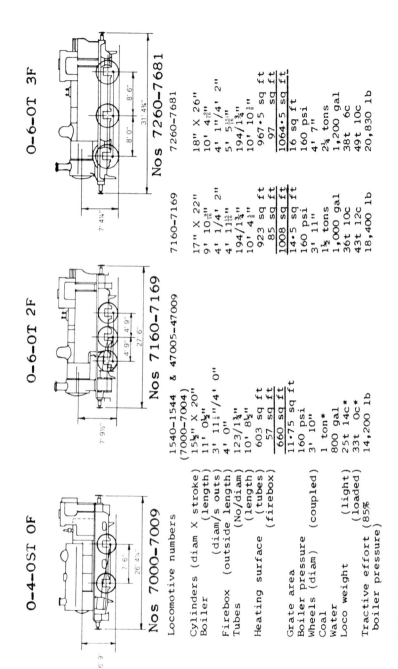

Nos 7000-7009

0-6-0T 2F

Nos 7160-7169 & 47005-47009

0-6-0T 3F

Nos 7260-7681

Locomotive numbers	1540-1544 (7000-7004)	7160-7169	7260-7681
Cylinders (diam X stroke)	15½" X 20"	17" X 22"	18" X 26"
Boiler (length)	11' 0½"	9' 10⅜"	10' 4⁹⁄₁₆"
Firebox (diam/s outs)	3' 11⅛"/4' 0"	4' 1/4' 2"	4' 1"/4' 2"
Firebox (outside length)	4' 0"	4' 1½"	5' 5¹⁵⁄₁₆"
Tubes (No/diam)	123/1¾"	194/1¹⁵⁄₁₆"	194/1¹³⁄₁₆"
(length)	10' 8½"	10' 4½"	10' 10½"
Heating surface (tubes)	603 sq ft	923 sq ft	967·5 sq ft
(firebox)	57 sq ft	85 sq ft	97 sq ft
	660 sq ft	1008 sq ft	1064·5 sq ft
Grate area	11·75 sq ft	14·5 sq ft	16 sq ft
Boiler pressure	160 psi	160 psi	160 psi
Wheels (diam) (coupled)	3' 10"	3' 11"	4' 7"
Coal	1 ton*	1½ tons	2¼ tons
Water	800 gal	1,000 gal	1,200 gal
Loco weight (light)	25t 14c*	36t 10c	38t 6c
(loaded)	33t 0c*	43t 12c	49t 10c
Tractive effort (85% boiler pressure)	14,200 lb	18,400 lb	20,830 lb

* Nos 47005-47009 2 tons; 26t 10c; 34t 16c.

DIESEL SHUNTING LOCOMOTIVES

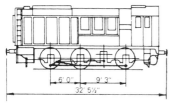

Nos 7080-7119

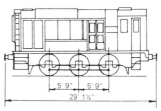

7120 Series

Locomotive numbers		7080-7099	7100-7119	7120 series
Engine horse power		350 hp	350 hp	350 hp
Fuel capacity		661 gal	661 gal	660 gal
Radiator capacity		89 gal	90 gal	89 gal
Tractive effort		35,000 lb	35,000 lb	35,000 lb
Wheel diam		4' 3"	4' 3"	4' 0½"
Weight	(light)	51t 14c	49t 16c	43t 12c
	(loaded)	55t 5c	53t 10c	47t 5c

DIESEL MAIN LINE LOCOMOTIVES
Nos 10000 & 10001

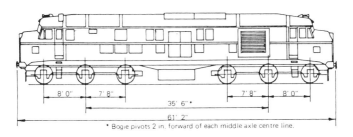

* Bogie pivots 2 in. forward of each middle axle centre line.

Locomotive numbers		10000-10001
Engine horse power		1,600 hp
Fuel capacity		900 gal
Radiator capacity		40 gal
Boiler water capacity		900 gal
Tractive effort		41,400 lb
Wheel diam		3' 6"
Weight	(loaded)	130t 13c

4–4–0 Class 2P No 563.   *LGRP 13844*

4–4–0 Class 2P No 653 fitted with Dabeg feed-water heater (fitted 1/34 to No 653 and 11/33 to No 633).   *LGRP 11289*

4–4–0 Class 4P Compounds Nos 939 and 922 near Larbert (July 1935).   *Author's collection*

4–4–0 Class 4P Compound No 936 with tender No 3677, an 'Old Standard' 3,500 gallons tender rebuilt in 1933 with a 'New Standard' body.   *Author's collection*

Above: 4–6–0 Class 5XP (later Patriot Class) No 5997 (renumbered 5535 in 1934) and later named *Sir Herbert Walker, K.C.B.*   *Author's collection*

Top right: 4–6–0 Class 6P No 5530 *Sir Frank Ree* (built as No 6022) as rebuilt with a taper boiler.   *LGRP 13038*

Centre right: 4–6–0 Class 5XP No 5552 *Silver Jubilee* (built as No 5642) at Bristol Temple Meads.   *LGRP 6343*

Bottom right: 4–6–0 Class 6P No 5736 *Phoenix* as rebuilt with a taper boiler (the cabside is still marked 5XP).   *LGRP 13039*

Below: 4–6–0 Class 5XP No 5520 *Llandudno* (built as No 5954).   *LGRP 13349*

Above: 4–6–0 Class 6P (Converted Scot) No 6109 *Royal Engineer* with a taper boiler. *LGRP 5385*

Top left: 4–6–0 Class 6P (Royal Scot) No 6145 *Condor* (later renamed *The Duke of Wellington's Regt. (West Riding).* *LGRP 9471*

Bottom left: 4–6–0 Class (Royal Scot) No 6100 *Royal Scot* as prepared for the 1933 American Tour. *British Railways*

Below: Late 'twenties West Coast Express Motive Power – Nos 10463 and 6127 with an unidentified Claughton (ex-LNWR) standing at Carlisle Upperby shed. *A. G. Dunbar*

Top: The experimental high pressure compound 4–6–0 No 6399 *Fury.*   *LGRP 5511*

Above: Fury converted to 4–6–0 Class 6P No 6170 *British Legion*   *LGRP 5514*

Below: 4–6–2 Class 7P (Princess Royal) No 6201 *Princess Elizabeth* (as fitted with a domed boiler)   *British Railways*

4–6–2 Class 7P (Princess Royal)
No 6208 *Princess Helena Victoria* with boiler in original domeless state. *British Railways*

Layout of footplate on Stanier locomotives – Princess Royal Class. *British Railways*

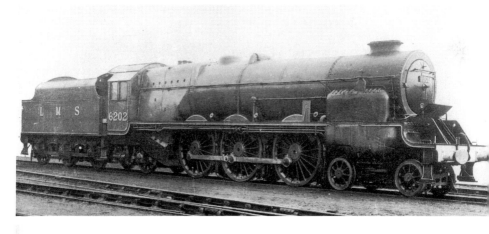

Top: Experimental turbine drive 4–6–2 No 6202.   *LGRP 5378*

Above: No 6202 rebuilt by British Railways as No 46202 *Princess Anne* with conventional four cylinder drive.   *Real Photographs*

Below: 4–6–2 Class 7P (streamlined Coronation) No 6227 *Duchess of Devonshire*.   *British Railways*

4–6–2 Class 7P (streamlined Coronation) Nos 6220 *Coronation*, 6221 *Queen Elizabeth* and 6222 *Queen Mary* ready to leave Crewe Works in June 1937. *British Railways*

4–6–2 Class 7P (non-streamlined Coronation) No 6234 *Duchess of Abercorn* shortly after the fitting of a double chimney in 1939. *R. N. Clements*

4–6–2 Class 7P No 46256 *Sir William A. Stanier F.R.S.* at the opening of Rugby Testing Station (October 1948). *J. M. Jarvis*

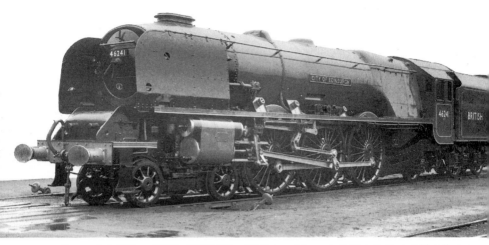

Above: 4–6–2 Class 7P No 46241 *City of Edinburgh* in early British Railways blue livery showing the front end and smokebox after the removal of the streamlining. *British Railways*

Top right: 2–6–0 Class 5P4F No 13174 (later No 2874). *Author's collection*

Centre right: 2–6–0 Class 5P4F No 13245 (later No 2945) with original arrangement of boiler clothing and style of dome cover. *Rail Archive Stephenson*

Bottom right: 4–6–0 Class 5P5F No 5157 *The Glasgow Highlander* with original pattern domeless boiler. *LGRP 13037*

Below: 4–6–2 Class 7P No 46220 *Coronation* in later days (reclassified 8P by British Railways) with a fully circular smokebox. *A. Swain*

4–6–0 Class 5 No M4748 with Caprotti valve gear and the boiler pattern adopted as standard for most of the class. *LGRP 13564*

2–6–2T Class 3P No 1 (built as No 15500). *LGRP 18824*

Three generations of St. Pancras suburban motive power: 2–6–2T Class 3P No 15530 (later No 31), 0–4–4T Class 1P No 1377 and 0–4–4WT No 1220, dating from 1931, 1893 and 1870 respectively. *LGRP 3277*

0–4–4T Class 2P No 6408 (later No 1908) fitted with vacuum control gear for motor trains. The initial pattern stove pipe chimney is still fitted. *LGRP 1391*

2–6–2T Class 3P No 104 (with domeless pattern boiler). *Rail Archive Stephenson*

Top: 2–6–2T Class 3P No 163 as fitted with larger domed boiler.   *LGRP 13154*

Above: 2–6–4T Class 4P No 2300.   *LGRP 22825*

Below: 2–6–4T Class 4P No 2501 (3-cylinder) on a down St. Albans train at Elstree in
1934.   *Rail Archive Stephenson*

2–6–4T Class 4P No 2673 (later shortened wheelbase version). *LGRP 5387*

2–6–2T Class 2P No 1200. *LGRP 4776*

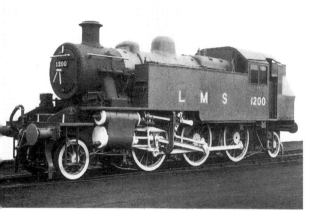

2–6–0 Class 2F No 6400. *LGRP 4777*

Five new 0–6–0T Class 2F
Nos 16715–9 (later Nos
7632–6) ready to leave
Beardmore's Dalmuir (Glasgow) factory in 1928. *A.
Dunbar collection*

0–6–0T Class 2F No 11278
(later No 7108 and then
7168). *LGRP 2384*

0–4–0ST Class 0F No 1541
(later No 7001). *LGRP 5460*

Sentinel shunter No 7164 (later No 7184) obtained for working at Clee Hill, Shropshire. *Real Photographs W7511*

0–6–0 Class 4F No 4065 (with early 1948 M prefix). *LGRP 13972*

0–6–0 Class 4F Nos 44053, 44217 and 44133, 2–8–0 Class 8F No 48205 and 4–4–0 Class 2P No 40691 stand around the turntable at 18C Hasland shed. *Author's collection*

0–8–0 Class 7F No 9557 (known as 'Austin Sevens' for many years). *LGRP 19496*

0–8–0 Class 7F No 9672 (built with ACFI feed water heater which was retained until about 1942 – Nos 9673 and 9674 were also fitted). *Real Photographs R6843*

2–6–6–2 Garratt No 4999 (later No 7999) at Derby when new.
Rail Archive Stephenson

–8–0 Class 8F No 8012.
GRP 18817

–6–0 Class 4F No 3000.
GRP 13563

Filling the tank – a rear view of a 'New Standard' 4,000 gallons tender. *Author's collection*

Sentinel steam railcar No 29910 (formerly No 4152). *Author's collection*

Sentinel-Doble compound No 7192 (the last steam shunting locomotive obtained by the LMS) and Hunslet diesel mechanical 0–6–0 No 7051. *Real Photographs W7514*

–6–0 diesel electric shunter
No 7128 (later British Railways No 12041). *LGRP 9507*

Britain's first main line diesel electric locomotive LMS No 10000. *LGRP 13089*

–6–0 Class 5P No 10460, built by the LMS to a Lancashire & Yorkshire Railway design. *British Railways*

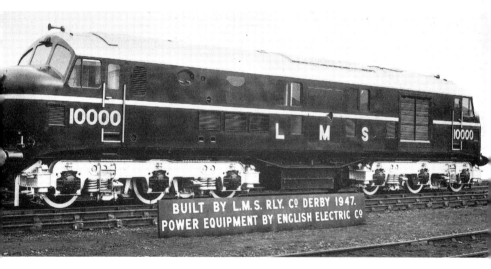

BUILT BY L.M.S. RLY. C? DERBY 1947.
POWER EQUIPMENT BY ENGLISH ELECTRIC C?

Above: 4–6–4T Class 5P No 11111 as built to a Lancashire & Yorkshire Railway design.
British Railways

Top right: 4–4–2T Class 3P No 2111 (later No 41929) built to a London Tilbury & Southend Railway design. *LGRP 10874*

Centre right: 4–6–0 Class 4P No 14638 built to a modified Caledonian Railway design.
Author's collection

Bottom right: 2–8–0 Class 7F No 9655 (later No 9482) acquired in 1927 as war surplus.
Real Photographs

Below: 4–6–0 Class 4P No 5845 *Princess of Wales*, the Wembley 1924 Exhibition locomotive (the name was only temporary for the exhibition). *British Railways*

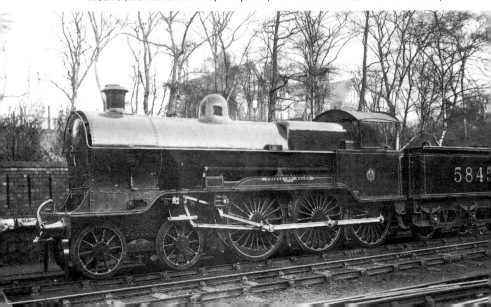

4–4–0 Northern Counties Committee Class U2 No 75 (later named *Antrim Castle*). *Real Photographs 88408*

2–6–0 Northern Counties Committee Class W No 92 (later named *The Bann*). *Real Photographs X252*

2–6–4T Northern Counties Committee Class WT No 7. *Real Photographs X145*

There were two periods when it was necessary to convert locomotives to burn oil
fuel when coal was in short supply.

The first in 1926 arose from a prolong-
ed miners strike and resulted in the following classes being fitted:-

```
4-4-0 Cl. 2   23 (ex-MR)
      Cl. 3    3 (ex-MR)
      Cl. 4   13 (ex-MR) and 48 (LMS)
4-6-0 Cl. 4   47 (ex-LNWR Prince of Wales)
      Cl. 5   39 (ex-LNWR Claughton)
      Cl. 5   12 (ex-LYR) and 7 (LMS)
```

All of these locomotives reverted to coal
later in 1926.

The second period of oil burning occurr-
ed in 1947 when the Socialist government
policies resulted in chronic coal shortages
and many users, including the railways were
encouraged to replace coal by oil. The LMS
was authorised to convert no less than 485
locomotives; at first the programme comprised all 33 Garratts, all 175 7F 0-8-0 and 266
8F 2-8-0, together with all 11 Somerset &
Dorset 2-8-0 engines. However 21 of the 8F
were replaced by 5 Cl. 5 4-6-0 and 16 4F
0-6-0 engines in the plans. Only 25 locomotives were actually converted before the
government discovered that it did not have
enough Dollars to pay for the oil and yet
again interfered by stopping the conversions!
Thus only the following were altered:-

```
4-6-0 Cl. 5    5
2-8-0 8F      11
0-8-0 7F       5
0-6-0 4F       5
```

Reversion to coal took place in 1948 other

than four 7F 0-8-0 which never ran again.

The depots selected for oil fuelling
were Cricklewood, Willesden, Northampton,
Wellingborough, Nuneaton, Shrewsbury, Toton,
Nottingham, Crewe, Swansea, Westhouses,
Kirkby, Hasland, Staveley, Normanton,
Mirfield, Wakefield, Leeds, Stourton, Newton
Heath, Aintree, Lostock Hall, Rose Grove
and Carlisle (Durran Hill).

Numbers of locomotives altered to burn oil
in 1926:

4-4-0 Cl. 2	362/4, 405/11/23/5/79/80/4/5/ 7/92/7/9, 500/4/18/27/33/55/7-9
4-4-0 Cl. 3	763/5/76
4-4-0 Cl. 4	1000/1/5/7/8/11/25/32/3/6/8/41/ 3/8-50/4/5/9/60/2/6/9/71/80/4/ 9/98/9, 1100/3/4/7/12/5/7/8/20- 9/31/6/7/9/49/51/5/63-5/8/73/9/ 82
4-6-0 Cl. 4	5600/2/7-10/6/20/2-4/6-8/30/8/ 41/5/51/5/51/5/61/6/71/80/9/96, 5702/3/11/2/7/8/26/31/9/41/50/ 62/71/2/4/5/80/91, 5829/36/41
4-6-0 Cl. 5	5900/1/4/7/9/11/2/8/22/4/6/31/ 6/9/41/3/7/50/3/9/60/2/4/72/80/ 3/4/6/9/90/2/4, 6003/5/9/12/5/ 24/8
4-6-0 Cl. 5	10412-4/7/9/21-3/5-7/31/44/5/ 50/2/9/62/74

Numbers of locomotives altered to burn oil
in 1946-7:

0-6-0 4F	4466, 4522/85/98
4-6-0 5	4826/7/9/30/44
2-8-0 8F	8064/79, 8191, 8269/73, 8370/ 85/6, 8606/53/96
0-8-0 7F	9511/33, 9613/42/70

No 8696 was altered in 1946, others in 1947.
(Nos 9533, 9613/42/70 never ran again).

The Second War affected the company's
locomotive stock in four ways apart from the
heavy onerous work and the effects of German
air raids. The simplest was the reinstate-
ment of old locomotives condemned in 1938-9
for further work, their numbers being:-
  4-6-0 (8), 2-6-0 (1), 0-8-0 (15),
  0-6-0 (22), 0-6-2T (6).
Concurrently the company lent no less than
43 of the 0-6-0 MR 2F goods engines to the
GWR in 1939-40, which apart from a few
which returned in 1939/40 stayed on the GWR
until 1945. The GWR also borrowed one diesel
electric shunter in 1939-41 (No 7069 and then
No 7076). The LNER lent the company four
Sentinel shunters in 1940 to 1944 but it was
the Southern Railway which helped the most
by sending 48 locomotives:-
  1941 (43) 4-4-0 (30), 0-4-4T (6),
            0-4-2T (7)
  1943 (5) 0-4-4T (3), 0-4-2T (2).
Apart from an early return in 1941 they stayed until 1944-5.

In December 1939 the 8F 2-8-0 design was
chosen for overseas military service and 240
were ordered from North British Locomotive
(100 Nos 300-99), Beyer, Peacock (100 Nos
400-99) and Vulcan Foundry (40 Nos 500-39).
Due to the course of events in France in
1940 only 100 were completed:-
  1940 300-37 (worked on LMS as Nos 8226-63)
       338-54
       400-14 (worked on LMS as Nos 8286-
               8300)
       415-20
  1941 355-59
       421-39
Further orders resulted in the following being built:-

           1941 360-99, 500-24 (North British)
                 440-47 (Beyer, Peacock)
           1942 540-71, 623 (North British)
                 448/49 (Beyer, Peacock)
The numbers 572 to 622 were used by the 51
requisitioned LMS locomotives. In addition
to those listed above several saw service on
the LMS whilst awaiting shipment; all but
33 were sent abroad and after a period of
loan the LMS took those that had stayed at
home in stock in 1943.

     Eight 0-6-0T requisitioned became WD
Nos 8-15 but all were lost in France in
1940; however five were recovered after the
war. Diesel locomotives lent or disposed
of to the government are mentioned in the
chapter on diesel locomotives.

     Apart from the diesels several steam
locomotives saw service on loan to the WD
in Britain:-
   1940 0-6-2T (1), 0-6-0T (7), 0-4-4T (2)
   1941 0-6-0 (1)
   1942 0-6-0 (3), 2-4-2T (4), 0-4-4T (2)
   1943 0-6-0 (4)
   1944 0-6-0 (2)
Some of these loans were short term and all
were back in LMS hands by 1945.

     Prior to their use in North West Europe
from late 1944 the LMS made use of no less
than 50 WD 2-8-0, 79 WD 2-10-0 and 50 American S160 class 2-8-0 locomotives, the last
being returned in 1945. In addition one of
the early Hunslet built 0-6-0ST locomotives,
WD No 5001, was put through a series of
trials at Leeds in April to June 1943.

     In March 1947 the LMS took on loan two
of the WD 2-10-0 locomotives completed after
the end of the war, Nos 73798/9.

The company made limited use of both steam and diesel powered railcars, having inherited 30 steam cars in 1923.

1925-6: Trials with Sentinel-Cammell steam cars were undertaken and one of these vehicles was purchased in 1927.

1927: Jun: 13 Sentinel-Cammell cars introduced on branches in the Midlands and Scotland. These were two-cylinder chain drive power bogie type with an articulated passenger saloon seating 44 thirds. In practice they proved under-powered on many branches and six new larger boilers were obtained to increase the power for some lines. None too successful, most were replaced in 1935 and the last in 1937. A further Sentinel type arrived on trial in 1927 (but was not taken into stock until 1929); it was a rigid framed car with an underfloor six-cylinder engine and cardan shaft drive. The seating was 44 thirds. This car survived on the Wanlochead branch in Scotland until 1939.

NEW RAILCARS
Sentinel 2233, 4143-54 (became 29900-12 in 1933)
Sentinel 4349 (became 29913 in 1933; this was the 6-cyl car).

1928: A four-car electric (dc) train originally built in 1916 (LYR) was taken out of the Manchester-Bury fleet and converted at Newton Heath carriage shops. Trials were concentrated between Blackpool and Preston, but in 1929 the equipment was removed and the vehicles ordered to be broken up in 1931. The vehicles were 14570 (power car), 14668/9 (trailers) and

14571 (driving trailer). The engine
was supplied by Beardmore and the
electrical gear by English Electric.
1929: Feb: A further, but larger, six-cylinder geared car was obtained for the
Axholme Joint line, the vehicle being
owned jointly with the LNER. Seating
was 64 thirds. Not taken into stock
until 1930 the car passed into sole
LNER ownership in 1933.
NEW RAILCAR
Sentinel 44 (allotted No 29987 in
   1933 but became LNER No 51915,
   lasting until 1944).
1931: A radical experiment using a motorbus
adopted to run on rails, known as the
'Ro-Railer', was tried on the Midland
branch to Hemel Hempstead before public service between Blisworth and
Stratford-upon-Avon where it then
took to the public roads to reach an
LMS owned hotel! Change over from
rail to road and vice versa took place
on a special siding at Stratford station, passengers not having to leave
their seats.
1934: Three two-axle diesel engined cars,
seating 40, were supplied by Leyland
Motors Ltd. The 6-cylinder 95 hp
engine drove through a torque con-
vertor. Two were based in Lancashire
at Lower Darwen and the other at
Hamilton, but all three ended their
days at the latter depot in 1951.
NEW RAILCARS
Leyland 29950-2
1938: A thoroughly modern streamlined light-
weight diesel hydraulic articulated
three car train was completed and after
trials entered regular service between
Oxford and Cambridge, providing an
express service, until sent to work

between St. Pancras and Nottingham, based at Bedford. Built at Derby the train anticipated by almost two decades the widespread use of diesel multiple units by British Railways. The outbreak of war prevented any further use and subsequently the two powered cars became an articulated service vehicle (for use on the Manchester South Junction & Altrincham electric line).
NEW TRAIN
80000/2 (powered cars) and 80001 (intermediate trailer)

In addition to the above four diesel powered railcars ran trials on the LMS:

1932: An Armstrong, Whitworth bogie car with 250 hp engine and GEC electrical transmission (later sold to the LNER).

1932: French built Michelin car with pneumatic tyred bogies.

1933: English Electric bogie car with 200 hp engine and electric transmission, capable of working with a drive-end trailer.

1935: Coventry-Pneumatic Rail Car Co (a subsidiary of Armstrong Siddely Motors Ltd) bogie car (having 8 axles) based on Michelin principle.

STEAM RAILCAR TOTALS 1922-48

	pre-Group	LMS*		pre-Group	LMS*		pre-Group	LMS*		pre-Group	LMS*
1922	28	-	1929	16	14	1934	8	14	1938	4	1
1923	30ø	-	1930	14	14	1935	7	2	1939	4	-
1926	27	-	1931	12	14	1936	7	2	1943	3	-
1927	21	13	1932	12	14	1937	5	1	1947	2	-
1928	19	13	1933	11	14						

The last two steam cars (1 LNWR and 1 LYR) were withdrawn by British Railways in 1948.

ø 2 ex-NSR not counted at the end of 1922 were reinstated in 1923.

* Totals exclude the Axholme Joint car (1929-33).

The company took the leading role in the development of non-steam shunting power in the United Kingdom and pioneered the introduction of main line diesel traction.

Actually the first diesel shunter used by the LMS was a narrow gauge (1ft 6in) obtained from Hudswell, Clarke in 1931 for use in Crewe Works. Only 20 hp it was soon moved to Horwich Works and lasted until 1957.

An investigation into shunting power in 1927-8 found that half of the total of goods engine-hours were spent in shunting (non-revenue earning work) which encouraged research into 'economical shunting units' in a move to reduce costs. Following the introduction of Sentinel steam shunters in 1930 further efforts involved diesel power.

1932: Mar: A Hunslet 0-6-0 mechanical locomotive gave a very impressive performance when shunting at Leeds.
Nov: Derby Works used the frames of an old MR 0-6-0T (No 1831) for a 400 hp hydraulic transmission locomotive. It was an expensive experiment and was discontinued in 1936.

1933: Jan: Authority given to purchase ten diesel mechanical shunting locomotives.
May: The Hunslet trial machine was purchased and became No 7401 (later 7051).

1934: The remaining diesel locomotives authorised in 1933 were delivered:-
Drewry/EE   0-4-0DM No 7050
Hunslet   0-6-0DM Nos 7402/3
                     (later 7052/3) and 7054
Hudswell, Clarke 0-6-0DM Nos 7055/6
Harland & Wolff   0-6-0DM No 7057
(Nos 7055/6 were not taken into stock until 1935 and No 7057 until 1936 -

the latter was the only locomotive
built in Ireland and used in the
United Kingdom).
Feb: A 250 hp diesel electric shunter
(No 7408, later 7058) was received
from Armstrong, Whitworth; the single
motor drove the six coupled wheels
through a jackshaft.
1936: Jan: First of ten larger 350 hp locomotives with English Electric equipment delivered. A similar machine
which had run trials on the LMS was
also taken into stock (after modification from 300 to 350 hp). These
were Nos 7069-78 and 7079 and were
geared for 35 mph maximum speed.
May: First of ten similar but single
motor locomotives supplied by Armstrong, Whitworth arrived, perpetua-
ting the jackshaft drive which limited the maximum speed to 20 mph and
soon found to be no disadvantage for
shunting.
NEW LOCOMOTIVES
7059-68 (Armstrong, Whitworth)
7069-79 (Hawthorn, Leslie/English
         Electric)
1939: May: The first LMS built diesel electric locomotive entered service, based on the jackshaft design. Eventually 40 were built. Derby Works became the centre for LMS diesel traction manufacture and overhaul.
1940-1944: The government requisitioned
many of the company's diesel locomotives for use at home and abroad, see-
ing service in France, Belgium, Italy,
North Africa and Egypt. Thus Nos
7050-4/9-73/5/7/8, 7100-9 were lost to
the company.
NEW LOCOMOTIVES
1939 7080-9

1940 7090-9
1941 7100-9 (sold to government)
1942 7110-9 (Nos 7110-5 used by the
    government for short while in
    1942)
1944: A new design had been prepared for a
    1940 order for 100 locomotives (can-
    celled in 1942); it was based on the
    1936 twin-motor type, but limited to
    20 mph. To meet military needs the
    first orders were placed by the gov-
    ernment, but only 14 of the 40 were
    delivered, becoming WD Nos 70260-73.
    Some of these locomotives were sold
    to the Netherlands Railways.
1945: Six of the locomotives ordered for
    the War Department were completed as
    LMS Nos 7120-5; the class was expand-
    ed to 106 by the LMS and British
    Railways, 36 being built at Darling-
    ton and allocated to the Eastern and
    North Eastern Regions.
    NEW LOCOMOTIVES
    1945 7120-5 (BR 12033-8)
    1947 7126-9 (BR 12039-42)
    1948 7130/1 (BR 12043/4), 12045-9
    1949 12050-66
    1950 12067-87
    1951 12088-97
    1952 12098-12136
    1953 12137/8
    (Nos 12045-68 were ordered as LMS Nos
    7132-55).
1947: Mar: The company announced that two
    main line locomotives were to be con-
    structed.
    Dec: The first of these locomotives,
    No 10000 made its appearance. Thus
    the LMS became the only railway com-
    pany in Britain to build and own a
    main line diesel locomotive.
    A smaller 800 hp machine was on order.

NEW LOCOMOTIVES
1947 10000
1948 10001

It should be added that the 800 hp locomotive was not completed until May 1950 and became British Railways No 10800.

To complete the notes on diesel traction mention should be made of the Vulcan Foundry 0-6-0 diesel mechanical machine which ran on trial in 1936. The company also obtained a standard John Fowler 0-4-0DM in 1936 for the use of the Civil Engineer, being No 2 (later ED1) and followed this with an order for five more which were delivered to British Railways in 1949.

DIESEL LOCOMOTIVE TOTALS 1933-72:

	0-6-0 DH	0-6-0 DE	0-6-0 DM	0-4-0 DH	Total		0-6-0 DE	Total
1933	-	-	1	-	1	1951	98	98
1934	1	1	4	1	7	1952	137	137
1935	1	1	6	1	9	1953	139	139
1936	1	22	7	1	31	1956	138	138
1939	-	32	5	1	38	1961	137	137
1940	-	34	5	1	40	1962	136	136
1941	-	44	5	1	50	1964	135	135
1942	-	40	4	1	45	1966	132	132
1943	-	40	2	-	42	1967	101	101
1944	-	34	1	-	35	1968	84	84
1945	-	40	-	-	40	1969	60	60
1947	-	44	-	-	44	1970	49	49
1948	-	51	-	-	51	1971	9	9
1949	-	67	-	-	67	1972	-	-
1950	-	88	-	-	88			

Totals for main line diesel locomotives:-

	CoCo	BoBo	Total
1947	1	-	1
1948	2	-	2
1950	2	1	3
1959	2	-	2
1963	1	-	1
1966	-	-	-

The company had two wholly owned out-
posts in Ireland and a joint share in the
County Donegal Railways Joint Committee
which had 21 narrow gauge locomotives in
1923. The smaller of the two owned railways was the Dundalk, Newry & Greenore
Railways which had six LNWR pattern
0-6-0ST, Nos 1-6 and all named; this line
was closed down by the British Transport
Commission at the end of 1951. The larger
Irish system was the Northern Counties
Committee and at the Grouping had 85 locomotives, 13 of them 3ft 0in gauge, comprising 24 4-4-0, 15 0-6-0, 26 2-4-0, 1 0-4-2,
4 2-4-0ST and 1 0-4-0ST on the 5ft 3in
section and 6 2-4-2T, 1 2-4-0T, 3 0-6-0T,
1 2-6-0ST and 2 0-4-2ST on the narrow
gauge. Some of the 4-4-0 locomotives, von
Borries compounds among them, had been
built by the Midland Railway at Derby Works.
After the Grouping the LMS(NCC) added the
following locomotives:-

1923	0-6-0	71-3 (soon numbered 13-5)
1924	4-4-0	1, 2, 74-8
1925	4-4-0	79-83
	Sentinel 91 (and Sentinel steam rail-car No 401)	
1926	4-4-0	3
1929	4-4-0	84
1931	4-4-0	4
1933	2-6-0	90-3
1934	4-4-0	85
	2-6-0	94/5
1935	4-4-0	86
	2-6-0	96/7
1936	4-4-0	87
1937	2-6-0	98
1938	2-6-0	99
1939	2-6-0	100/1
1940	2-6-0	102

```
1942 2-6-0    103/4
1944 0-6-0T   18/9 (transferred from LMS)
1946 2-6-4T   5-8
1947 2-6-4T   1-4, 9, 10
```
These locomotives were built by:-

LMS Derby	71-3, 90-3, 1-10 (2-6-4T)
NCC Belfast	1-4 (4-4-0), 79-81, 84-7, 94-104
Sentinel	91, 401
North British	74-8, 82/3

The only additions to the narrow gauge stock were two 4-4-2T, Nos 113/4, taken over with the Ballycastle Railway in 1924.

Naming became quite extensive on the NCC and the following new locomotives were named (and renamed in one case):-

1	Glenhesk	87	Queen Alexandra
2	Glendun	90	Duke of Abercorn
3	Glenaan*	91	The Bush
4	Glenariff	92	The Bann
74	Dunluce Castle	93	The Foyle
75	Antrim Castle	94	The Maine
76	Olderfleet Castle	95	The Braid
78	Chichester Castle	96	Silver Jubilee
79	Kenbaan Castle	97	Earl of Ulster
80	Dunseverick Castle	98	King Edward VIII
81	Carrickfergus Castle	99	King George VI
		100	Queen Elizabeth
82	Dunananie Castle	101	Lord Masserene
83	Carra Castle	103	Thomas Somerset
84	Lisanoure Castle		

* Originally Galgorm Castle

At the end of LMS ownership there were 54 5ft 3in and 4 narrow gauge locomotives. This small system serving the north east corner of Ulster was sold to Ulster Transport Authority in 1949, but Derby Works supplied eight more 2-6-4T, Nos 50-3 in 1949 and Nos 54-7 in 1950. The last of all these locomotives ceased working in 1971.

The major workshops of the company constit-
ed some of the largest factories and employ-
ment of labour in the United Kingdom.

Crewe (formerly LNWR): commenced repairs in
1843 and the first new engines
were completed in late 1843. The
works grew in size until it covered some 160 acres and employed
over 10,000 persons. In its time
it has produced virtually every-
thing needed for the manufacture
and repair of locomotives, including steel making. Officially the
the number of steam locomotives
built is 7,331, the last in 1958.
The most famous of its products
are undoubtedly the Webb Compounds of the LNWR and the LMS
streamlined Pacifics designed by
Sir William Stanier.

Derby (formerly MR): repairs commenced in
1840 but it was not until 1851
that the first locomotive was
built. Eventually the locomotive works covered 13 acres with
some 3,800 staff. The official
number of steam locomotives from
1851 to 1957 is 2,995 (including
some for the Somerset & Dorset
Joint Committee and the Northern
Counties Committee). The preserved Midland compound repre-
sents what is probably Derby's
most famous class of steam
locomotive.

Horwich (formerly LYR): replaced an older
establishment in Manchester and
started repairs in 1887 and completed its first new locomotive
in 1889. The site covered 116

118

acres and included a steel foundry. The best known Horwich
steam product of LMS days is the
2-6-0 class dating from 1926.
The number of steam locomotives
built up to 1957 was 1,840.

St. Rollox (formerly CR); commenced business
in 1854 and eventually employed
about 3,000 staff. New construction ceased in 1928 but without
doubt 4-6-0 No 903 Cardean of
1906 (LMS No 14752) can be regarded as the work's most famous
engine.

With the exception of Stoke which completed
four locomotives of NSR design in early 1923
none of the other workshops taken over by
the LMS built any locomotives after the
Grouping; these works were Bow (LNWR ex NLR),
Plaistow (MR ex LTSR), Stoke (NSR), Barrow
(FR), Maryport (MCR), Kilmarnock (G&SWR) and
Inverness (HR). In addition there were various lifting shops attached to some of the
major engine sheds which for a few years
carried out extensive overhauls of locomotives, but in LMS days they became part of
the adjacent sheds.

It should be noted that locomotives of
LMS design were constructed to British Railways orders at Swindon, Brighton, Doncaster
and Darlington works, which together with
Eastleigh and Ashford had also built 313
locomotives (2-8-0 8F) to meet government
and London & North Eastern Railway wartime
orders.

Apart from its own workshops the LMS
placed orders on a number of contractors,
as indicated by the list of locomotive
builders.

Works	Type	Numbers	Total
Crewe (1,435)	2-8-0	8000-26, 8096-8175, 8301-30	137
	0-8-0	9500-9674	175
	4-6-2	6200-12/20-56, 46257	51
	4-6-0	44658-67, 44718-47, 4748-53, 44754-7, 4758-82, 4826-4931, 4967-81, 5000-19, 5070-4, 5452-71, 5502-19/23/4/9-32/6-56, 5607-54/65-99, 5700-5742	412
	2-6-0	13030-13109, 13150-13284, 6400-19, 46420-64	280
	0-6-0	4107-76, 4302-11, 4437-56, 4507-56/62-76	165
	4-4-0	636-60, 686-700	40
	0-8-4T	7930-59	30
	2-6-2T	185-209, 1200-9, 41210-41319	145
Derby (1,229)	4-6-0	4800-25, 5472-99, 5500/1/20-2/5-8/33-5, 5655-64, 6150-69	96
	0-6-0	4027-56, 4207-4301, 4407-36, 4577-4606	185
	4-4-0	563-632, 575/6/80 (2nd Nos), 661-85, 935-9, 1045-1114	173
	2-6-4T	42050-65, 42107-86, 2187-2494, 2500-44, 2618-99	531
	2-6-2T	15500-69, 71-184, 41320-9	194
	0-6-0T	11270-9	10
	0-4-4T	6400-9	10
	4-4-2T	2110-9/25-34/51-60	30
Horwich (441)	2-8-0	8331-99, 8490-5	75
	4-6-0	44668-44717, 4783-99, 4932-66/82-99, 10434-74	161
	2-6-0	13000-29, 13110-49, 3000-10, 43011-49, 43112-36	145
	0-6-0	4457-66	10
	4-4-0	1115-34	20
	0-6-0T	16750-64	15
	0-4-0ST	47005-9	5
	4-6-4T	11110-9	10
St. Rollox (80)	4-6-0	14630-49	20
	0-6-0	4177-4206, 4312-31, 4467-76	60
Stoke (4)	0-6-2T	2270-3	4

Total built in LMS workshops 3,189 (404 by British Railways)

Works	Type	Numbers	Total
Swindon (105)	2-8-0	8400-79	80
	2-6-0	46503-27	25
Doncaster (100)	2-8-0	8510-39, LNER 3148-67	50
	2-6-0	43050-69, 43107-11/37-61	50
Darlington (128)	2-8-0	8500-9/40-59, LNER 3125-47	53
	2-6-0	43070-43106, 46465-46502	75
Ashford (14)	2-8-0	8610-2/8-24/71-4	14

Works	Type	Number	Total
Brighton (134)	2-8-0	8613-7/25-49/63-70/5-99, 8700-4, LNER 7651-75	93
	2-6-4T	42066--42106	41
Eastleigh (23)	2-8-0	8600-9/50-62	23

Total built in other railways' workshops 504 (191 by British Railways)

LOCOMOTIVES BUILT BY OUTSIDE CONTRACTORS

Contractor	Type	Numbers	Total
Armstrong, Whitworth	4-6-0	5125-5451	327
Bagnall	0-6-0T	16535-49, 16675-84	25
Barclay	0-6-0	4357-81	25
Beardmore (91)	4-6-0	5845	1
	0-6-0T	16600-24, 16685-16749	90
Beyer, Peacock	Garratt	4967-99	33
Hunslet	0-6-0T	7135-49, 16510-34, 16625-74	90
Kerr, Stuart	0-6-0	4082-4106, 4332-56	50
Kitson	0-4-0ST	1540-4	5
Nasmyth, Wilson (15)	4-4-2T	2120-4	5
	0-4-4T	15260-9	10
North British (404)	2-8-0	8176-8225	50
	4-6-0	5557-5606, 6100-49, 6399	101
	0-6-0	4057-81, 4382-4406, 4477-4506	80
	4-4-0	1135-59	25
	2-6-4T	2545-2617	73
	0-6-0T	7120-34, 16400-59	75
Vulcan Foundry (364)	2-8-0	8027-95	69
	4-6-0	5020-69, 5075-5124	100
	4-4-0	900-34, 1160-99	75
	0-6-0T	7100-19, 16460-16509, 16550-99	120
Sentinel	0-4-0T	7160-4, 7192	6

Total built by outside contractors 1,435

LOCOMOTIVES BUILT TO GOVERNMENT ORDERS

Contractor	Type	Numbers	Total
Beyer, Peacock	2-8-0	WD 400-49	50
Kitson	2-8-0	9661 (purchased 1927)	1
North British	2-8-0	9646-60/2-5 (purchased 1927)	19
	2-8-0	WD 300-99, 500-24/40-71, 623	158

Total built 20 (First War), 208 (Second War)

DIESEL LOCOMOTIVES BUILT IN LMS AND BRITISH RAILWAYS WORKSHOPS

Works	Type	Numbers	Total
Derby (113)	CoCo 0-6-0DH 0-6-0DE	10000/1 1831 (Conversion) 7080-7131, 12045-12102	2 1 110
Darlington (36)	0-6-0DE	12103-38	36

Total built in railway workshops 149 (96 by British Railways);
Derby also built 14 0-6-0DE for the Government

DIESEL LOCOMOTIVES BUILT BY OUTSIDE CONTRACTORS

Contractor	Type	Numbers	Total
Armstrong Whitworth	0-6-0DE	7408, 7059-68	11
English Electric	0-4-0DM	7050	1
Harland & Wolff	0-6-0DM	7057	1
Hawthorne Leslie	0-6-0DE	7069-79	11
Hudswell, Clarke	0-6-0DM	7055/6	2
Hunslet	0-6-0DM	7401-3, 7054	4
North British	BoBo	10800	1

Total built by outside contractors 31 (one delivered to British
Railways

LOCOMOTIVE CONSTRUCTION **PROGRAMMES**

(continued from page 54)

The following orders were placed by British Railways in other region
lot lists:-

1949 Programme	Southern Region	3491	2-6-4T	42096-42106
1950 Programme	Southern Region	3536	2-6-4T	42066-95
	Eastern Region	1276	2-6-0	43050-69
	Eastern Region	1278	2-6-0	43070-43106
1951 Programme	Eastern Region	1308	2-6-0	43137-61
	Eastern Region	1309	2-6-0	46465-82
	Eastern Region	1310	2-6-0	46483-46502
	Eastern Region	1312	0-6-0DE	12103-38
1950 Programme	Eastern Region	1352	2-6-0	43107-11
1952 Programme	Western Region	394	2-6-0	46503-27

The LMS company allotted C&W series Lot Numbers to the following ra
car orders:-

312 Sentinel cars 2233, 4143-54 (see locomotive Lot No 40).
576 Sentinel car 4349 (see locomotive Lot No 64).
760 Leyland diesel cars 29950-2.
989 Articulated diesel hydraulic train Nos 80000-2.

1A WILLESDEN	12A CARLISLE KINGMOOR	22C Bath
1B Camden	12B Upperby	22D Templecombe
1C Watford	12C Durran Hill	22E Highbridge
	12D Workington	
2A RUGBY	12E Moor Row	23A BANK HALL
2B Bletchley	12F Beattock	23B Aintree
2C Northampton	12G Dumfries	23C Southport
2D Nuneaton	12H Stranraer	23D Wigan (Central)
2E Warwick		23E Lostock Hall
2F Coventry	13A PLAISTOW	23F Walton-on-the-Hill
	13B Devons Road	23G Ormskirk
3A BESCOT	13C Tilbury	
3B Bushbury	13D Shoeburyness	24A ACCRINGTON
3C Walsall	13E Upminster	24B Rose Grove
3D Aston		24C Colne
3E Monument Lane	14A CRICKLEWOOD	24D Lower Darwen
	14B Kentish Town	24E Blackpool
4A SHREWSBURY	14C St. Albans	24F Fleetwood
4B Swansea		
4C Upper Bank	15A WELLINGBORO'	25A WAKEFIELD
4D Abergavenny	15B Kettering	25B Huddersfield
4E Tredegar	15C Leicester	25C Goole
	15D Bedford	25D Mirfield
5A CREWE NORTH		25E Sowerby Bridge
5B Crewe South	16A NOTTINGHAM	25F Low Moor
5C Stafford	16B Peterboro'	25G Farnley Junction
5D Stoke	16C Kirkby	
5E Alsager	16D Mansfield	26A NEWTON HEATH
5F Uttoxeter		26B Agecroft
	17A DERBY	26C Bolton
6A CHESTER	17B Burton	26D Bury
6B Mold Junction	17C Coalville	26E Bacup
6C Birkenhead	17D Rowsley	26F Lees
6D Birkenhead North		
	18A TOTON	27A POLMADIE
7A LLANDUDNO JUNCTION	18B Westhouses	27B Hurlford
7B Bangor	18C Hasland	27C Edinburgh
7C Holyhead	18D Staveley	27D Carstairs
7D Rhyl		27E Girvan
	19A SHEFFIELD	27F Ayr
8A EDGE HILL	19B Millhouses	27G Greenock
8B Warrington	19C Canklow	27H Ardrossan
8C Speke Junction	19D Heaton Mersey	27J Corkerhill
8D Widnes	19E Belle Vue	27K Dawsholm
	19F York	27L St. Enoch
9A LONGSIGHT	19G Trafford Park	
9B Stockport		28A Motherwell
9C Macclesfield	20A LEEDS	28B Hamilton
9D Buxton	20B Stourton	28C Grangemouth
	20C Carlton	
10A SPRINGS BRANCH	20D Normanton	29A PERTH
10B Preston	20E Manningham	29B Stirling
10C Patricroft	20F Skipton	29C Dundee
10D Plodder Lane	20G Hellifield	29D Forfar
10E Sutton Oak		29E Oban
	21A SALTLEY	29F Aberdeen
11A CARNFORTH	21B Bourneville	29G St. Rollox
11B Barrow	21C Bromsgrove	29H Inverness
11C Lancaster	21D Stratford-on-Avon	29J Aviemore
11D Oxenholme		29K Forres
11E Tebay	22A BRISTOL	
	22B Gloucester	

The shed numbers shown were those that came
into use at the beginning of 1935. Only
the main sheds are given, there being numerous minor sheds.

A few numbers were changed by the LMS as
follows:-

11C	Lancaster	became	20H
19G	Trafford Park		19F
23E	Lostock Hall		24C
27B	Hurlford		30B
27C	Edinburgh		28B
27D	Carstairs		28C
27F	Ayr		30D
27G	Greenock		27B
27H	Ardrossan		30C
27J	Corkerhill		30A
27K	Dawsholm		31E
28B	Hamilton		27C
28C	Grangemouth		31D
29B	Stirling		31B
29E	Oban		31C
29F	Aberdeen		29B
29G	St. Rollox		31A
29H	Inverness		32A
29J	Aviemore		32B
29K	Forres		32C

About 1940 20C Carlton became known as
Royston.

Prior to the above numbers coming into
use the old company numbers were retained
for former MR, LNWR and LYR sheds; numbers
in the appropriate divisions were added by
the LMS for LTSR, NLR, Wirral, NSR, FR and
MCR sheds. No numbering system was used
in the Northern Division before 1935.

All LMS built locomotives (and those built by other railways and by British Railways) are listed by:-

No = number carried at the end of 1947; where the LMS had used another series beforehand details are given at the head of each class, but individual renumbering dates are not given.

New = date into service.

Wdn = date of withdrawal.

Supplementary notes give details of major rebuildings and certain other changes and any other relevant information.

It should be noted that a number of LMS locomotives were withdrawn before Nationalisation, many for wartime military service.

Under British Railways from 2/2/48 to 15/3/48 some 160 locomotives had a temporary 'M' prefix to the number. General renumbering then commenced by the addition of 40000 to existing numbers, exceptions being the 4-4-2T Class 3P which were renumbered directly to Nos 41928-52/69-78 in accordance with the already announced intention and the following which were condemned unrenumbered:-

7930/2/3/6/8/9/48/51/4/6/8/9, 9504/7/12/4/ 7/8/21/2/7-30/3/4/42/6/9/50/9/65/72/3/6/7/ 88/97/9, 9601/4/6/13/4/6/9/21/6/9/32/3/9/ 42/4-6/52/4/6/8/69/70.

Diesel locomotives were completely renumbered with the exception of No 10000 (and one not renumbered to its allotted number 13000).

4-4-2T Class 3P

35 locomotives built as Nos 2110-34 and 2151-60 and renumbered 41928-52/69-78 by British Railways in 1948-9.

No	New	Wdn	No	New	Wdn	No	New	Wdn	No	New	Wdn
2110	5/23	2/59	2119	8/23	3/52	2128	6/27	2/59	2153	2/30	2/55
2111	6/23	8/51	2120	8/25	2/55	2129	6/27	11/60	2154	2/30	2/55
2112	6/23	8/52	2121	8/25	2/59	2130	6/27	2/59	2155	2/30	2/55
2113	7/23	3/51	2122	8/25	4/56	2131	6/27	4/60	2156	2/30	2/55
2114	7/23	8/51	2123	8/25	2/59	2132	7/27	2/59	2157	2/30	11/59
2115	7/23	8/51	2124	8/25	11/56	2133	7/27	11/56	2158	2/30	11/56
2116	7/23	8/51	2125	5/27	2/56	2134	7/27	11/56	2159	3/30	2/59
2117	8/23	9/51	2126	5/27	11/56	2151	1/30	4/60	2160	3/30	2/59
2118	8/23	9/58	2127	6/27	2/59	2152	1/30	11/56			

0-6-2T Class 4F

4 locomotives built as North Staffordshire Railway Nos 1, 2, 10 and 48 in early 1923 and renumbered 2270-3.

No	New	Wdn	No	New	Wdn	No	New	wdn	No	New	Wdn
2270	-/23	10/37	2271	-/23	10/37	2272	-/23	8/35	2273	-/23	2/37

All four were built with superheater boilers but No 2272 was fitted with a saturated boiler in 6/32.

0-8-4T Class 7F

30 locomotives built to LNWR design.

No	New	Wdn	No	New	Wdn	No	New	Wdn	No	New	Wdn
7930	2/23	8/48	7938	6/23	2/48	7946	8/23	12/47	7953	10/23	5/45
7931	2/23	12/51	7939	6/23	11/50	7947	8/23	8/44	7954	11/23	10/48
7932	2/23	9/49	7940	7/23	1/46	7948	9/23	7/48	7955	10/23	8/46
7933	5/23	6/50	7941	7/23	12/46	7949	9/23	10/46	7956	11/23	11/48
7934	5/23	5/46	7942	7/23	11/44	7950	10/23	6/46	7957	11/23	12/45
7935	5/23	9/46	7943	8/23	2/47	7951	10/23	1/49	7958	11/23	12/48
7936	5/23	6/49	7944	8/23	11/47	7952	10/23	8/45	7959	1/24	6/48
7937	5/23	10/50	7945	8/23	9/46						

Nos 7930-42 entered service as LNWR Nos 380, 782, 1189, 1677, 1976, 256 731, 739, 1908, 1956, 468, 792, 793 respectively; Nos 7943/4 were allotted LNWR series numbers 1904 and 609.
No 7957 was altered to No 27957 erroneously in 4/34 but immediately reverted to 7957; No 7943 became No 27943 in 2/45.

4-6-0 Class 4P

1 locomotive built to LNWR design.

No	New	Wdn
5845	3/24	11/47

- became No 25845 in 9/34

2-8-0 Class 7F

20 Government surplus locomotives purchased in 1927.

ROD No	LMS No	New	LMS date	1931 No	Wdn	ROD No	LMS No	New	LMS date	1931 No	Wdn
1891	9646	7/18	9/27	-	12/29	1865	9649	4/18	9/27	9479	11/31
1835	9647	12/17	10/27	9477	8/31	1871	9650	4/18	11/27	-	11/29
1837	9648	12/17	4/28	9478	8/31	1924	9651	6/18	4/28	-	12/29

ROD No	LMS No	New	LMS date	1931 No	Wdn		ROD No	LMS No	New	LMS date	1931 No	Wdn
1926	9652	6/18	10/27	9480	9/31		1803	9659	9/17	4/28	-	11/29
1938	9653	8/18	10/27	-	12/30		1877	9660	5/18	5/28	-	10/31
1832	9654	11/17	12/27	9481	2/32		1602	9661	1/18	4/28	-	11/31
1912	9655	4/18	3/28	9482	10/31		1801	9662	8/17	3/28	-	2/32
1851	9656	2/18	11/27	-	12/29		1888	9663	7/18	3/28	-	12/30
1934	9657	7/18	2/28	-	12/29		1918	9664	5/18	4/28	-	12/30
1850	9658	2/18	4/28	-	11/29		1853	9665	3/18	7/28	-	12/29

os 9649/52/4/5 became Nos 9479-82 in 9/31 (Nos 9647/8 were not alt-
red to Nos 9477/8).

4-6-0 Class 5P

1 locomotives built to LYR design.

No	New	Wdn	No	New	Wdn	No	New	Wdn	No	New	Wdn
0434	1/23	8/34	10445	5/23	2/36	10455	6/24	10/51	10465	10/24	1/37
0435	1/23	2/36	10446	5/23	6/46	10456	6/24	3/36	10466	10/24	8/35
0436	2/23	11/36	10447	6/23	11/34	10457	8/24	8/36	10467	11/24	1/37
0437	2/23	10/46	10448	6/23	10/49	10458	8/24	11/35	10468	11/24	2/36
0438	2/23	6/36	10449	7/23	3/36	10459	8/24	2/36	10469	11/24	10/35
0439	4/23	10/35	10450	7/23	6/36	10460	8/24	12/47	10470	12/24	8/35
0440	4/23	5/36	10451	7/23	8/36	10461	9/24	5/35	10471	1/25	2/36
0441	4/23	11/34	10452	7/23	6/36	10462	9/24	10/35	10472	1/25	2/35
0442	4/23	8/50	10453	7/23	4/34	10463	9/24	9/35	10473	1/25	2/37
0443	4/23	4/36	10454	7/23	3/36	10464	10/24	6/39	10474	2/25	12/35
0444	5/23	2/37									

os 10434-46 entered service as LYR Nos 1663-75 (Nos 10447-74 were to
ave been LYR Nos 1676-83/94-9, 1700-13).
o 10456 was rebuilt as a four-cylinder compound in 7/26.

4-6-4T Class 5P

0 locomotives built to LYR design.

No	New	Wdn	No	New	Wdn	No	New	Wdn	No	New	Wdn
1110	3/24	1/42	11113	4/24	2/39	11116	5/24	8/38	11118	5/24	11/41
1111	3/24	1/40	11114	4/24	7/41	11117	5/24	6/41	11119	6/24	11/41
1112	4/24	7/38	11115	4/24	6/38						

4-6-0 Class 4P

0 locomotives built to Caledonian Railway design.

No	New	Wdn	No	New	Wdn	No	New	Wdn	No	New	Wdn
4630	7/25	1/51	14635	6/26	1/52	14640	8/26	10/52	14645	11/26	7/50
4631	11/25	5/48	14636	6/26	2/53	14641	9/26	11/48	14646	11/26	3/49
4632	1/26	7/47	14637	7/26	3/48	14642	9/26	10/49	14647	11/26	3/51
4633	1/26	3/46	14638	7/26	5/51	14643	10/26	2/48	14648	12/26	11/51
4634	5/26	11/52	14639	8/26	12/53	14644	10/26	4/48	14649	12/26	9/51

0-4-4T Class 2P

No	New	Wdn	No	New	Wdn	No	New	Wdn	No	New	Wdn
5260	5/25	12/62	15263	5/25	11/61	15266	6/25	9/61	15268	6/25	9/61
5261	5/25	9/61	15264	6/25	9/61	15267	6/25	10/61	15269	6/25	3/62
5262	5/25	10/61	15265	6/25	9/61						

2-6-2T Class 3P

70 locomotives built as Nos 15500-69 and renumbered 1-70 in 1934.

No	New	Wdn	No	New	Wdn	No	New	Wdn	No	New	Wdn
1	3/30	1/61	19	12/30	12/59	37	5/31	7/61	54	9/31	2/6
2	3/30	11/59	20	12/30	7/61	38	5/31	7/61	55	9/31	11/5
3	3/30	2/61	21	12/30	9/59	39	5/31	12/59	56	10/31	11/5
4	3/30	11/59	22	1/31	12/62	40	5/31	12/59	57	10/31	3/6
5	4/30	2/59	23	1/31	11/59	41	5/31	9/60	58	10/31	11/5
6	4/30	10/62	24	1/31	3/62	42	6/31	7/61	59	10/31	11/5
7	4/30	7/61	25	1/31	12/59	43	6/31	11/59	60	11/31	12/5
8	4/30	11/59	26	2/31	11/62	44	6/31	11/59	61	9/32	12/5
9	4/30	5/62	27	2/31	11/59	45	7/31	11/59	62	10/32	11/6
10	5/30	7/61	28	2/31	12/60	46	7/31	11/59	63	10/32	9/6
11	5/30	8/60	29	2/31	7/61	47	7/31	11/59	64	10/32	7/6
12	5/30	11/60	30	3/31	8/59	48	7/31	11/59	65	10/32	11/5
13	5/30	12/59	31	3/31	11/62	49	8/31	7/61	66	10/32	11/5
14	5/30	5/60	32	3/31	7/61	50	8/31	5/61	67	10/32	12/5
15	6/30	3/61	33	3/31	9/61	51	8/31	4/61	68	11/32	12/5
16	11/30	7/61	34	4/31	7/61	52	8/31	9/59	69	11/32	12/5
17	11/30	11/59	35	4/31	7/61	53	9/31	2/61	70	11/32	3/6
18	12/30	7/61	36	4/31	6/60						

Nos 21-40 were built with condensing gear (No 21 had this gear removed in 6/44).
The following were fitted with vacuum control gear for motor trains:-
10 9/37; 12 3/47; 17 12/54; 20 5/35; 43 4/35; 45 12/54; 56 9/39;
57 11/39; 58 3/39; 59 5/39; 60 4/39; 61 5/39.
(No 12 was fitted with gear removed fron No 58).

2-6-2T Class 3P

139 locomotives.

No	New	Wdn	No	New	Wdn	No	New	Wdn	No	New	Wdn
71	2/35	12/61	100	6/35	8/62	129	9/35	10/61	158	10/37	1/6
72	2/35	8/62	101	6/35	10/61	130	9/35	10/61	159	10/37	12/6
73	2/35	8/62	102	6/35	10/61	131	9/35	10/61	160	10/37	11/5
74	3/35	11/61	103	6/35	10/61	132	9/35	10/61	161	11/37	11/6
75	3/35	7/61	104	6/35	9/62	133	10/35	10/61	162	11/37	10/6
76	3/35	10/61	105	6/35	7/62	134	10/35	10/61	163	11/37	11/59
77	3/35	7/61	106	6/35	11/62	135	10/35	11/62	164	11/37	10/6
78	3/35	11/62	107	6/35	9/61	136	10/35	10/61	165	11/37	10/6
79	3/35	10/61	108	7/35	11/61	137	10/35	11/62	166	12/37	10/6
80	3/35	9/62	109	7/35	7/62	138	10/35	9/62	167	12/37	10/6
81	3/35	10/61	110	7/35	5/62	139	10/35	10/59	168	12/37	10/6
82	3/35	2/62	111	7/35	10/61	140	10/35	11/61	169	12/37	10/59
83	3/35	11/62	112	7/35	11/62	141	11/35	10/61	170	12/37	1/6
84	4/35	11/59	113	8/35	7/62	142	11/35	7/61	171	12/37	5/61
85	4/35	7/62	114	8/35	11/62	143	11/35	10/61	172	12/37	11/59
86	4/35	11/62	115	8/35	10/61	144	11/35	12/61	173	1/38	7/6
87	4/35	11/62	116	8/35	11/62	145	7/37	9/62	174	1/38	6/6
88	4/35	7/62	117	8/35	11/62	146	8/37	8/62	175	3/38	10/61
89	4/35	8/62	118	8/35	8/61	147	8/37	11/62	176	3/38	12/6
90	4/35	7/62	119	8/35	8/62	148	8/37	8/62	177	4/38	10/6
91	5/35	10/61	120	8/35	10/62	149	8/37	10/61	178	4/38	10/6
92	5/35	5/61	121	8/35	10/61	150	9/37	12/62	179	4/38	2/6
93	5/35	1/62	122	8/35	6/62	151	9/37	12/62	180	4/38	1/6
94	5/35	10/61	123	9/35	10/61	152	9/37	1/62	181	4/38	3/6
95	5/35	10/61	124	9/35	8/61	153	9/37	12/62	182	5/38	10/6
96	5/35	11/59	125	9/35	11/59	154	9/37	1/62	183	5/38	10/6
97	5/35	6/61	126	9/35	5/61	155	10/37	5/61	184	5/38	10/6
98	6/35	11/62	127	9/35	11/59	156	10/37	10/61	185	10/37	2/6
99	6/35	10/62	128	9/35	7/62	157	10/37	11/62	186	10/37	12/6

No	New	Wdn	No	New	Wdn	No	New	Wdn	No	New	Wdn
187	10/37	12/62	193	12/37	8/62	199	1/38	10/61	205	3/38	11/62
188	10/37	12/62	194	12/37	10/61	200	1/38	12/62	206	3/38	2/62
189	11/37	12/62	195	12/37	11/61	201	2/38	7/62	207	4/38	2/62
190	11/37	11/62	196	1/38	12/62	202	2/38	9/62	208	4/38	10/61
191	12/37	9/62	197	1/38	7/62	203	2/38	7/62	209	4/38	10/61
192	12/37	12/61	198	1/38	7/62	204	3/38	11/59			

e following were fitted with 6A boilers (longer firebox):
83 7/43; 87 6/37; 114 8/38; 139 11/38.
e following were fitted with 6B boilers (larger barrel and superheater):
42 6/56; 148 11/42; 163 2/41; 167 4/56; 169 12/40; 203 7/42.

4-4-0 Class 2P

8 locomotives (including 3 replacements for those transferred to the merset & Dorset Joint Committee).

No	New	Wdn	No	New	Wdn	No	New	Wdn	No	New	Wdn
563	3/28	5/62	598	10/28	11/59	633	6/28	11/59	667	1/32	11/59
564	4/28	2/62	599	11/28	5/59	634	6/28	5/62	668	1/32	10/61
565	4/28	11/59	600	11/28	4/59	635	7/28	2/61	669	1/32	9/61
566	4/28	9/61	601	5/28	12/59	636	8/31	11/59	670	1/32	12/62
567	4/28	8/59	602	11/28	10/61	637	8/31	9/61	671	1/32	11/60
568	4/28	11/59	603	11/28	7/61	638	8/31	5/62	672	2/32	10/62
569	5/28	11/61	604	11/28	6/61	639	8/31	11/34	673	2/32	11/59
570	5/28	8/61	605	11/28	10/59	640	8/31	9/61	674	2/32	11/59
571	5/28	7/61	606	11/28	5/59	641	8/31	10/61	675	2/32	8/59
572	11/28	7/61	607	11/28	7/59	642	8/31	10/61	676	2/32	8/57
573	5/28	5/59	608	11/28	9/59	643	8/31	10/61	677	2/32	11/59
574	6/28	4/61	609	11/28	10/61	644	8/31	11/59	678	3/32	7/61
575	10/29	8/61	610	12/28	5/59	645	8/31	10/61	679	3/32	11/59
576	10/29	11/59	611	12/28	9/59	646	9/31	5/62	680	3/32	11/59
577	6/28	7/61	612	12/28	10/61	647	9/31	10/61	681	4/32	8/62
578	7/28	11/61	613	10/29	10/61	648	9/31	9/61	682	4/32	2/61
579	7/28	7/61	614	10/29	10/61	649	9/31	11/59	683	4/32	3/61
580	10/29	2/61	615	11/29	10/61	650	9/31	9/61	684	4/32	7/61
581	7/28	10/60	616	11/29	7/59	651	9/31	11/61	685	4/32	7/61
582	7/28	12/59	617	11/29	11/59	652	9/31	5/60	686	10/32	10/61
583	7/28	9/60	618	11/29	9/61	653	9/31	11/59	687	10/32	10/61
584	8/28	10/60	619	11/29	10/61	654	10/31	12/59	688	10/32	7/59
585	8/28	2/61	620	11/29	10/61	655	10/31	11/59	689	10/32	10/61
586	8/28	4/61	621	11/29	10/61	656	10/31	11/59	690	11/32	10/60
587	8/28	8/59	622	11/29	5/61	657	10/31	10/62	691	11/32	2/61
588	8/28	11/60	623	12/29	8/61	658	10/31	11/59	692	11/32	7/61
589	8/28	11/59	624	12/29	8/61	659	10/31	7/61	693	11/32	7/59
590	9/28	6/59	625	12/29	10/61	660	12/31	11/59	694	11/32	11/62
591	9/28	11/34	626	12/29	10/61	661	12/31	11/61	695	11/32	3/61
592	9/28	12/61	627	12/29	2/61	662	12/31	9/54	696	11/32	5/62
593	9/28	8/61	628	12/29	1/61	663	12/31	9/61	697	11/32	2/62
594	9/28	11/59	629	1/30	4/61	664	12/31	7/62	698	11/32	7/60
595	9/28	6/61	630	1/30	10/60	665	12/31	6/62	699	12/32	12/59
596	9/28	9/61	631	1/30	8/60	666	1/32	7/59	700	12/32	8/62
597	10/28	8/61	632	1/30	2/61						

s 633-5 were built as Nos 575/6/80 but became SDJC Nos 44-6 before en-
ing traffic; the 1929 built Nos 575/6/80 were their repalcements.

4-4-0 Class 4P

locomotives.

o	New	Wdn	No	New	Wdn	No	New	Wdn	No	New	Wdn
00	4/27	4/56	901	4/27	6/54	902	4/27	8/56	903	4/27	8/55

No	New	Wdn	No	New	Wdn	No	New	Wdn	No	New	Wdn
904	4/27	3/57	1057	5/24	4/53	1105	11/25	9/57	1153	9/25	10/57
905	4/27	11/53	1058	5/24	2/54	1106	11/25	7/58	1154	9/25	8/55
906	4/27	1/55	1059	6/24	11/55	1107	11/25	9/55	1155	9/25	2/57
907	4/27	9/60	1060	6/24	2/58	1108	11/25	1/57	1156	9/25	8/58
908	5/27	7/55	1061	6/24	5/55	1109	11/25	12/52	1157	9/25	5/60
909	5/27	6/56	1062	6/24	5/59	1110	11/25	8/54	1158	9/25	8/59
910	6/27	5/56	1063	7/24	10/60	1111	11/25	5/58	1159	10/25	4/58
911	6/27	12/52	1064	7/24	1/57	1112	11/25	10/57	1160	9/25	10/56
912	6/27	4/55	1065	7/24	3/56	1113	11/25	12/58	1161	9/25	11/59
913	6/27	8/55	1066	8/24	5/58	1114	12/25	5/58	1162	9/25	6/60
914	6/27	8/54	1067	8/24	2/55	1115	6/25	5/54	1163	9/25	11/58
915	6/27	12/55	1068	8/24	11/58	1116	7/25	11/57	1164	9/25	10/58
916	6/27	7/55	1069	9/24	11/55	1117	8/25	4/55	1165	9/25	2/59
917	6/27	12/56	1070	9/24	11/55	1118	8/25	1/58	1166	9/25	9/56
918	6/27	12/52	1071	9/24	3/58	1119	9/25	11/58	1167	10/25	10/58
919	7/27	1/54	1072	9/24	10/55	1120	10/25	6/59	1168	10/25	7/61
920	7/27	5/58	1073	10/24	8/57	1121	10/25	2/59	1169	10/25	7/59
921	7/27	11/55	1074	10/24	2/54	1122	11/25	12/58	1170	11/25	4/56
922	7/27	12/52	1075	10/24	5/57	1123	11/25	12/59	1171	11/25	12/52
923	7/27	10/54	1076	11/24	5/55	1124	11/25	1/55	1172	11/25	8/57
924	7/27	3/55	1077	11/24	4/57	1125	12/25	1/53	1173	11/25	1/59
925	5/27	11/59	1078	11/24	9/58	1126	12/25	10/56	1174	11/25	2/54
926	5/27	7/57	1079	11/24	10/56	1127	12/25	8/55	1175	11/25	4/59
927	5/27	7/57	1080	11/24	1/54	1128	12/25	3/56	1176	11/25	1/59
928	6/27	3/58	1081	11/24	11/55	1129	12/25	5/55	1177	11/25	11/59
929	5/27	6/56	1082	11/24	3/54	1130	1/26	8/55	1178	11/25	12/53
930	5/27	4/57	1083	12/24	12/58	1131	1/26	3/26	1179	11/25	3/57
931	5/27	10/58	1084	12/24	6/54	1132	2/26	10/56	1180	11/25	3/57
932	5/27	5/56	1085	5/25	1/57	1133	2/26	9/54	1181	11/25	10/57
933	6/27	4/58	1086	5/25	4/58	1134	2/26	9/54	1182	11/25	12/52
934	6/27	3/57	1087	6/25	10/54	1135	6/25	8/55	1183	11/25	2/59
935	8/32	3/58	1088	6/25	12/56	1136	6/25	10/55	1184	12/25	6/53
936	8/32	1/61	1089	6/25	7/57	1137	7/25	4/56	1185	2/27	10/57
937	8/32	4/58	1090	7/25	12/58	1138	7/25	12/54	1186	2/27	9/57
938	9/32	8/56	1091	7/25	4/55	1139	7/25	9/54	1187	2/27	7/56
939	9/32	10/56	1092	7/25	7/53	1140	7/25	4/57	1188	3/27	11/53
1045	2/24	6/57	1093	7/25	6/58	1141	7/25	9/54	1189	3/27	6/58
1046	2/24	1/53	1094	7/25	1/59	1142	7/25	6/56	1190	3/27	1/58
1047	2/24	2/54	1095	8/25	1/58	1143	7/25	2/59	1191	3/27	3/56
1048	3/24	10/57	1096	8/25	4/54	1144	7/25	2/58	1192	3/27	5/57
1049	3/24	2/59	1097	8/25	5/56	1145	7/25	9/53	1193	3/27	10/58
1050	3/24	5/56	1098	8/25	5/57	1146	7/25	10/54	1194	3/27	9/57
1051	3/24	11/54	1099	9/25	11/53	1147	8/25	3/56	1195	3/27	11/57
1052	4/24	3/53	1100	9/25	3/59	1148	8/25	3/53	1196	3/27	6/54
1053	4/24	5/56	1101	9/25	8/59	1149	8/25	8/55	1197	3/27	5/57
1054	4/24	9/54	1102	10/25	12/58	1150	8/25	9/57	1198	3/27	11/5.
1055	4/24	3/53	1103	10/25	11/57	1151	8/25	1/57	1199	4/27	1/58
1056	5/24	10/53	1104	10/25	8/55	1152	9/25	3/58			

2-6-2T Class 2P

130 locomotives.

No	New	Wdn	No	New	Wdn	No	New	Wdn	No	New	Wdn
1200	12/46	7/65	1209	12/46	7/65	41218	9/48	7/65	41227	10/48	9/6
1201	12/46	7/65	41210	8/48	5/64	41219	9/48	10/65	41228	10/48	6/6
1202	12/46	11/66	41211	8/48	9/66	41220	9/48	11/66	41229	10/48	11/6
1203	12/46	9/63	41212	8/48	10/65	41221	9/48	7/65	41230	8/49	4/6
1204	12/46	12/66	41213	9/48	12/63	41222	9/48	12/66	41231	8/49	5/6
1205	12/46	2/64	41214	9/48	7/65	41223	10/48	3/66	41232	8/49	8/6
1206	12/46	3/66	41215	9/48	1/65	41224	10/48	7/67	41233	8/49	11/6
1207	12/46	12/66	41216	9/48	3/66	41225	10/48	9/64	41234	8/49	11/6
1208	12/46	7/65	41217	9/48	12/66	41226	10/48	9/64	41235	8/49	11/6

No	New	Wdn	No	New	Wdn	No	New	Wdn	No	New	Wdn
41236	9/49	10/62	41260	6/50	9/64	41284	11/50	3/67	41307	4/52	3/66
41237	9/49	9/64	41261	7/50	7/65	41285	11/50	12/66	41308	4/52	2/65
41238	9/49	4/65	41262	7/50	1/64	41286	11/50	11/66	41309	5/52	12/63
41239	9/49	5/64	41263	7/50	12/62	41287	11/50	7/66	41310	5/52	9/64
41240	9/49	9/63	41264	7/50	12/66	41288	12/50	10/62	41311	5/52	1/64
41241	9/49	12/66	41265	8/50	12/62	41289	12/50	1/63	41312	5/52	7/67
41242	9/49	7/65	41266	8/50	11/62	41290	9/51	3/66	41313	5/52	10/65
41243	10/49	7/65	41267	8/50	11/62	41291	9/51	2/66	41314	5/52	6/65
41244	10/49	11/66	41268	8/50	7/64	41292	9/51	9/63	41315	5/52	6/64
41245	10/49	12/63	41269	8/50	12/62	41293	10/51	3/65	41316	6/52	10/66
41246	10/49	9/62	41270	9/50	4/65	41294	10/51	9/66	41317	6/52	12/64
41247	10/49	11/62	41271	9/50	10/62	41295	10/51	4/67	41318	6/52	10/63
41248	11/49	11/64	41272	9/50	10/65	41296	10/51	3/66	41319	6/52	7/67
41249	11/49	3/66	41273	9/50	12/63	41297	10/51	10/63	41320	1/52	7/67
41250	11/49	11/63	41274	9/50	1/63	41298	10/51	7/67	41321	2/52	7/65
41251	11/49	11/66	41275	10/50	10/65	41299	11/51	10/66	41322	2/52	6/64
41252	11/49	11/62	41276	10/50	12/63	41300	3/52	9/64	41323	3/52	6/64
41253	11/49	4/64	41277	10/50	11/62	41301	3/52	9/66	41324	3/52	10/65
41254	11/49	11/62	41278	10/50	11/62	41302	3/52	10/63	41325	3/52	5/65
41255	11/49	6/62	41279	10/50	12/63	41303	3/52	9/64	41326	4/52	5/64
41256	12/49	6/62	41280	10/50	12/62	41304	3/52	11/66	41327	4/52	5/64
41257	12/49	6/62	41281	10/50	11/63	41305	4/52	5/65	41328	5/52	6/64
41258	12/49	9/62	41282	10/50	11/63	41306	4/52	12/63	41329	5/52	6/64
41259	12/49	6/62	41283	11/50	3/66						

0-4-4T Class 2P

10 locomotives built as Nos 6400-9 and renumbered 1900-9 in 1946.

No	New	Wdn	No	New	Wdn	No	New	Wdn	No	New	Wdn
1900	12/32	3/62	1903	12/32	11/59	1906	12/32	11/59	1908	12/32	11/59
1901	12/32	11/59	1904	12/32	11/59	1907	12/32	11/59	1909	1/33	11/59
1902	12/32	11/59	1905	12/32	11/59						

All were fitted with vacuum control gear for motor trains:-
1900 9/50; 1902   9/50; 1904 9/50; 1906 3/57; 1908 7/34; 1909 3/34
1901 2/51; 1903 9/50; 1905 1/51; 1907 4/51

2-6-4T Class 4P

645 locomotives (Nos 2300-2424 were parallel boiler type, remainder taper boilered; Nos 2500-36 had three-cylinders).

No	New	Wdn	No	New	Wdn	No	New	Wdn	No	New	Wdn
2050	9/50	4/65	42070	11/50	6/65	42090	4/51	6/64	42110	5/49	6/66
2051	9/50	7/65	42071	11/50	3/67	42091	4/51	10/63	42111	6/49	12/62
2052	9/50	5/67	42072	11/50	9/67	42092	5/51	7/64	42112	6/49	7/65
2053	10/50	6/65	42073	11/50	9/67	42093	5/51	9/67	42113	6/49	7/65
2054	10/50	7/64	42074	11/50	9/66	42094	5/51	11/62	42114	6/49	6/65
2055	10/50	7/64	42075	11/50	5/65	42095	6/51	6/66	42115	7/49	11/66
2066	11/50	10/64	42076	12/50	3/67	42096	7/50	12/66	42116	7/49	6/67
2067	11/50	7/64	42077	12/50	6/64	42097	7/50	12/66	42117	8/49	12/62
2058	11/50	8/66	42078	12/50	6/66	42098	7/50	2/63	42118	8/49	9/65
2059	11/50	6/64	42079	1/51	5/67	42099	8/50	12/64	42119	8/49	8/65
2060	12/50	4/65	42080	1/51	1/67	42100	8/50	2/63	42120	8/49	9/63
2061	12/50	9/65	42081	1/51	5/67	42101	9/50	2/63	42121	9/49	7/66
2062	12/50	5/65	42082	1/51	6/65	42102	9/50	12/66	42122	9/49	12/62
2063	12/50	10/63	42083	2/51	4/67	42103	9/50	5/65	42123	10/49	2/64
2064	12/50	6/65	42084	2/51	12/64	42104	9/50	9/65	42124	10/49	1/64
2065	12/50	7/65	42085	2/51	9/67	42105	9/50	12/66	42125	10/49	12/66
2066	10/50	8/67	42086	3/51	3/67	42106	10/50	5/65	42126	11/49	10/64
2067	10/50	2/63	42087	3/51	10/66	42107	3/49	2/66	42127	11/49	10/64
2068	10/50	12/63	42088	3/51	10/62	42108	3/49	12/66	42128	11/49	11/66
2069	10/50	11/66	42089	4/51	10/64	42109	4/49	6/65	42129	12/49	9/65

No	New	Wdn	No	New	Wdn	No	New	Wdn	No	New	Wdn
42130	12/49	12/62	2194	2/48	8/65	2258	11/46	12/62	2322	5/28	7/65
42131	12/49	8/65	2195	2/48	4/66	2259	12/46	10/65	2323	6/28	6/62
42132	12/49	6/66	2196	2/48	5/67	2260	12/46	5/66	2324	6/28	11/62
42133	1/50	3/67	2197	3/48	5/66	2261	12/46	2/64	2325	1/29	9/61
42134	1/50	3/67	2198	3/48	5/65	2262	12/46	10/64	2326	2/29	6/60
42135	1/50	2/64	2199	3/48	9/65	2263	12/46	7/64	2327	2/29	8/65
42136	2/50	1/63	2200	10/45	6/64	2264	12/46	7/66	2328	2/29	9/61
42137	2/50	1/64	2201	11/45	7/64	2265	1/47	10/65	2329	2/29	9/61
42138	3/50	9/67	2202	11/45	5/65	2266	1/47	3/66	2330	2/29	12/61
42139	3/50	12/65	2203	11/45	12/62	2267	1/47	5/67	2331	3/29	8/62
42140	4/50	6/63	2204	11/45	12/66	2268	1/47	12/62	2332	3/29	9/61
42141	4/50	9/67	2205	11/45	12/62	2269	2/47	6/67	2333	3/29	5/63
42142	5/50	6/66	2206	11/45	4/63	2270	2/47	1/63	2334	3/29	12/65
42143	5/50	10/64	2207	11/45	12/62	2271	2/47	12/66	2335	3/29	4/64
42144	6/50	12/62	2208	12/45	7/64	2272	3/47	12/62	2336	4/29	10/62
42145	6/50	8/67	2209	12/45	2/65	2273	5/47	9/66	2337	3/29	12/63
42146	8/50	10/62	2210	12/45	5/67	2274	6/47	5/67	2338	4/29	1/64
42147	4/48	4/65	2211	12/45	12/62	2275	6/47	6/64	2339	4/29	9/63
42148	5/48	12/64	2212	12/45	8/65	2276	7/47	12/62	2340	4/29	6/62
42149	5/48	6/67	2213	12/45	1/66	2277	7/47	8/66	2341	4/29	10/59
42150	5/48	12/66	2214	12/45	2/65	2278	7/47	4/64	2342	4/29	6/62
42151	5/48	9/63	2215	12/45	12/62	2279	8/47	7/63	2343	4/29	10/65
42152	5/48	9/67	2216	12/45	7/66	2280	8/47	3/64	2344	5/29	5/61
42153	6/48	8/64	2217	12/45	9/61	2281	8/47	4/63	2345	5/29	5/60
42154	6/48	1/67	2218	1/46	10/64	2282	8/47	9/64	2346	5/29	9/60
42155	6/48	5/65	2219	1/46	6/62	2283	9/47	9/67	2347	5/29	9/62
42156	6/48	2/66	2220	2/46	12/61	2284	9/47	12/64	2348	5/29	9/61
42157	6/48	7/63	2221	2/46	9/64	2285	9/47	8/65	2349	6/29	7/61
42158	7/48	4/65	2222	3/46	5/65	2286	9/47	12/64	2350	6/29	2/65
42159	7/48	6/66	2223	4/46	6/62	2287	10/47	6/67	2351	6/29	8/62
42160	7/48	5/65	2224	4/46	1/67	2288	10/47	9/63	2352	6/29	4/62
42161	8/48	12/66	2225	4/46	6/66	2289	10/47	5/65	2353	6/29	6/64
42162	8/48	12/62	2226	5/46	6/64	2290	10/47	9/62	2354	6/29	11/59
42163	8/48	6/64	2227	5/46	12/62	2291	10/47	12/64	2355	6/29	11/63
42164	8/48	12/62	2228	5/46	9/63	2292	11/47	5/64	2356	7/29	9/61
42165	9/48	2/65	2229	5/46	1/64	2293	11/47	4/63	2357	7/29	3/62
42166	9/48	10/63	2230	6/46	8/65	2294	11/47	5/63	2358	7/29	10/62
42167	9/48	6/64	2231	6/46	6/63	2295	11/47	10/65	2359	7/29	10/64
42168	9/48	3/64	2232	6/46	1/66	2296	11/47	7/65	2360	7/29	8/61
42169	9/48	2/66	2233	6/46	4/67	2297	12/47	5/67	2361	7/29	1/64
42170	10/48	10/65	2234	7/46	2/64	2298	12/47	11/62	2362	8/29	5/62
42171	10/48	6/64	2235	7/46	6/67	2299	12/47	3/65	2363	8/29	12/61
42172	10/48	12/62	2236	7/46	5/67	2300	11/27	11/60	2364	8/29	9/61
42173	10/48	12/62	2237	8/46	12/62	2301	12/27	10/63	2365	8/29	10/60
42174	10/48	8/65	2238	8/46	10/63	2302	12/27	9/61	2366	8/29	4/64
42175	11/48	12/62	2239	9/46	4/64	2303	12/27	10/62	2367	9/29	8/62
42176	11/48	6/66	2240	9/46	4/66	2304	1/28	9/62	2368	9/29	6/65
42177	11/48	12/66	2241	9/46	11/65	2305	1/28	8/62	2369	9/29	5/65
42178	11/48	6/63	2242	9/46	7/64	2306	1/28	12/62	2370	9/29	6/62
42179	12/48	3/65	2243	9/46	8/65	2307	1/28	7/61	2371	9/29	4/62
42180	12/48	11/63	2244	9/46	6/64	2308	1/28	8/59	2372	9/29	12/62
42181	12/48	10/66	2245	10/46	10/64	2309	2/28	9/64	2373	10/29	11/60
42182	12/48	4/63	2246	10/46	6/64	2310	2/28	2/63	2374	10/29	9/65
42183	1/49	9/66	2247	10/46	8/65	2311	2/28	4/64	2375	5/32	2/62
42184	1/49	12/66	2248	10/46	12/62	2312	2/28	11/59	2376	5/32	11/62
42185	2/49	4/64	2249	10/46	7/66	2313	3/28	11/63	2377	5/32	5/61
42186	2/49	6/64	2250	10/46	12/64	2314	3/28	12/62	2378	6/32	4/64
2187	12/47	5/67	2251	10/46	9/67	2315	3/28	12/62	2379	6/32	7/64
2188	12/47	5/63	2252	11/46	9/67	2316	3/28	2/63	2380	6/32	12/60
2189	12/47	9/67	2253	11/46	6/63	2317	3/28	8/65	2381	6/32	5/65
2190	1/48	6/64	2254	11/46	6/62	2318	4/28	9/62	2382	7/32	9/61
2191	1/48	12/62	2255	11/46	6/62	2319	4/28	10/63	2383	7/32	9/61
2192	1/48	5/64	2256	11/46	6/64	2320	4/28	11/62	2384	7/32	8/63
2193	1/48	12/62	2257	11/46	6/62	2321	5/28	11/59	2385	5/33	9/62

No	New	Wdn	No	New	Wdn	No	New	Wdn	No	New	Wdn
2386	5/33	9/61	2450	7/36	6/60	2519	9/34	6/62	2583	10/36	10/66
2387	5/33	3/62	2451	7/36	10/64	2520	9/34	6/62	2584	10/36	7/64
2388	5/33	11/62	2452	7/36	3/62	2521	9/34	11/61	2585	10/36	11/62
2389	6/33	3/63	2453	8/36	5/64	2522	9/34	6/62	2586	10/36	11/64
2390	6/33	9/60	2454	8/36	12/62	2523	9/34	6/62	2587	10/36	6/67
2391	6/33	2/63	2455	8/36	3/66	2524	9/34	9/61	2588	10/36	10/64
2392	6/33	2/63	2456	8/36	4/65	2525	9/34	6/62	2589	10/36	9/64
2393	6/33	5/62	2457	8/36	11/62	2526	10/34	6/62	2590	10/36	2/65
2394	6/33	6/66	2458	9/36	10/63	2527	10/34	6/62	2591	10/36	9/62
2395	9/33	11/61	2459	9/36	1/65	2528	10/34	6/62	2592	10/36	5/63
2396	9/33	7/62	2460	9/36	8/65	2529	10/34	6/62	2593	10/36	6/62
2397	9/33	1/61	2461	9/36	3/64	2530	11/34	6/62	2594	11/36	4/64
2398	9/33	11/60	2462	10/36	5/66	2531	11/34	9/61	2595	11/36	9/63
2399	9/33	8/60	2463	10/36	1/64	2532	11/34	6/62	2596	11/36	8/62
2400	9/33	1/65	2464	10/36	8/65	2533	11/34	6/62	2597	11/36	10/65
2401	9/33	6/63	2465	10/36	2/65	2534	11/34	12/61	2598	11/36	11/63
2402	9/33	10/62	2466	10/36	1/63	2535	11/34	6/62	2599	11/36	9/62
2403	9/33	12/62	2467	11/36	10/61	2536	12/34	6/62	2600	11/36	11/62
2404	9/33	10/61	2468	11/36	9/65	2537	12/35	9/62	2601	11/36	3/65
2405	10/33	10/64	2469	11/36	5/63	2538	12/35	6/62	2602	11/36	12/64
2406	10/33	8/65	2470	11/36	9/62	2539	12/35	2/61	2603	12/36	5/63
2407	10/33	11/62	2471	12/36	10/61	2540	12/35	10/62	2604	12/36	5/65
2408	10/33	3/64	2472	12/36	10/62	2541	12/35	12/62	2605	12/36	12/64
2409	10/33	1/64	2473	12/36	10/62	2542	12/35	7/65	2606	12/36	10/66
2410	10/33	9/66	2474	12/36	10/64	2543	12/35	5/63	2607	12/36	1/64
2411	10/33	7/64	2475	12/36	10/61	2544	12/35	11/62	2608	12/36	8/64
2412	11/33	1/62	2476	1/37	9/62	2545	6/36	10/61	2609	12/36	2/65
2413	11/33	5/64	2477	1/37	6/65	2546	6/36	3/67	2610	1/37	4/66
2414	11/33	10/64	2478	1/37	2/65	2547	7/36	5/63	2611	1/37	5/67
2415	11/33	12/62	2479	1/37	10/61	2548	7/36	2/67	2612	1/37	1/64
2416	11/33	6/64	2480	2/37	1/63	2549	7/36	11/61	2613	1/37	4/67
2417	11/33	4/64	2481	2/37	9/64	2550	7/36	4/64	2614	1/37	5/64
2418	11/33	4/60	2482	2/37	4/65	2551	7/36	12/64	2615	2/37	9/62
2419	12/33	11/63	2483	2/37	9/62	2552	7/36	10/61	2616	2/37	9/67
2420	12/33	5/62	2484	3/37	1/66	2553	7/36	11/62	2617	2/37	11/63
2421	12/33	8/64	2485	3/37	6/63	2554	7/36	4/65	2618	6/38	7/65
2422	12/33	12/62	2486	3/37	5/63	2555	7/36	5/65	2619	6/38	5/64
2423	12/33	9/61	2487	3/37	9/63	2556	7/36	7/63	2620	7/38	9/64
2424	1/34	9/64	2488	4/37	2/65	2557	8/36	10/63	2621	7/38	10/62
2425	2/36	9/63	2489	4/37	11/64	2558	8/36	4/65	2622	7/38	2/67
2426	2/36	12/65	2490	4/37	5/60	2559	8/36	9/64	2623	7/38	2/64
2427	2/36	10/61	2491	4/37	9/63	2560	8/36	4/64	2624	7/38	11/62
2428	2/36	10/61	2492	5/37	6/65	2561	8/36	11/63	2625	8/38	5/66
2429	2/36	9/62	2493	5/37	4/64	2562	8/36	1/64	2626	8/38	10/65
2430	3/36	3/65	2494	5/37	8/65	2563	8/36	11/63	2627	8/38	10/61
2431	3/36	5/66	2500	4/34	6/62	2564	8/36	5/65	2628	9/38	1/64
2432	3/36	8/65	2501	4/34	6/62	2565	8/36	11/64	2629	9/38	10/64
2433	3/36	5/62	2502	4/34	6/62	2566	8/36	5/65	2630	9/38	9/64
2434	3/36	3/64	2503	4/34	6/62	2567	8/36	3/65	2631	9/38	9/64
2435	3/36	3/65	2504	4/34	5/62	2568	9/36	12/62	2632	9/38	6/63
2436	4/36	5/66	2505	6/34	6/62	2569	9/36	1/64	2633	9/38	1/64
2437	4/36	5/64	2506	6/34	8/61	2570	9/36	10/61	2634	9/38	1/65
2438	4/36	2/61	2507	6/34	5/61	2571	9/36	11/63	2635	9/38	10/61
2439	4/36	8/65	2508	6/34	6/62	2572	9/36	1/64	2636	10/38	5/63
2440	5/36	9/63	2509	6/34	6/62	2573	9/36	11/64	2637	10/38	10/61
2441	5/36	1/64	2510	6/34	8/61	2574	9/36	9/67	2638	10/38	12/62
2442	5/36	8/65	2511	6/34	6/62	2575	9/36	10/62	2639	11/38	9/64
2443	5/36	11/62	2512	7/34	11/60	2576	9/36	6/62	2640	11/38	9/64
2444	5/36	5/64	2513	7/34	6/62	2577	9/36	1/67	2641	11/38	9/62
2445	5/36	10/64	2514	7/34	4/62	2578	9/36	10/62	2642	11/38	9/62
2446	6/36	4/64	2515	8/34	6/62	2579	9/36	6/62	2643	11/38	12/63
2447	6/36	3/65	2516	8/34	6/62	2580	10/36	11/62	2644	11/38	3/67
2448	6/36	1/62	2517	8/34	6/62	2581	10/36	3/66	2645	12/38	9/65
2449	6/36	11/64	2518	8/34	6/62	2582	10/36	5/63	2646	12/38	9/62

No	New	Wdn	No	New	Wdn	No	New	Wdn	No	New	Wdn
2647	12/38	5/67	2661	5/41	9/62	2674	4/45	11/62	2687	7/45	6/62
2648	12/38	10/61	2662	6/41	12/64	2675	4/45	9/65	2688	8/45	5/65
2649	12/38	2/65	2663	6/42	3/67	2676	4/45	5/66	2689	8/45	9/67
2650	12/38	6/67	2664	7/42	11/66	2677	5/45	6/62	2690	8/45	12/66
2651	12/38	9/64	2665	8/42	6/67	2678	5/45	6/62	2691	8/45	10/66
2652	1/39	4/64	2666	8/42	9/62	2679	5/45	6/62	2692	9/45	12/62
2653	12/40	9/62	2667	10/42	2/65	2680	5/45	3/65	2693	9/45	9/66
2654	1/41	11/64	2668	11/42	8/63	2681	6/45	6/63	2694	9/45	12/66
2655	2/41	1/63	2669	12/42	10/61	2682	6/45	7/64	2695	10/45	6/64
2656	2/41	5/67	2670	12/42	12/64	2683	6/45	10/61	2696	10/45	8/64
2657	2/41	11/64	2671	1/43	12/62	2684	6/45	6/62	2697	10/45	1/67
2658	2/41	9/62	2672	2/43	6/62	2685	7/45	6/62	2698	10/45	9/63
2659	3/41	4/63	2673	3/45	8/65	2686	7/45	5/64	2699	10/45	5/67
2660	4/41	4/65									

The following were fitted with longer firebox (domed) boilers:-
2505 12/37; 2513 12/37; 2523 3/43; 2538 1/49.

2-6-0 Class 5P4F

285 locomotives built as Nos 13000-13284 and renumbered 2700-2984 in 1934-6 (Nos 2945-84 had taper boilers).

No	New	Wdn	No	New	Wdn	No	New	Wdn	No	New	Wdn
2700	5/26	3/66	2741	3/27	5/65	2782	9/27	11/66	2823	10/29	2/64
2701	7/26	12/64	2742	3/27	7/62	2783	9/27	8/65	2824	10/29	7/62
2702	9/26	1/66	2743	6/27	12/62	2784	9/27	12/62	2825	10/29	6/62
2703	10/26	9/64	2744	4/27	12/62	2785	10/27	11/63	2826	11/29	9/64
2704	10/26	9/63	2745	5/27	12/62	2786	10/27	11/62	2827	11/29	8/65
2705	12/26	12/64	2746	5/27	11/63	2787	10/27	4/65	2828	11/29	10/65
2706	12/26	11/63	2747	5/27	2/63	2788	10/27	9/64	2829	12/29	6/62
2707	1/27	9/64	2748	5/27	10/64	2789	10/27	11/66	2830	5/30	11/62
2708	2/27	7/64	2749	6/27	7/62	2790	10/27	7/63	2831	5/30	12/65
2709	2/27	4/64	2750	6/27	8/63	2791	10/27	1/65	2832	5/30	3/65
2710	2/27	8/65	2751	6/27	4/65	2792	10/27	10/63	2833	5/30	12/62
2711	3/27	8/63	2752	6/27	12/62	2793	10/27	12/64	2834	6/30	12/62
2712	3/27	2/66	2753	6/27	8/65	2794	11/27	11/63	2835	6/30	12/62
2713	3/27	11/62	2754	6/27	11/64	2795	11/27	11/66	2836	7/30	12/62
2714	3/27	9/62	2755	6/27	10/64	2796	11/27	10/63	2837	7/30	12/62
2715	4/27	2/66	2756	6/27	6/64	2797	11/27	3/62	2838	8/30	3/63
2716	5/27	4/65	2757	7/27	6/64	2798	12/27	11/63	2839	8/30	6/64
2717	5/27	10/64	2758	8/27	10/63	2799	12/27	1/65	2840	8/30	9/64
2718	5/27	5/63	2759	6/27	1/63	2800	12/28	10/65	2841	9/30	3/65
2719	6/27	1/64	2760	6/27	8/64	2801	12/28	6/66	2842	9/30	6/64
2720	6/27	12/62	2761	6/27	6/64	2802	12/28	6/64	2843	10/30	3/63
2721	8/27	10/63	2762	6/27	11/63	2803	12/28	11/66	2844	10/30	8/65
2722	8/27	1/65	2763	7/27	6/64	2804	12/28	12/62	2845	10/30	8/64
2723	9/27	8/63	2764	7/27	1/62	2805	12/28	10/63	2846	11/30	9/64
2724	10/27	8/62	2765	8/27	12/66	2806	12/28	12/63	2847	11/30	6/62
2725	10/27	10/64	2766	7/27	11/62	2807	12/28	12/62	2848	11/30	3/65
2726	11/27	10/62	2767	7/27	3/63	2808	1/29	12/62	2849	12/30	7/65
2727	11/27	1/67	2768	7/27	12/63	2809	1/29	12/62	2850	2/30	7/62
2728	11/27	2/63	2769	7/27	2/64	2810	4/29	12/63	2851	2/30	5/64
2729	12/27	10/63	2770	7/27	11/63	2811	5/29	7/62	2852	3/30	5/63
2730	12/26	6/65	2771	7/27	11/63	2812	5/29	6/66	2853	3/30	6/63
2731	12/26	2/64	2772	8/27	5/65	2813	6/29	11/63	2854	3/30	11/63
2732	12/26	6/65	2773	8/27	11/62	2814	6/29	8/65	2855	3/30	9/64
2733	12/26	2/65	2774	8/27	11/63	2815	6/29	9/64	2856	3/30	11/62
2734	12/26	3/66	2775	9/27	10/62	2816	6/29	9/64	2857	3/30	12/62
2735	12/26	11/63	2776	9/27	6/64	2817	7/29	4/65	2858	3/30	4/64
2736	2/27	11/66	2777	8/27	8/65	2818	7/29	5/62	2859	3/30	12/66
2737	1/27	11/66	2778	9/27	4/65	2819	8/29	9/65	2860	3/30	9/64
2738	2/27	5/64	2779	9/27	5/62	2820	8/29	4/64	2861	3/30	6/66
2739	2/27	11/66	2780	9/27	10/65	2821	8/29	3/63	2862	4/30	11/62
2740	3/27	1/66	2781	9/27	11/62	2822	9/29	6/62	2863	4/30	8/66

No	New	Wdn	No	New	Wdn	No	New	Wdn	No	New	Wdn
2864	4/30	7/61	2895	8/30	1/63	2925	5/31	11/64	2955	12/33	4/66
2865	4/30	11/63	2896	8/30	3/65	2926	5/31	10/64	2956	12/33	9/64
2866	4/30	10/62	2897	8/30	4/64	2927	5/31	7/62	2957	12/33	1/66
2867	4/30	6/64	2898	8/30	9/65	2928	5/31	2/63	2958	1/34	11/65
2868	4/30	6/62	2899	8/30	12/66	2929	5/31	8/62	2959	1/34	12/65
2869	5/30	7/65	2900	8/30	10/65	2930	5/31	7/61	2960	12/33	1/66
2870	5/30	3/63	2901	8/30	5/65	2931	6/31	9/64	2961	1/34	8/65
2871	5/30	9/63	2902	9/30	2/64	2932	6/31	4/65	2962	1/34	2/64
2872	5/30	12/63	2903	9/30	8/62	2933	6/31	3/63	2963	12/33	7/66
2873	5/30	8/63	2904	9/30	5/65	2934	6/31	10/64	2964	1/34	11/65
2874	5/30	10/62	2905	9/30	7/65	2935	12/32	1/63	2965	1/34	8/64
2875	5/30	12/62	2906	9/30	12/62	2936	12/32	7/65	2966	1/34	7/64
2876	5/30	12/62	2907	9/30	10/64	2937	12/32	5/65	2967	1/34	4/66
2877	5/30	12/62	2908	9/30	8/66	2938	12/32	9/65	2968	1/34	12/66
2878	6/30	9/65	2909	9/30	1/66	2939	12/32	6/62	2969	1/34	11/64
2879	6/30	9/65	2910	10/30	11/63	2940	12/32	9/65	2970	1/34	10/64
2880	6/30	11/64	2911	10/30	11/63	2941	12/32	5/65	2971	1/34	12/64
2881	6/30	11/62	2912	10/30	9/65	2942	12/32	1/67	2972	1/34	4/65
2882	6/30	12/62	2913	10/30	6/66	2943	12/32	5/64	2973	1/34	11/63
2883	6/30	12/62	2914	10/30	12/63	2944	12/32	4/63	2974	1/34	9/65
2884	6/30	12/62	2915	10/30	12/62	2945	10/33	3/66	2975	1/34	3/66
2885	7/30	12/63	2916	10/30	6/65	2946	11/33	11/65	2976	1/34	7/63
2886	7/30	3/65	2917	10/30	8/66	2947	11/33	12/65	2977	1/34	6/66
2887	7/30	9/62	2918	11/30	12/62	2948	11/33	10/65	2978	1/34	4/66
2888	7/30	2/64	2919	11/30	10/66	2949	12/33	11/63	2979	2/34	12/64
2889	7/30	5/62	2920	11/30	12/64	2950	12/33	10/65	2980	2/34	1/66
2890	7/30	5/63	2921	11/30	2/63	2951	11/33	3/66	2981	2/34	5/66
2891	8/30	10/62	2922	11/30	3/64	2952	12/33	9/64	2982	2/34	11/65
2892	8/30	5/65	2923	11/30	1/64	2953	12/33	1/66	2983	3/34	1/66
2893	8/30	7/61	2924	12/30	2/66	2954	12/33	2/67	2984	3/34	9/63
2894	8/30	12/64									

The following locomotives were modified with Lentz rotary cam poppet valves, replaced by Reidinger valve gear at the second date given:-
2818 12/31 11/53; 2824 1/32 1/54; 2825 2/32 11/52; 2829 1/32 6/53
2822 2/32 4/53

2-6-0 Class 4F

162 locomotives.

No	New	Wdn	No	New	Wdn	No	New	Wdn	No	New	Wdn
3000	12/47	9/67	43024	1/49	5/67	43048	11/49	5/67	43072	9/50	11/64
3001	12/47	9/67	43025	1/49	9/65	43049	11/49	8/67	43073	9/50	8/67
3002	12/47	12/67	43026	2/49	9/66	43050	7/50	9/67	43074	9/50	6/66
3003	1/48	9/67	43027	2/49	5/68	43051	8/50	1/67	43075	9/50	4/65
3004	1/48	9/67	43028	3/49	11/67	43052	8/50	11/66	43076	10/50	9/67
3005	1/48	11/65	43029	3/49	9/67	43053	8/50	4/64	43077	10/50	4/67
3006	1/48	2/68	43030	3/49	10/66	43054	8/50	12/66	43078	10/50	12/66
3007	1/48	9/67	43031	4/49	3/66	43055	9/50	7/67	43079	10/50	10/66
3008	1/48	2/68	43032	4/49	1/65	43056	9/50	12/66	43080	10/50	6/65
3009	3/48	11/66	43033	5/49	2/68	43057	9/50	12/66	43081	10/50	1/65
3010	3/48	12/67	43034	5/49	5/67	43058	9/50	12/64	43082	11/50	11/65
43011	3/48	2/67	43035	5/49	11/65	43059	9/50	1/65	43083	11/50	12/63
43012	4/48	4/67	43036	6/49	5/66	43060	9/50	12/64	43084	11/50	9/67
43013	4/48	10/65	43037	6/49	4/65	43061	9/50	1/64	43085	11/50	1/65
43014	4/48	4/66	43038	6/49	5/64	43062	11/50	6/65	43086	11/50	12/64
43015	5/48	7/67	43039	7/49	12/66	43063	11/50	9/67	43087	11/50	12/64
43016	5/48	1/66	43040	7/49	11/66	43064	11/50	6/65	43088	12/50	12/67
43017	5/48	11/67	43041	8/49	8/67	43065	11/50	1/65	43089	12/50	11/65
43018	5/48	10/66	43042	8/49	2/66	43066	12/50	1/67	43090	12/50	4/65
43019	6/48	5/68	43043	9/49	9/67	43067	12/50	4/65	43091	12/50	6/65
43020	12/48	10/66	43044	9/49	9/67	43068	12/50	1/64	43092	12/50	4/65
43021	12/48	9/67	43045	10/49	8/66	43069	12/50	9/66	43093	12/50	1/65
43022	12/48	11/66	43046	10/49	11/67	43070	8/50	9/67	43094	12/50	1/64
43023	1/49	12/67	43047	11/49	12/67	43071	9/50	3/67	43095	12/50	11/66

No	New	Wdn	No	New	Wdn	No	New	Wdn	No	New	Wdn
43096	12/50	2/67	43113	4/51	8/66	43130	11/51	6/67	43146	9/51	1/65
43097	1/51	1/67	43114	5/51	11/63	43131	11/51	12/63	43147	10/51	12/64
43098	2/51	5/67	43115	5/51	5/67	43132	12/51	12/66	43148	10/51	4/65
43099	2/51	12/66	43116	6/51	5/66	43133	12/51	12/66	43149	10/51	11/65
43100	2/51	2/67	43117	6/51	7/67	43134	12/51	2/65	43150	11/51	1/65
43101	2/51	3/67	43118	6/51	11/67	43135	12/51	10/66	43151	11/51	2/67
43102	3/51	12/66	43119	6/51	8/67	43136	1/52	7/64	43152	11/51	1/64
43103	3/51	11/66	43120	7/51	8/67	43137	7/51	9/67	43153	12/51	6/65
43104	3/51	1/64	43121	8/51	11/67	43138	7/51	3/67	43154	12/51	12/64
43105	3/51	5/67	43122	8/51	3/67	43139	7/51	9/67	43155	12/51	1/65
43106	4/51	6/68	43123	8/51	7/67	43140	8/51	5/67	43156	1/52	1/65
43107	5/51	12/63	43124	9/51	12/66	43141	8/51	10/66	43157	7/52	1/65
43108	5/51	11/65	43125	9/51	9/67	43142	8/51	12/63	43158	7/52	1/65
43109	6/51	11/65	43126	9/51	4/66	43143	8/51	6/65	43159	8/52	6/65
43110	6/51	12/63	43127	10/51	1/65	43144	9/51	4/65	43160	8/52	1/65
43111	7/51	6/65	43128	10/51	7/65	43145	9/51	1/65	43161	9/52	6/65
43112	3/51	9/67	43129	11/51	6/67						

0-6-0 Class 4F

575 locomotives (Nos 4557-61 were allotted to former SDJC locomotives of similar earlier Midland Railway type).

No	New	Wdn	No	New	Wdn	No	New	Wdn	No	New	Wdn
4027	11/24	11/64	4067	10/25	4/61	4107	12/24	8/61	4147	11/25	8/61
4028	11/24	10/65	4068	10/25	11/63	4108	1/25	12/59	4148	11/25	5/61
4029	12/24	7/60	4069	10/25	10/63	4109	2/25	5/64	4149	11/25	11/64
4030	12/24	3/64	4070	11/25	6/62	4110	3/25	3/64	4150	11/25	1/63
4031	12/24	4/60	4071	11/25	4/63	4111	3/25	8/61	4151	12/25	12/63
4032	12/24	11/59	4072	11/25	11/59	4112	3/25	1/63	4152	12/25	8/61
4033	12/24	10/61	4073	11/25	11/59	4113	5/25	1/66	4153	12/25	4/63
4034	12/24	6/63	4074	11/25	8/63	4114	5/25	5/63	4154	12/25	4/62
4035	1/25	2/65	4075	11/25	11/65	4115	5/25	7/65	4155	12/25	10/65
4036	1/25	6/62	4076	11/25	7/65	4116	5/25	11/59	4156	12/25	2/64
4037	1/25	8/61	4077	11/25	3/60	4117	6/25	9/64	4157	12/25	7/65
4038	1/25	4/64	4078	11/25	4/64	4118	6/25	5/65	4158	12/25	7/62
4039	1/25	5/64	4079	11/25	11/64	4119	6/25	12/63	4159	2/26	10/62
4040	1/25	11/64	4080	11/25	7/64	4120	7/25	11/59	4160	2/26	12/65
4041	2/25	6/64	4081	11/25	9/65	4121	7/25	1/65	4161	2/26	12/59
4042	2/25	10/64	4082	9/25	8/61	4122	7/25	9/62	4162	2/26	12/63
4043	2/25	6/65	4083	9/25	12/63	4123	7/25	6/65	4163	2/26	7/60
4044	2/25	7/65	4084	10/25	12/59	4124	7/25	5/64	4164	2/26	7/63
4045	3/25	11/64	4085	10/25	10/63	4125	8/25	3/65	4165	2/26	7/64
4046	3/25	8/63	4086	11/25	11/65	4126	8/25	8/63	4166	2/26	1/62
4047	3/25	10/63	4087	11/25	2/62	4127	8/25	1/65	4167	3/26	1/64
4048	3/25	7/64	4088	11/25	11/61	4128	8/25	12/62	4168	3/26	11/63
4049	3/25	12/64	4089	11/25	12/63	4129	8/25	9/62	4169	3/26	8/65
4050	3/25	11/59	4090	11/25	10/61	4130	9/25	12/64	4170	3/26	10/65
4051	4/25	12/64	4091	11/25	2/64	4131	9/25	11/64	4171	3/26	5/64
4052	4/25	6/60	4092	11/25	9/64	4132	9/25	8/63	4172	3/26	5/64
4053	4/25	3/63	4093	11/25	3/60	4133	9/25	11/63	4173	4/26	12/59
4054	5/25	12/64	4094	11/25	5/63	4134	9/25	11/64	4174	4/26	12/63
4055	5/25	10/63	4095	11/25	12/59	4135	9/25	4/65	4175	4/26	12/59
4056	5/25	10/65	4096	11/25	9/64	4136	10/25	12/59	4176	4/26	7/63
4057	8/25	11/65	4097	11/25	6/63	4137	10/25	2/65	4177	12/24	11/64
4058	8/25	11/59	4098	11/25	12/63	4138	10/25	7/62	4178	12/24	11/64
4059	9/25	7/64	4099	12/25	2/65	4139	10/25	8/65	4179	1/25	12/64
4060	9/25	3/64	4100	12/25	3/63	4140	10/25	12/59	4180	2/25	4/64
4061	9/25	6/65	4101	12/25	5/63	4141	11/25	7/61	4181	2/25	8/65
4062	9/25	8/62	4102	12/25	9/64	4142	11/25	12/59	4182	2/25	9/64
4063	9/25	6/65	4103	12/25	12/59	4143	11/25	10/62	4183	3/25	10/63
4064	10/25	11/59	4104	12/25	5/62	4144	11/25	8/59	4184	3/25	10/63
4065	10/25	1/65	4105	12/25	10/61	4145	11/25	2/59	4185	3/25	11/64
4066	10/25	9/63	4106	1/26	2/64	4146	11/25	11/64	4186	3/25	10/63

No	New	Wdn	No	New	Wdn	No	New	Wdn	No	New	Wdn
4187	4/25	7/62	4251	6/26	10/62	4315	12/27	5/64	4379	12/27	9/64
4188	4/25	11/65	4252	7/26	5/63	4316	12/27	12/59	4380	1/28	8/64
4189	4/25	12/62	4253	7/26	10/62	4317	12/27	12/57	4381	1/28	9/64
4190	5/25	9/63	4254	7/26	10/62	4318	1/28	10/62	4382	9/26	11/59
4191	5/25	8/64	4255	7/26	12/62	4319	1/28	11/61	4383	9/26	11/59
4192	6/25	4/65	4256	7/26	4/62	4320	1/28	10/62	4384	9/26	10/64
4193	6/25	10/62	4257	7/26	10/62	4321	1/28	4/64	4385	10/26	8/59
4194	6/25	12/62	4258	8/26	5/62	4322	1/28	12/62	4386	10/26	5/65
4195	7/25	3/65	4259	8/26	7/64	4323	1/28	10/62	4387	10/26	10/63
4196	7/25	1/62	4260	8/26	10/64	4324	1/28	11/61	4388	10/26	12/62
4197	10/25	9/64	4261	9/26	10/63	4325	2/28	10/62	4389	10/26	7/65
4198	10/25	12/62	4262	9/26	8/63	4326	2/28	12/59	4390	10/26	11/65
4199	10/25	12/62	4263	10/26	3/65	4327	2/28	5/64	4391	10/26	3/60
4200	10/25	7/65	4264	10/26	10/65	4328	2/28	12/62	4392	10/26	6/64
4201	10/25	9/59	4265	10/26	12/62	4329	3/28	7/62	4393	10/26	11/62
4202	10/25	9/63	4266	10/26	3/65	4330	3/28	10/62	4394	10/26	7/66
4203	11/25	3/66	4267	10/26	5/62	4331	3/28	12/62	4395	10/26	11/63
4204	11/25	12/59	4268	10/26	3/63	4332	10/26	9/64	4396	10/26	5/64
4205	11/25	3/63	4269	10/26	12/65	4333	10/26	4/64	4397	12/26	3/62
4206	11/25	6/61	4270	11/26	11/63	4334	10/26	6/65	4398	12/26	7/63
4207	11/25	11/63	4271	11/26	12/65	4335	10/26	2/63	4399	12/26	2/64
4208	11/25	9/63	4272	11/26	6/63	4336	10/26	12/63	4400	1/27	10/65
4209	11/25	5/63	4273	11/26	9/62	4337	10/26	4/64	4401	1/27	6/65
4210	11/25	10/65	4274	11/26	12/63	4338	10/26	8/62	4402	1/27	1/65
4211	12/25	3/65	4275	11/26	10/64	4339	10/26	12/65	4403	1/27	6/64
4212	12/25	12/63	4276	12/26	5/65	4340	10/26	12/62	4404	1/27	12/62
4213	12/25	5/64	4277	12/26	5/65	4341	12/26	2/63	4405	1/27	6/66
4214	12/25	12/64	4278	12/26	1/66	4342	12/26	10/63	4406	1/27	3/60
4215	12/25	2/65	4279	12/26	1/64	4343	1/27	3/60	4407	8/27	9/62
4216	12/25	8/62	4280	12/26	12/63	4344	1/27	12/64	4408	8/27	10/65
4217	1/26	12/59	4281	12/26	12/62	4345	1/27	12/63	4409	8/27	12/61
4218	1/26	3/66	4282	12/26	7/63	4346	1/27	11/65	4410	8/27	3/60
4219	1/26	11/63	4283	12/26	12/62	4347	3/27	3/65	4411	9/27	9/63
4220	1/26	9/64	4284	12/26	8/64	4348	4/27	7/64	4412	9/27	3/60
4221	1/26	5/64	4285	12/26	12/59	4349	4/27	7/65	4413	9/27	3/63
4222	1/26	11/64	4286	12/26	4/64	4350	4/27	12/65	4414	9/27	5/65
4223	1/26	11/63	4287	12/26	12/63	4351	5/27	4/63	4415	9/27	3/60
4224	1/26	2/62	4288	1/27	3/64	4352	5/27	9/63	4416	9/27	6/63
4225	2/26	11/59	4289	1/27	6/64	4353	5/27	2/65	4417	9/27	11/62
4226	2/26	8/64	4290	1/27	6/64	4354	5/27	11/63	4418	9/27	11/63
4227	2/26	12/59	4291	1/27	11/59	4355	6/27	9/65	4419	9/27	8/63
4228	2/26	12/62	4292	1/27	8/63	4356	6/27	11/65	4420	10/27	10/65
4229	2/26	11/64	4293	1/27	12/59	4357	1/27	11/59	4421	10/27	12/64
4230	2/26	12/59	4294	2/27	11/65	4358	1/27	1/65	4422	10/27	6/65
4231	2/26	6/63	4295	2/27	2/64	4359	1/27	7/63	4423	10/27	11/59
4232	3/26	11/63	4296	2/27	1/64	4360	2/27	3/60	4424	10/27	10/63
4233	3/26	11/64	4297	2/27	8/63	4361	2/27	11/59	4425	10/27	2/65
4234	3/26	10/62	4298	2/27	12/59	4362	4/27	10/64	4426	10/27	12/63
4235	3/26	12/64	4299	2/27	5/63	4363	4/27	11/63	4427	10/27	3/60
4236	3/26	10/64	4300	2/27	12/65	4364	4/27	1/64	4428	10/27	2/64
4237	3/26	10/63	4301	3/27	3/64	4365	5/27	11/59	4429	10/27	5/65
4238	3/26	12/63	4302	10/26	3/64	4366	5/27	3/60	4430	11/27	3/60
4239	4/26	11/63	4303	10/26	8/63	4367	6/27	9/64	4431	11/27	9/64
4240	4/26	9/64	4304	10/26	5/64	4368	7/27	8/62	4432	11/27	11/63
4241	4/26	7/63	4305	10/26	4/65	4369	7/27	12/59	4433	11/27	12/64
4242	4/26	4/64	4306	10/26	11/59	4370	7/27	8/63	4434	11/27	9/63
4243	4/26	9/65	4307	10/26	10/62	4371	8/27	5/67	4435	12/27	10/62
4244	4/26	10/64	4308	9/26	10/63	4372	9/27	11/59	4436	11/27	4/64
4245	4/26	5/62	4309	10/26	7/63	4373	10/27	12/64	4437	11/27	12/63
4246	5/26	12/64	4310	10/26	2/66	4374	10/27	2/63	4438	12/27	3/60
4247	5/26	12/65	4311	10/26	2/66	4375	11/27	10/60	4439	12/27	4/64
4248	5/26	9/64	4312	11/27	10/62	4376	11/27	12/64	4440	12/27	3/64
4249	6/26	11/61	4313	11/27	12/59	4377	12/27	10/66	4441	12/27	8/64
4250	6/26	5/65	4314	12/27	7/62	4378	12/27	5/63	4442	12/27	7/63

No	New	Wdn	No	New	Wdn	No	New	Wdn	No	New	Wdn
4443	12/27	8/65	4483	12/27	3/60	4523	8/28	7/63	4568	8/37	10/63
4444	12/27	8/63	4484	12/27	11/64	4524	8/28	1/63	4569	8/37	7/64
4445	12/27	6/63	4485	12/27	4/63	4525	8/28	10/66	4570	8/37	10/65
4446	12/27	10/65	4486	12/27	1/65	4526	8/28	11/63	4571	8/37	12/64
4447	1/28	7/63	4487	12/27	4/62	4527	8/28	3/65	4572	9/37	9/64
4448	1/28	11/63	4488	12/27	3/60	4528	8/28	5/65	4573	9/37	5/62
4449	1/28	8/65	4489	12/27	8/65	4529	8/28	9/64	4574	9/37	11/63
4450	2/28	5/65	4490	12/27	8/65	4530	9/28	11/63	4575	9/37	11/64
4451	2/28	12/65	4491	12/27	10/62	4531	9/28	4/64	4576	10/37	5/62
4452	2/28	6/64	4492	10/27	4/64	4532	9/28	4/63	4577	4/39	9/64
4453	2/28	3/60	4493	11/27	10/63	4533	9/28	2/64	4578	4/39	2/64
4454	2/28	11/63	4494	11/27	6/63	4534	9/28	11/64	4579	4/39	11/62
4455	2/28	3/63	4495	11/27	3/60	4535	9/28	9/63	4580	5/39	11/64
4456	2/28	3/65	4496	11/27	3/60	4536	9/28	8/65	4581	5/39	9/64
4457	3/28	12/63	4497	11/27	11/64	4537	9/28	10/62	4582	5/39	11/63
4458	3/28	10/65	4498	11/27	3/60	4538	10/28	1/64	4583	6/39	7/64
4459	4/28	3/60	4499	11/27	9/64	4539	10/28	9/63	4584	7/39	11/63
4460	5/28	10/64	4500	11/27	7/66	4540	10/28	5/64	4585	7/39	8/60
4461	5/28	9/64	4501	11/27	12/64	4541	10/28	11/63	4586	9/39	9/64
4462	5/28	11/65	4502	11/27	3/60	4542	11/28	6/63	4587	9/39	5/65
4463	5/28	9/64	4503	11/27	3/60	4543	11/28	5/64	4588	9/39	9/64
4464	5/28	5/64	4504	11/27	11/63	4544	11/28	4/65	4589	9/39	11/64
4465	6/28	6/63	4505	11/27	9/65	4545	11/28	3/63	4590	9/39	8/61
4466	7/28	5/65	4506	12/27	3/60	4546	11/28	3/60	4591	10/39	11/64
4467	5/28	4/64	4507	6/28	3/60	4547	11/28	8/61	4592	10/39	11/63
4468	5/28	9/64	4508	6/28	8/62	4548	11/28	1/65	4593	10/39	12/64
4469	5/28	3/63	4509	6/28	9/62	4549	12/28	5/64	4594	10/39	10/62
4470	5/28	6/63	4510	6/28	2/60	4550	12/28	3/62	4595	10/39	9/63
4471	6/28	3/60	4511	6/28	3/60	4551	12/28	5/63	4596	11/39	8/63
4472	6/28	5/63	4512	6/28	2/64	4552	12/28	9/64	4597	3/40	10/65
4473	7/28	3/60	4513	6/28	3/60	4553	12/28	10/62	4598	3/40	9/63
4474	7/28	12/61	4514	6/28	9/64	4554	12/28	7/64	4599	4/40	10/65
4475	8/28	2/63	4515	6/28	3/60	4555	12/28	3/60	4600	7/40	3/60
4476	8/28	5/63	4516	6/28	8/64	4556	12/28	12/63	4601	8/40	11/65
4477	12/27	7/61	4517	7/28	11/63	4562	5/37	11/63	4602	8/40	8/64
4478	12/27	11/64	4518	7/28	8/62	4563	7/37	3/60	4603	9/40	10/64
4479	12/27	5/64	4519	7/28	1/63	4564	7/37	9/64	4604	9/40	1/64
4480	11/27	3/60	4520	7/28	1/64	4565	7/37	9/64	4605	2/41	10/64
4481	12/27	11/64	4521	7/28	9/62	4566	7/37	9/64	4606	3/41	3/62
4482	12/27	5/62	4522	7/28	10/65	4567	7/37	5/64			

4-6-0 Class 5P5F

842 locomotives.

No	New	Wdn	No	New	Wdn	No	New	Wdn	No	New	Wdn
44658	5/49	11/67	44676	4/50	7/64	44694	12/50	9/67	44712	10/48	11/66
44659	5/49	6/67	44677	4/50	10/67	44695	12/50	6/67	44713	11/48	8/68
44660	5/49	8/64	44678	5/50	11/67	44696	12/50	5/67	44714	11/48	11/66
44661	6/49	8/67	44679	5/50	9/67	44697	12/50	11/67	44715	11/48	1/68
44662	6/49	9/67	44680	6/50	9/67	44698	7/48	7/66	44716	11/48	7/65
44663	6/49	5/68	44681	6/50	9/67	44699	7/48	5/67	44717	12/48	8/67
44664	6/49	5/68	44682	6/50	11/67	44700	7/48	7/66	44718	3/49	11/66
44665	6/49	3/68	44683	7/50	4/68	44701	8/48	6/64	44719	3/49	10/64
44666	7/49	2/67	44684	7/50	9/67	44702	8/48	6/65	44720	3/49	10/66
44667	7/49	9/67	44685	8/50	4/67	44703	8/48	12/66	44721	3/49	8/65
44668	12/49	4/66	44686	4/51	10/65	44704	9/48	9/66	44722	4/49	4/67
44669	12/49	10/67	44687	5/51	1/66	44705	9/48	9/66	44723	4/49	10/66
44670	1/50	1/66	44688	8/50	8/66	44706	9/48	12/63	44724	4/49	10/66
44671	2/50	2/67	44689	9/50	3/67	44707	9/48	1/66	44725	4/49	10/67
44672	2/50	3/68	44690	10/50	8/68	44708	10/48	1/68	44726	5/49	10/67
44673	2/50	5/65	44691	10/50	3/67	44709	10/48	8/68	44727	5/49	10/67
44674	3/50	12/67	44692	10/50	5/66	44710	10/48	12/66	44728	1/49	1/68
44675	3/50	9/67	44693	11/50	5/67	44711	10/48	5/68	44729	1/49	10/66

No	New	Wdn	No	New	Wdn	No	New	Wdn	No	New	Wdn
44730	1/49	11/67	4794	8/47	4/67	4858	12/44	12/67	4922	1/46	6/64
44731	2/49	4/66	4795	8/47	7/67	4859	12/44	11/67	4923	1/46	6/64
44732	2/49	7/67	4796	9/47	5/67	4860	12/44	1/67	4924	2/46	7/65
44733	2/49	6/67	4797	9/47	9/66	4861	1/45	11/67	4925	2/46	9/66
44734	2/49	12/67	4798	10/47	9/66	4862	1/45	7/67	4926	2/46	4/68
44735	2/49	8/68	4799	10/47	7/65	4863	1/45	5/67	4927	2/46	9/67
44736	3/49	9/67	4800	5/44	3/68	4864	1/45	5/68	4928	3/46	5/67
44737	3/49	1/67	4801	5/44	6/64	4865	2/45	9/67	4929	3/46	6/68
44738	6/48	6/64	4802	6/44	6/68	4866	2/45	9/67	4930	3/46	5/67
44739	6/48	1/65	4803	6/44	5/68	4867	2/45	6/67	4931	4/46	10/65
44740	5/48	4/63	4804	6/44	3/68	4868	2/45	5/68	4932	9/45	8/68
44741	6/48	3/65	4805	6/44	9/67	4869	3/45	9/66	4933	10/45	10/67
44742	6/48	4/64	4806	7/44	8/68	4870	3/45	6/67	4934	10/45	9/67
44743	6/48	1/66	4807	9/44	3/68	4871	3/45	8/68	4935	10/45	10/66
44744	7/48	11/63	4808	9/44	12/66	4872	3/45	9/67	4936	11/45	8/67
44745	7/48	10/64	4809	9/44	8/68	4873	3/45	11/67	4937	11/45	5/67
44746	8/48	1/64	4810	10/44	8/66	4874	4/45	8/68	4938	11/45	10/67
44747	7/48	5/63	4811	10/44	10/66	4875	4/45	5/67	4939	11/45	12/65
4748	2/48	9/64	4812	10/44	9/67	4876	4/45	11/67	4940	11/45	3/68
4749	2/48	9/64	4813	10/44	8/66	4877	4/44	8/68	4941	12/45	11/66
4750	2/48	8/63	4814	10/44	9/67	4878	5/45	7/68	4942	12/45	6/68
4751	3/48	10/64	4815	11/44	2/68	4879	5/45	4/67	4943	12/45	9/67
4752	3/48	4/64	4816	11/44	7/68	4880	5/45	11/66	4944	1/46	9/67
4753	3/48	7/65	4817	11/44	8/67	4881	5/45	7/66	4945	1/46	10/66
44754	4/48	4/64	4818	11/44	6/68	4882	6/45	7/67	4946	1/46	5/67
44755	4/48	11/63	4819	11/44	12/67	4883	6/45	7/67	4947	2/46	6/68
44756	6/48	10/64	4820	12/44	12/66	4884	6/45	6/68	4948	2/46	9/67
44757	12/48	11/65	4821	12/44	6/67	4885	7/45	12/63	4949	2/46	6/68
4758	9/47	7/68	4822	12/44	10/67	4886	7/45	10/67	4950	3/46	8/68
4759	9/47	11/67	4823	12/44	11/65	4887	8/45	12/67	4951	3/46	11/66
4760	9/47	10/66	4824	12/44	9/67	4888	8/45	8/68	4952	3/46	10/66
4761	10/47	4/68	4825	12/44	10/67	4889	8/45	1/68	4953	3/46	12/66
4762	10/47	11/66	4826	7/44	9/67	4890	8/45	6/68	4954	4/46	9/66
4763	10/47	9/65	4827	7/44	6/65	4891	8/45	6/68	4955	4/46	8/65
4764	11/47	9/65	4828	7/44	9/67	4892	9/45	4/67	4956	4/46	6/66
4765	12/47	9/67	4829	8/44	5/68	4893	9/45	11/67	4957	5/46	6/64
4766	12/47	8/66	4830	8/44	8/67	4894	9/45	8/68	4958	5/46	3/67
4767	12/47	12/67	4831	8/44	12/67	4895	9/45	12/67	4959	5/46	7/65
4768	4/47	5/67	4832	8/44	11/67	4896	9/45	9/67	4960	5/46	1/66
4769	4/47	6/65	4833	8/44	9/67	4897	9/45	8/67	4961	6/46	6/64
4770	4/47	11/67	4834	8/44	9/67	4898	9/45	10/67	4962	6/46	12/67
4771	5/47	3/67	4835	9/44	7/67	4899	9/45	7/68	4963	6/46	7/68
4772	5/47	11/67	4836	9/44	5/68	4900	10/45	6/67	4964	7/46	10/67
4773	5/47	12/67	4837	9/44	9/67	4901	10/45	8/65	4965	8/46	3/68
4774	5/47	8/67	4838	9/44	3/68	4902	10/45	11/67	4966	8/46	9/66
4775	6/47	11/67	4839	9/44	12/66	4903	10/45	4/68	4967	4/46	6/64
4776	6/47	10/67	4840	10/44	11/67	4904	10/45	12/65	4968	4/46	6/64
4777	6/47	6/68	4841	10/44	10/66	4905	10/45	11/67	4969	4/46	12/63
4778	6/47	11/67	4842	10/44	1/68	4906	10/45	3/68	4970	4/46	9/65
4779	7/47	12/66	4843	10/44	9/67	4907	11/45	11/67	4971	4/46	8/68
4780	7/47	6/68	4844	10/44	11/67	4908	11/45	6/66	4972	4/46	11/66
4781	8/47	8/68	4845	10/44	6/68	4909	11/45	9/67	4973	5/46	9/65
4782	8/47	12/66	4846	11/44	1/68	4910	11/45	6/68	4974	5/46	6/66
4783	3/47	6/64	4847	11/44	11/66	4911	11/45	11/67	4975	5/46	9/65
4784	4/47	5/64	4848	11/44	2/68	4912	11/45	9/67	4976	5/46	2/64
4785	4/47	6/64	4849	11/44	12/64	4913	11/45	7/67	4977	6/46	11/66
4786	4/47	8/66	4850	11/44	7/66	4914	12/45	8/67	4978	6/46	7/65
4787	5/47	11/67	4851	11/44	3/68	4915	12/45	12/67	4979	6/46	7/65
4788	5/47	11/66	4852	11/44	9/67	4916	12/45	12/67	4980	6/46	7/65
4789	5/47	12/64	4853	12/44	6/67	4917	12/45	11/67	4981	7/46	1/67
4790	6/47	3/67	4854	12/44	9/67	4918	12/45	1/67	4982	9/46	5/67
4791	6/47	11/66	4855	12/44	5/68	4919	12/45	12/66	4983	9/46	9/67
4792	7/47	9/67	4856	12/44	2/67	4920	12/45	11/67	4984	9/46	11/66
4793	8/47	12/64	4857	12/44	9/67	4921	1/46	2/65	4985	10/46	11/67

No	New	Wdn	No	New	Wdn	No	New	Wdn	No	New	Wdn
4986	10/46	5/67	5050	11/34	8/67	5114	6/35	1/68	5178	9/35	1/65
4987	11/46	10/66	5051	11/34	11/66	5115	6/35	11/66	5179	9/35	12/62
4988	12/46	12/67	5052	11/34	9/67	5116	6/35	7/67	5180	9/35	9/65
4989	12/46	2/67	5053	11/34	11/66	5117	6/35	10/65	5181	9/35	1/66
4990	12/46	9/67	5054	11/34	2/68	5118	6/35	10/66	5182	9/35	3/66
4991	12/46	5/67	5055	11/34	8/68	5119	6/35	12/62	5183	9/35	10/64
4992	1/47	12/66	5056	11/34	8/67	5120	6/35	7/67	5184	9/35	9/65
4993	1/47	12/67	5057	12/34	8/67	5121	6/35	6/64	5185	9/35	6/66
4994	1/47	7/64	5058	12/34	10/66	5122	6/35	4/64	5186	9/35	9/67
4995	2/47	11/66	5059	12/34	7/67	5123	7/35	9/63	5187	9/35	5/68
4996	2/47	4/64	5060	12/34	3/67	5124	7/35	5/67	5188	9/35	7/67
4997	3/47	5/67	5061	12/34	11/67	5125	5/35	12/62	5189	9/35	7/63
4998	3/47	4/67	5062	12/34	4/67	5126	5/35	5/67	5190	10/35	5/68
4999	3/47	9/66	5063	12/34	10/66	5127	5/35	11/66	5191	10/35	7/67
5000	2/35	10/67	5064	12/34	3/67	5128	5/35	9/66	5192	10/35	8/65
5001	3/35	3/68	5065	12/34	4/68	5129	5/35	9/66	5193	10/35	9/67
5002	3/35	7/65	5066	1/35	2/64	5130	5/35	11/67	5194	10/35	4/65
5003	3/35	5/67	5067	1/35	10/67	5131	5/35	4/68	5195	10/35	7/66
5004	3/35	9/66	5068	1/35	12/65	5132	5/35	3/67	5196	10/35	12/67
5005	3/35	1/68	5069	1/35	6/67	5133	5/35	2/68	5197	10/35	1/67
5006	3/35	9/67	5070	5/35	5/67	5134	5/35	8/68	5198	10/35	9/67
5007	3/35	7/64	5071	5/35	7/67	5135	5/35	10/64	5199	10/35	8/63
5008	3/35	6/64	5072	6/35	9/67	5136	6/35	12/66	5200	10/35	7/68
5009	3/35	11/65	5073	6/35	8/68	5137	6/35	9/66	5201	10/35	4/68
5010	3/35	8/63	5074	6/35	9/65	5138	6/35	8/67	5202	10/35	6/68
5011	4/35	12/65	5075	2/35	9/67	5139	6/35	9/66	5203	11/35	6/68
5012	4/35	10/66	5076	3/35	6/68	5140	6/35	9/66	5204	11/35	1/67
5013	4/35	4/68	5077	3/35	8/65	5141	6/35	3/67	5205	11/35	10/66
5014	4/35	6/67	5078	3/35	10/65	5142	6/35	4/65	5206	11/35	8/68
5015	4/35	9/67	5079	3/35	3/67	5143	6/35	12/65	5207	11/35	9/66
5016	5/35	7/66	5080	3/35	9/67	5144	6/35	6/64	5208	11/35	10/67
5017	5/35	8/68	5081	3/35	10/65	5145	6/35	11/67	5209	11/35	6/68
5018	5/35	12/66	5082	3/35	7/66	5146	6/35	6/65	5210	11/35	4/66
5019	5/35	5/67	5083	3/35	12/67	5147	6/35	5/67	5211	11/35	5/67
5020	8/34	12/65	5084	3/35	11/66	5148	6/35	12/65	5212	11/35	8/68
5021	8/34	9/67	5085	3/35	12/62	5149	6/35	6/68	5213	11/35	12/66
5022	8/34	9/63	5086	3/35	12/62	5150	6/35	3/68	5214	11/35	12/66
5023	8/34	9/63	5087	3/35	7/63	5151	6/35	12/62	5215	11/35	10/67
5024	8/34	5/67	5088	3/35	9/64	5152	6/35	12/62	5216	11/35	2/66
5025	8/34	8/68	5089	4/35	8/67	5153	6/35	6/64	5217	11/35	11/66
5026	9/34	10/65	5090	4/35	12/65	5154	6/35	11/66	5218	11/35	4/66
5027	9/34	5/68	5091	4/35	9/66	5155	7/35	11/66	5219	11/35	9/67
5028	9/34	3/67	5092	4/35	12/67	5156	7/35	8/68	5220	11/35	9/66
5029	9/34	10/66	5093	4/35	11/65	5157	7/35	12/62	5221	11/35	12/67
5030	9/34	12/62	5094	4/35	2/67	5158	7/35	7/64	5222	12/35	2/67
5031	9/34	6/67	5095	4/35	8/68	5159	7/35	12/62	5223	12/35	12/66
5032	9/34	2/64	5096	4/35	8/68	5160	7/35	9/66	5224	12/35	11/66
5033	9/34	12/66	5097	4/35	6/66	5161	7/35	11/66	5225	8/36	10/67
5034	9/34	2/68	5098	4/35	12/62	5162	8/35	11/66	5226	8/36	9/67
5035	9/34	11/64	5099	4/35	9/63	5163	8/35	5/65	5227	8/36	1/68
5036	9/34	12/62	5100	5/35	9/63	5164	8/35	8/66	5228	8/36	3/67
5037	9/34	11/65	5101	5/35	3/68	5165	8/35	12/62	5229	8/36	9/65
5038	9/34	2/68	5102	5/35	1/65	5166	8/35	9/63	5230	8/36	8/65
5039	10/34	8/67	5103	5/35	10/64	5167	8/35	5/67	5231	8/36	8/68
5040	10/34	7/67	5104	5/35	6/68	5168	8/35	9/66	5232	8/36	11/66
5041	10/34	12/67	5105	5/35	10/66	5169	8/35	12/62	5233	8/36	5/66
5042	10/34	9/67	5106	5/35	1/67	5170	8/35	3/64	5234	8/36	9/67
5043	10/34	11/67	5107	5/35	9/67	5171	8/35	10/65	5235	8/36	1/66
5044	10/34	11/66	5108	5/35	12/65	5172	8/35	6/64	5236	8/36	12/67
5045	10/34	10/66	5109	5/35	3/67	5173	8/35	7/64	5237	8/36	9/65
5046	10/34	6/68	5110	6/35	8/68	5174	8/35	12/62	5238	8/36	12/66
5047	10/34	7/66	5111	6/35	10/67	5175	8/35	7/63	5239	8/36	9/67
5048	10/34	11/67	5112	6/35	10/66	5176	8/35	8/66	5240	8/36	1/67
5049	10/34	8/63	5113	6/35	6/65	5177	9/35	7/66	5241	9/36	9/67

No	New	Wdn	No	New	Wdn	No	New	Wdn	No	New	Wdn
5242	9/36	6/67	5306	1/37	1/65	5370	6/37	8/66	5434	11/37	8/66
5243	9/36	9/67	5307	1/37	10/67	5371	6/37	4/67	5435	11/37	6/68
5244	9/36	7/63	5308	1/37	8/67	5372	6/37	11/66	5436	11/37	4/68
5245	9/36	8/65	5309	1/37	9/66	5373	6/37	9/67	5437	11/37	10/67
5246	9/36	12/67	5310	1/37	8/68	5374	6/37	11/67	5438	11/37	8/66
5247	9/36	4/67	5311	2/37	10/66	5375	6/37	1/68	5439	11/37	10/65
5248	9/36	2/66	5312	2/37	6/68	5376	6/37	3/68	5440	11/37	9/67
5249	9/36	12/66	5313	2/37	2/65	5377	6/37	12/67	5441	12/37	2/67
5250	9/36	3/67	5314	2/37	11/65	5378	7/37	3/65	5442	12/37	8/66
5251	9/36	12/63	5315	2/37	8/63	5379	7/37	7/65	5443	12/37	8/65
5252	9/36	3/66	5316	2/37	3/68	5380	7/37	3/65	5444	12/37	8/68
5253	9/36	3/68	5317	2/37	11/63	5381	7/37	5/68	5445	12/37	6/68
5254	9/36	4/68	5318	2/37	8/68	5382	7/37	6/68	5446	12/37	2/67
5255	10/36	6/68	5319	2/37	5/67	5383	7/37	2/67	5447	12/37	8/68
5256	10/36	8/67	5320	2/37	10/63	5384	7/37	6/64	5448	12/37	8/67
5257	10/36	11/65	5321	2/37	10/67	5385	7/37	11/66	5449	12/37	11/67
5258	10/36	3/68	5322	2/37	9/66	5386	7/37	8/68	5450	12/37	11/67
5259	10/36	12/67	5323	2/37	9/67	5387	7/37	3/65	5451	12/37	11/66
5260	10/36	8/68	5324	2/37	8/67	5388	7/37	8/68	5452	9/38	12/62
5261	10/36	10/67	5325	3/37	8/66	5389	7/37	10/65	5453	9/38	12/62
5262	10/36	8/68	5326	3/37	3/67	5390	8/37	8/68	5454	9/38	8/67
5263	10/36	10/67	5327	3/37	1/65	5391	8/37	2/68	5455	9/38	8/67
5264	10/36	9/67	5328	3/37	9/67	5392	8/37	5/68	5456	10/38	12/64
5265	10/36	5/62	5329	3/37	11/66	5393	8/37	9/66	5457	10/38	9/63
5266	10/36	12/62	5330	3/37	8/68	5394	8/37	7/68	5458	10/38	12/62
5267	10/36	10/67	5331	3/37	11/67	5395	8/37	3/68	5459	10/38	5/64
5268	10/36	8/68	5332	3/37	11/66	5396	8/37	2/66	5460	10/38	6/65
5269	11/36	8/68	5333	3/37	6/66	5397	8/37	8/68	5461	10/38	8/66
5270	11/36	9/67	5334	3/37	6/65	5398	8/37	9/65	5462	11/38	6/64
5271	11/36	9/67	5335	3/37	7/62	5399	8/37	12/66	5463	11/38	11/66
5272	11/36	10/65	5336	3/37	1/67	5400	8/37	5/64	5464	11/38	10/66
5273	11/36	9/67	5337	4/37	2/65	5401	8/37	11/61	5465	11/38	2/64
5274	11/36	5/67	5338	4/37	10/66	5402	8/37	4/67	5466	11/38	2/67
5275	11/36	10/67	5339	4/37	6/67	5403	8/37	9/66	5467	11/38	12/66
5276	11/36	1/67	5340	4/37	4/67	5404	8/37	5/67	5468	12/38	6/64
5277	11/36	2/67	5341	4/37	1/67	5405	9/37	8/67	5469	12/38	11/66
5278	11/36	6/67	5342	4/37	8/68	5406	9/37	7/67	5470	12/38	9/64
5279	11/36	3/68	5343	4/37	6/67	5407	9/37	8/68	5471	12/38	7/65
5280	11/36	11/67	5344	4/37	8/66	5408	9/37	11/66	5472	4/43	9/66
5281	11/36	12/67	5345	4/37	5/68	5409	9/37	8/67	5473	5/43	11/66
5282	11/36	5/68	5346	4/37	6/67	5410	9/37	9/66	5474	5/43	9/66
5283	11/36	1/67	5347	4/37	11/67	5411	9/37	5/68	5475	6/43	9/66
5284	12/36	5/68	5348	4/37	8/66	5412	9/37	8/67	5476	7/43	1/64
5285	12/36	12/67	5349	5/37	11/67	5413	9/37	9/64	5477	7/43	8/66
5286	12/36	3/65	5350	5/37	8/68	5414	10/37	2/65	5478	8/43	12/66
5287	12/36	8/68	5351	5/37	8/65	5415	10/37	11/67	5479	8/43	6/64
5288	12/36	11/67	5352	5/37	4/67	5416	10/37	7/65	5480	8/43	8/66
5289	12/36	11/66	5353	5/37	7/68	5417	10/37	7/67	5481	9/43	9/67
5290	12/36	6/68	5354	5/37	11/65	5418	10/37	2/66	5482	9/43	6/64
5291	12/36	10/65	5355	5/37	12/62	5419	10/37	9/66	5483	9/43	2/66
5292	12/36	11/67	5356	5/37	6/64	5420	10/37	6/68	5484	10/43	2/64
5293	12/36	8/65	5357	5/37	12/66	5421	10/37	2/68	5485	10/43	10/63
5294	12/36	3/68	5358	5/37	12/63	5422	10/37	9/66	5486	10/43	12/65
5295	12/36	12/67	5359	5/37	5/67	5423	10/37	5/67	5487	11/43	6/64
5296	12/36	2/68	5360	5/37	9/65	5424	10/37	4/68	5488	11/43	11/66
5297	12/36	9/67	5361	5/37	2/64	5425	10/37	10/67	5489	11/43	11/66
5298	12/36	9/67	5362	5/37	10/65	5426	10/37	3/68	5490	12/43	12/66
5299	1/37	11/67	5363	6/37	10/66	5427	10/37	8/66	5491	12/43	7/65
5300	1/37	12/65	5364	6/37	8/66	5428	10/37	9/67	5492	1/44	12/66
5301	1/37	7/65	5365	6/37	12/66	5429	11/37	8/65	5493	1/44	1/68
5302	1/37	7/67	5366	6/37	4/64	5430	11/37	9/66	5494	1/44	9/67
5303	1/37	6/67	5367	6/37	11/63	5431	11/37	12/67	5495	2/44	3/67
5304	1/37	8/67	5368	6/37	11/67	5432	11/37	10/66	5496	2/44	6/64
5305	1/37	8/68	5369	6/37	3/67	5433	11/37	3/66	5497	4/44	6/64

No	New	Wdn		No	New	Wdn
5498	4/44	6/65		5499	4/44	8/65

The following locomotives were fitted with sloping throatplate boilers
(in place of the original vertical throatplate type):-
5002 12/37; 5007 1/60; 5008 1/60; 5011 1/49: 5020 6/39; 5022 12/39;
5023 12/37; 5026 2/37; 5027 12/36; 5040 3/40; 5045 11/54; 5047 5/38;
5049 7/54; 5054 1/37; 5057 12/37; 5058 11/37; 5059 7/45; 5066 4/60;
5082 12/56; 5087 9/55; 5097 3/37; 5108 6/45; 5109 5/48; 5142 12/37;
5151 3/51; 5163 5/61; 5165 1/46; 5197 5/60.
(Nos 5023/6/49 and 5165 reverted to original boiler type in 3/53, 1/59,
3/57 and 8/49 respectively).

4-6-0 Class 5XP

52 locomotives (42 built with the numbers shown below and renumbered in
1934).

5971	5500	5936	5507	5983	5514	5933	5521	5996	5528	5997	5535
5902	5501	6010	5508	5992	5515	5973	5522	5926	5529	6018	5536
5959	5502	6005	5509	5982	5516	6026	5523	6022	5530	6015	5537
5985	5503	6012	5510	5952	5517	5907	5524	6027	5531	6000	5538
5987	5504	5942	5511	6006	5518	5916	5525	6011	5532	5925	5539
5946	5505	5966	5512	6008	5519	5963	5526	5905	5533	5901	5540
5974	5506	5958	5513	5954	5520	5944	5527	5935	5534	5903	5541

No	New	Wdn		No	New	Wdn		No	New	Wdn		No	New	Wdn
5500	11/30	3/61		5513	9/32	9/62		5526	3/33	10/64		5539	7/33	9/61
5501	11/30	8/61		5514	9/32	5/61		5527	4/33	12/64		5540	8/33	4/63
5502	7/32	9/60		5515	10/32	6/62		5528	4/33	1/63		5541	8/33	6/62
5503	7/32	8/61		5516	10/32	7/61		5529	4/33	2/64		5542	3/34	6/62
5504	7/32	3/62		5517	2/33	6/62		5530	4/33	12/65		5543	3/34	11/62
5505	7/32	6/62		5518	2/33	10/62		5531	4/33	10/65		5544	3/34	12/61
5506	8/32	3/62		5519	2/33	3/62		5532	4/33	1/64		5545	3/34	5/64
5507	8/32	10/62		5520	2/33	5/62		5533	4/33	9/62		5546	3/34	6/62
5508	8/32	11/60		5521	3/33	9/63		5534	4/33	5/64		5547	4/34	9/62
5509	8/32	8/61		5522	3/33	9/64		5535	5/33	10/63		5548	4/34	6/62
5510	8/32	6/62		5523	3/33	1/64		5536	5/33	12/62		5549	4/34	6/62
5511	9/32	2/61		5524	3/33	9/62		5537	7/33	6/62		5550	5/34	11/62
5512	9/32	3/65		5525	3/33	5/63		5538	7/33	9/62		5551	5/34	6/62

The following locomotives were rebuilt and fitted 2A type taper boilers:
5512 6/48; 5514 3/47; 5521 10/46; 5522 2/49; 5523 10/48; 5525 7/48;
5526 2/47; 5527 8/48; 5528 8/47; 5529 6/47; 5530 10/46; 5531 11/47;
5532 7/48; 5534 12/48; 5535 8/48; 5536 10/48; 5540 10/47; 5545 10/48.
Following rebuilding these 18 locomotives were reclassified 6P.

4-6-0 Class 5XP

191 locomotives.

No	New	Wdn		No	New	Wdn		No	New	Wdn		No	New	Wdn
5552	5/34	9/64		5567	8/34	1/65		5582	11/34	12/62		5597	1/35	1/65
5553	6/34	11/64		5568	8/34	4/64		5583	11/34	10/64		5598	2/35	10/64
5554	6/34	11/64		5569	8/34	4/64		5584	12/34	9/64		5599	1/35	8/64
5555	6/34	8/63		5570	8/34	12/62		5585	12/34	5/64		5600	2/35	12/65
5556	6/34	9/64		5571	9/34	5/64		5586	12/34	1/65		5601	4/35	9/64
5557	6/34	9/64		5572	9/34	1/64		5587	12/34	12/62		5602	4/35	3/65
5558	7/34	8/64		5573	9/34	9/65		5588	12/34	4/65		5603	3/35	12/62
5559	7/34	10/62		5574	9/34	3/66		5589	12/34	3/65		5604	3/35	7/65
5560	7/34	11/63		5575	9/34	6/63		5590	12/34	12/65		5605	4/35	2/64
5561	7/34	9/64		5576	9/34	12/62		5591	12/34	10/63		5606	4/35	6/64
5562	8/34	11/67		5577	9/34	9/64		5592	12/34	9/64		5607	6/34	11/62
5563	8/34	11/65		5578	9/34	5/64		5593	12/34	10/67		5608	7/34	9/65
5564	8/34	7/64		5579	10/34	8/64		5594	1/35	12/64		5609	7/34	9/60
5565	8/34	1/64		5580	10/34	12/64		5595	1/35	1/65		5610	7/34	1/64
5566	8/34	11/62		5581	10/34	8/66		5596	1/35	7/66		5611	7/34	9/64

No	New	Wdn	No	New	Wdn	No	New	Wdn	No	New	Wdn
5612	8/34	3/64	5645	12/34	10/63	5678	12/35	12/62	5711	6/36	12/62
5613	8/34	9/64	5646	12/24	12/63	5679	12/35	12/62	5712	6/36	11/63
5614	8/34	1/64	5647	1/35	4/67	5680	12/35	1/63	5713	7/36	10/62
5615	8/34	12/62	5648	1/35	2/63	5681	12/35	9/64	5714	7/36	7/63
5616	8/34	1/61	5649	1/35	10/63	5682	1/36	6/64	5715	7/36	12/62
5617	9/34	11/64	5650	1/35	1/63	5683	1/36	12/62	5716	7/36	9/64
5618	10/34	2/64	5651	1/35	11/62	5684	2/36	12/65	5717	7/36	10/63
5619	10/34	8/61	5652	1/35	1/65	5685	2/36	4/64	5718	8/36	10/62
5620	10/34	9/64	5653	1/35	3/65	5686	2/36	11/62	5719	8/36	3/63
5621	10/34	12/62	5654	2/35	6/66	5687	2/36	12/62	5720	8/36	12/62
5622	10/34	9/64	5655	12/34	4/65	5688	2/36	12/62	5721	8/36	10/65
5623	10/34	7/64	5656	12/34	12/62	5689	2/36	12/64	5722	8/36	11/62
5624	10/34	11/63	5657	12/34	9/64	5690	3/36	3/64	5723	8/36	8/64
5625	10/34	9/63	5658	12/34	9/65	5691	3/36	12/62	5724	9/36	10/62
5626	11/34	10/65	5659	12/34	5/63	5692	3/36	12/62	5725	9/36	12/62
5627	11/34	9/66	5660	12/34	6/66	5693	3/36	12/62	5726	10/36	3/65
5628	11/34	12/62	5661	12/34	5/65	5694	3/36	1/67	5727	10/36	12/62
5629	11/34	4/65	5662	12/34	11/62	5695	3/36	1/64	5728	10/36	10/62
5630	11/34	11/61	5663	1/35	10/64	5696	4/36	7/64	5729	10/36	10/62
5631	11/34	8/64	5664	1/35	5/65	5697	4/36	9/67	5730	10/36	10/63
5632	11/34	10/65	5665	11/35	12/62	5698	4/36	10/65	5731	10/36	10/62
5633	11/34	10/65	5666	11/35	4/65	5699	4/36	11/64	5732	10/36	2/64
5634	11/34	5/63	5667	11/35	1/65	5700	4/36	7/64	5733	11/36	9/64
5635	11/34	9/64	5668	12/35	12/63	5701	4/36	2/63	5734	11/36	12/63
5636	12/34	12/62	5669	12/35	5/63	5702	5/36	4/63	5735	11/36	10/64
5637	12/34	12/52	5670	12/35	10/64	5703	5/36	11/64	5736	11/36	9/64
5638	12/34	3/64	5671	12/35	11/63	5704	5/36	1/65	5737	11/36	5/64
5639	12/34	9/63	5672	12/35	11/64	5705	5/36	11/65	5738	12/36	12/63
5640	12/34	3/64	5673	12/35	12/62	5706	5/36	9/63	5739	12/36	1/67
5641	12/34	9/64	5674	12/35	10/64	5707	5/36	12/62	5740	12/36	10/63
5642	12/34	1/65	5675	12/35	6/67	5708	6/36	2/64	5741	12/36	1/64
5643	12/34	1/66	5676	12/35	9/64	5709	6/36	11/63	5742	12/36	5/65
5644	12/34	11/63	5677	12/35	12/62	5710	6/36	6/64			

Nos 5552 and 5642 exchanged numbers in 4/35.
The following locomotives were fitted with sloping throatplate boilers
(in place of the original vertical throatplate type);-
5567 4/37; 5590 4/37; 5607 6/36; 5608 4/37; 5610 2/37; 5616 7/36;
5621 6/37; 5622 7/36; 5639 3/37; 5640 8/36; 5657 4/37.
(Nos 5607/16/22 reverted to original boiler type in 4/38, 2/38 and 7/38).
The following locomotives were fitted with 2A type taper boiler:-
5735 5/42; 5736 4/42.
Following rebuilding these two locomotives were reclassified 6P.

4-6-0 Class 6P

71 locomotives (including No 6170 reconstructed from the 1929 high pressure experimental locomotive).

No	New	Wdn	No	New	Wdn	No	New	Wdn	No	New	Wdn
6100	7/27	10/62	6115	9/27	12/65	6130	8/27	12/62	6145	10/27	12/62
6101	8/27	8/63	6116	9/27	8/63	6131	9/27	11/62	6146	10/27	12/62
6102	8/27	12/62	6117	10/27	11/62	6132	9/27	2/64	6147	10/27	12/62
6103	8/27	12/62	6118	10/27	6/64	6133	9/27	2/63	6148	11/27	11/64
6104	8/27	12/62	6119	10/27	11/63	6134	9/27	12/62	6149	11/27	8/63
6105	8/27	12/62	6120	10/27	7/63	6135	9/27	12/62	6150	5/30	11/63
6106	8/27	12/62	6121	10/27	12/62	6136	9/27	3/64	6151	6/30	12/62
6107	8/27	12/62	6122	10/27	10/64	6137	9/27	11/62	6152	7/30	4/65
6108	8/27	1/63	6123	10/27	11/62	6138	9/27	2/63	6153	7/30	12/62
6109	9/27	12/62	6124	11/27	12/62	6139	10/27	10/62	6154	7/30	12/62
6110	9/27	2/64	6125	8/27	10/64	6140	10/27	10/65	6155	7/30	12/64
6111	9/27	9/63	6126	8/27	10/63	6141	10/27	4/64	6156	7/30	10/64
6112	9/27	5/64	6127	8/27	12/62	6142	10/27	1/64	6157	8/30	1/64
6113	9/27	12/62	6128	8/27	5/65	6143	10/27	12/63	6158	8/30	10/63
6114	9/27	9/63	6129	8/27	6/64	6144	10/27	1/64	6159	8/30	12/62

No	New	Wdn	No	New	Wdn	No	New	Wdn	No	New	Wdn
6160	8/30	5/65	6163	9/30	8/64	6166	10/30	9/64	6169	11/30	5/6.
6161	9/30	11/62	6164	9/30	12/62	6167	10/30	4/64	6170	11/35	12/6:
6162	9/30	5/64	6165	10/30	11/64	6168	10/30	5/64			

No 6170 was built as No 6399 in 12/29 and rebuilt with a taper boiler shown (it was not taken into stock as No 6399).

Nos 6100-69 were converted with a taper boiler (2A type):-

6100 6/50; 6101 11/45; 6102 10/49; 6103 6/43; 6104 3/46; 6105 5/4
6106 9/49; 6107 2/50; 6108 8/43; 6109 7/43; 6110 1/53; 6111 10/4
6112 9/43; 6113 12/50; 6114 6/46; 6115 8/47; 6116 5/44; 6117 12/4
6118 12/46; 6119 9/44; 6120 11/44; 6121 8/46; 6122 9/45; 6123 5/4
6124 12/43; 6125 8/43; 6126 6/45; 6127 8/44; 6128 6/46; 6129 12/4
6130 12/49; 6131 10/44; 6132 11/43; 6133 7/44; 6134 12/53; 6135 1/4
6136 3/50; 6137 3/55; 6138 6/44; 6139 11/46; 6140 5/52; 6141 10/5
6142 2/51; 6143 6/49; 6144 6/45; 6145 1/44; 6146 10/43; 6147 9/4
6148 7/54; 6149 4/45; 6150 12/45; 6151 4/53; 6152 8/45; 6153 8/4
6154 3/48; 6155 8/50; 6156 5/54; 6157 1/46; 6158 9/52; 6159 10/4
6160 2/45; 6161 10/46; 6162 1/48; 6163 10/53; 6164 6/51; 6165 6/5.
6166 1/45; 6167 12/48; 6168 4/46; 6169 5/45.

4-6-2 Class 7P

13 locomotives.

No	New	Wdn	No	New	Wdn	No	New	Wdn	No	New	Wdn
6200	7/33	11/62	6204	7/35	10/61	6207	8/35	11/61	6210	9/35	10/6
6201	11/33	10/62	6205	7/35	11/61	6208	8/35	10/62	6211	9/35	10/6
6202	6/35	5/54	6206	8/35	11/62	6209	8/35	9/62	6212	10/35	10/6
6203	7/35	10/62									

No 6202 was built with turbine drive (ceased working as such in 3/50) and was rebuilt as a conventional 4-cylinder locomotive in 8/52.

4-6-2 Class 7P

38 locomotives.

No	New	Wdn	No	New	Wdn	No	New	Wdn	No	New	Wdn
6220	6/37	4/63	6230	7/38	11/63	6240	3/40	9/64	6249	4/44	11/6
6221	6/37	5/63	6231	7/38	12/62	6241	4/40	9/64	6250	5/44	9/6
6222	6/37	10/63	6232	7/38	12/62	6242	5/40	10/63	6251	6/44	9/6
6223	7/37	10/63	6233	7/38	2/64	6243	6/40	9/64	6252	6/44	5/6
6224	7/37	10/63	6234	8/38	1/63	6244	7/40	9/64	6253	9/46	1/6
6225	5/38	9/64	6235	7/39	9/64	6245	6/43	9/64	6254	9/46	9/6
6226	5/38	9/64	6236	7/39	3/64	6246	8/43	1/63	6255	10/46	9/6
6227	6/38	12/62	6237	8/39	9/64	6247	9/43	5/63	6256	12/47	10/6
6228	6/38	9/64	6238	9/39	9/64	6248	10/43	9/64	46257	5/48	9/6
6229	9/38	2/64	6239	9/39	9/64						

Nos 6220-9/35-48 were built as streamlined locomotives; the casing was removed as follows:-

6220 9/46; 6221 5/46; 6222 5/46; 6223 8/46; 6224 5/46; 6225 2/4
6226 6/47; 6227 2/47; 6228 7/47; 6229 11/47; 6235 4/46; 6236 12/4
6237 1/47; 6238 11/46; 6239 6/47; 6240 6/47; 6241 1/47; 6242 3/4
6243 5/49; 6244 8/47; 6245 8/47; 6246 9/46; 6247 5/47; 6248 12/4

2-6-0 Class 2F

128 locomotives

No	New	Wdn	No	New	Wdn	No	New	Wdn	No	New	Wdn
6400	12/46	5/67	6402	12/46	7/67	6404	12/46	5/65	6406	12/46	1/6
6401	12/46	5/66	6403	12/46	6/64	6405	12/46	11/66	6407	12/46	12/6

No	New	Wdn	No	New	Wdn	No	New	Wdn	No	New	Wdn
6408	12/46	10/62	46438	1/50	1/63	46468	7/51	10/65	46498	2/52	9/65
6409	12/46	7/64	46439	1/50	3/67	46469	7/51	8/62	46499	3/52	5/67
6410	1/47	3/66	46440	2/50	3/67	46470	7/51	5/67	46500	3/52	1/67
6411	1/47	1/67	46441	2/50	4/67	46471	7/51	10/62	46501	3/52	5/67
6412	1/47	8/66	46442	2/50	10/66	46472	7/51	1/65	46502	3/52	2/67
6413	2/47	10/65	46443	2/50	3/67	46473	8/51	12/63	46503	11/52	5/67
6414	2/47	6/66	46444	2/50	7/65	46474	8/51	7/64	46504	11/52	10/66
6415	2/47	10/62	46445	2/50	6/66	46475	8/51	7/64	46505	11/52	6/67
6416	2/47	4/66	46446	3/50	12/66	46476	9/51	1/62	46506	11/52	5/67
6417	3/47	2/67	46447	3/50	12/66	46477	9/51	12/62	46507	11/52	6/65
6418	3/47	1/67	46448	3/50	5/67	46478	9/51	4/62	46508	12/52	12/66
6419	3/47	8/66	46449	3/50	5/67	46479	9/51	7/65	46509	12/52	10/66
6420	11/48	1/65	46450	4/50	1/66	46480	9/51	5/67	46510	12/52	9/65
6421	11/48	10/66	46451	4/50	11/66	46481	10/51	12/62	46511	12/52	9/65
6422	11/48	12/66	46452	4/50	5/67	46482	10/51	8/65	46512	12/52	11/66
6423	11/48	1/65	46453	4/50	4/62	46483	10/51	11/63	46513	12/52	7/66
6424	11/48	12/66	46454	4/50	10/66	46484	10/51	6/67	46514	12/52	6/66
6425	11/48	9/65	46455	4/50	5/67	46485	11/51	6/67	46515	1/53	5/67
6426	12/48	9/66	46456	5/50	9/65	46486	11/51	5/67	46516	1/53	4/67
6427	12/48	10/66	46457	5/50	5/67	46487	11/51	5/67	46517	1/53	11/65
6428	12/48	11/66	46458	5/50	12/66	46488	11/51	6/65	46518	1/53	3/66
6429	12/48	6/66	46459	5/50	9/65	46489	11/51	11/63	46519	2/53	10/66
6430	12/48	10/65	46460	5/50	8/66	46490	11/51	5/67	46520	2/53	5/67
6431	12/48	3/67	46461	6/50	7/64	46491	12/51	5/67	46521	2/53	10/66
6432	12/48	5/67	46462	6/50	8/66	46492	12/51	6/67	46522	3/53	5/67
6433	12/48	5/67	46463	6/50	2/66	46493	12/51	10/62	46523	3/53	5/67
6434	12/48	9/66	46464	6/50	8/66	46494	12/51	9/62	46524	3/53	2/65
6435	1/50	7/64	46465	6/51	3/67	46495	1/52	10/66	46525	3/53	12/64
6436	1/50	5/67	46466	6/51	8/62	46496	2/52	3/66	46526	3/53	7/66
6437	1/50	5/67	46467	6/51	7/64	46497	2/52	4/65	46527	3/53	10/65

0-4-0ST Class OF

locomotives built as Nos 1540-4 and renumbered 7000-4 in 1935-6.
locomotives built as Nos 47005-9.

No	New	Wdn	No	New	Wdn	No	New	Wdn	No	New	Wdn
7000	11/32	10/66	7003	12/32	4/64	47006	11/53	8/66	47008	12/53	9/64
7001	11/32	12/66	7004	12/32	1/64	47007	11/53	12/63	47009	1/54	9/64
7002	11/32	9/64	47005	10/53	12/66						

0-6-0T Class 2F

) locomotives built as Nos 11270-9 and renumbered 7100-9 in 1935-8 and
urther renumbered 7160-9 in 1939.

No	New	Wdn	No	New	Wdn	No	New	Wdn	No	New	Wdn
7160	12/28	10/63	7163	12/28	12/62	7166	12/28	5/63	7168	1/29	10/62
7161	12/28	8/63	7164	12/28	9/64	7167	1/29	7/60	7169	1/29	9/59
7162	12/28	12/59	7165	12/28	9/64						

Sentinel locomotives

locomotives (2-cylinder chain drive) built as Nos 7160-3 and renumbered
180-3 in 1939;
locomotive (2-cylinder chain drive industrial type) built as No 7164
nd renumbered 7184 in 1939;
locomotive (2-cylinder Doble compound) built as No 7192.

No	New	Wdn	No	New	Wdn	No	New	Wdn	No	New	Wdn
7180	6/30	8/53	7182	6/30	2/56	7184	1/32	12/55	7192	12/34	6/43
7181	6/30	11/56	7183	6/30	9/55						

415 locomotives built as Nos 7100-49 and 16400-16764 and renumbered 7260
7309 and 7317-7681 in 1934-8.

No	New	Wdn	No	New	Wdn	No	New	Wdn	No	New	Wdn
7260	7/24	6/60	7326	7/26	12/66	7385	10/26	3/64	7444	5/27	11/66
7261	7/24	6/62	7327	7/26	12/66	7386	10/26	4/63	7445	5/27	3/66
7262	7/24	11/60	7328	7/26	6/62	7387	11/26	12/59	7446	6/27	12/60
7263	7/24	9/61	7329	7/26	5/59	7388	11/26	12/66	7447	6/27	12/66
7264	7/24	4/63	7330	7/26	8/65	7389	11/26	6/66	7448	6/27	9/61
7265	7/24	9/60	7331	7/26	4/59	7390	11/26	9/64	7449	7/27	3/63
7266	7/24	9/66	7332	7/26	5/62	7391	11/26	11/66	7450	7/27	3/66
7267	7/24	11/63	7333	7/26	11/64	7392	11/26	8/62	7451	7/27	9/65
7268	7/24	7/61	7334	7/26	9/61	7393	11/26	2/66	7452	10/26	3/65
7269	7/24	9/62	7335	7/26	12/60	7394	11/26	12/59	7453	10/26	4/66
7270	8/24	9/62	7336	7/26	5/66	7395	11/26	4/65	7454	10/26	7/65
7271	8/24	12/60	7337	8/26	12/59	7396	11/26	10/66	7455	10/26	5/62
7272	8/24	6/66	7338	8/26	10/65	7397	11/26	10/66	7456	10/26	8/44
7273	8/24	11/66	7339	8/26	12/59	7398	11/26	5/61	7457	11/26	8/62
7274	8/24	12/59	7340	8/26	3/62	7399	11/26	8/65	7458	11/26	8/63
7275	8/24	3/62	7341	8/26	7/66	7400	11/26	8/65	7459	12/26	1/63
7276	8/24	3/66	7342	8/26	5/62	7401	11/26	11/60	7460	12/26	5/63
7277	8/24	4/61	7343	8/26	9/64	7402	12/26	12/62	7461	4/27	9/64
7278	8/24	6/63	7344	8/26	9/64	7403	12/26	9/61	7462	4/27	9/61
7279	8/24	12/66	7345	9/26	9/64	7404	12/26	2/62	7463	4/27	11/60
7280	8/24	4/66	7346	9/26	12/59	7405	12/26	9/61	7464	5/27	9/65
7281	8/24	3/63	7347	7/26	11/60	7406	12/26	12/66	7465	5/27	6/63
7282	9/24	12/60	7348	7/26	9/62	7407	12/26	12/59	7466	6/27	9/62
7283	9/24	4/63	7349	7/26	7/64	7408	12/26	11/65	7467	1/28	9/64
7284	9/24	9/64	7350	7/26	12/65	7409	12/26	12/59	7468	1/28	1/65
7285	9/24	8/65	7351	7/26	6/62	7410	12/26	9/66	7469	1/28	1/64
7286	9/24	8/65	7352	7/26	3/60	7411	12/26	12/59	7470	1/28	6/62
7287	10/24	10/63	7353	7/26	2/62	7412	12/26	9/63	7471	1/28	12/66
7288	10/24	11/64	7354	7/26	10/64	7413	12/26	5/63	7472	12/27	11/66
7289	10/24	10/67	7355	7/26	9/64	7414	12/26	5/62	7473	12/27	2/62
7290	10/24	6/62	7356	7/26	8/62	7415	12/26	4/66	7474	12/27	8/62
7291	10/24	12/59	7357	7/26	12/66	7416	12/26	6/66	7475	12/27	2/62
7292	10/24	12/62	7358	7/26	12/62	7417	12/26	11/62	7476	12/27	5/64
7293	10/24	12/66	7359	7/26	7/65	7418	12/26	6/61	7477	12/27	12/59
7294	10/24	10/63	7360	7/26	7/63	7419	12/26	12/63	7478	1/28	4/64
7295	10/24	4/65	7361	7/26	4/65	7420	12/26	9/61	7479	1/28	8/62
7296	10/24	12/59	7362	8/26	11/65	7421	12/26	9/61	7480	1/28	9/65
7297	10/24	6/64	7363	8/26	12/59	7422	12/26	7/62	7481	1/28	3/63
7298	10/24	12/66	7364	7/26	12/59	7423	12/26	6/65	7482	1/28	10/66
7299	11/24	11/59	7365	7/26	12/64	7424	12/26	5/62	7483	1/28	3/62
7300	12/24	8/63	7366	7/26	4/62	7425	12/26	5/62	7484	1/28	2/61
7301	12/24	12/59	7367	8/26	11/66	7426	12/26	8/62	7485	1/28	1/65
7302	1/25	9/62	7368	8/26	2/64	7427	10/26	9/66	7486	1/28	3/60
7303	1/25	8/60	7369	9/26	2/61	7428	10/26	10/65	7487	1/28	8/65
7304	1/25	6/62	7370	9/26	10/59	7429	10/26	12/65	7488	1/28	11/66
7305	2/25	2/65	7371	9/26	9/65	7430	10/26	1/64	7489	1/28	12/59
7306	2/25	12/64	7372	9/26	9/64	7431	10/26	10/62	7490	2/28	7/63
7307	3/25	8/66	7373	9/26	12/66	7432	10/26	8/65	7491	2/28	12/62
7308	3/25	8/64	7374	9/26	3/60	7433	10/26	9/62	7492	2/28	7/64
7309	3/25	11/59	7375	9/26	8/64	7434	11/26	4/64	7493	2/28	12/66
7317	6/26	4/66	7376	9/26	12/62	7435	11/26	10/66	7494	2/28	10/66
7318	6/26	10/66	7377	9/26	10/66	7436	4/27	12/60	7495	2/28	9/65
7319	6/26	8/62	7378	10/26	11/65	7437	4/27	8/66	7496	2/28	11/63
7320	6/26	5/64	7379	10/26	11/63	7438	4/27	9/61	7497	4/28	9/62
7321	6/26	10/65	7380	10/26	4/64	7439	5/27	9/65	7498	4/28	3/60
7322	6/26	7/63	7381	10/26	9/62	7440	5/27	12/59	7499	4/28	8/65
7323	6/26	3/60	7382	10/26	12/59	7441	5/27	12/63	7500	4/28	6/65
7324	6/26	12/66	7383	10/26	10/67	7442	5/27	3/65	7501	4/28	9/64
7325	6/26	9/65	7384	10/26	10/66	7443	5/27	12/60	7502	4/28	8/63

No	New	Wdn	No	New	Wdn	No	New	Wdn	No	New	Wdn
7503	4/28	3/64	7548	12/27	8/62	7593	8/28	8/62	7638	12/28	7/63
7504	4/28	4/62	7549	12/27	7/64	7594	9/28	7/64	7639	12/28	3/60
7505	4/28	8/65	7550	1/28	3/64	7595	9/28	3/60	7640	12/28	10/64
7506	4/28	3/66	7551	1/28	2/63	7596	9/28	6/65	7641	1/29	12/66
7507	4/28	8/66	7552	1/28	11/62	7597	10/28	10/65	7642	1/29	5/62
7508	4/28	9/61	7553	2/28	8/44	7598	11/28	7/66	7643	1/29	11/66
7509	4/28	12/60	7554	2/28	8/62	7599	11/28	12/66	7644	1/29	11/62
7510	5/28	11/60	7555	2/28	6/62	7600	11/28	3/60	7645	2/29	4/65
7511	5/28	4/64	7556	2/28	12/62	7601	11/28	3/62	7646	2/29	8/65
7512	5/28	5/65	7557	3/28	2/64	7602	9/28	1/66	7647	2/29	5/65
7513	5/28	5/61	7558	3/28	3/64	7603	9/28	11/66	7648	2/29	4/64
7514	5/28	5/62	7559	3/28	5/61	7604	9/28	8/62	7649	2/29	10/66
7515	5/28	7/64	7560	3/28	7/60	7605	10/28	5/61	7650	2/29	3/60
7516	5/28	2/62	7561	4/28	8/60	7606	10/28	6/65	7651	2/29	12/63
7517	2/28	6/64	7562	4/28	11/62	7607	10/28	1/61	7652	3/29	6/60
7518	2/28	10/63	7563	4/28	3/60	7608	10/28	11/62	7653	3/29	10/64
7519	2/28	9/65	7564	4/28	3/65	7609	10/28	1/64	7654	3/29	12/63
7520	2/28	11/65	7565	5/28	3/66	7610	10/28	8/62	7655	3/29	11/65
7521	2/28	10/66	7566	5/28	11/66	7611	10/28	5/66	7656	3/29	12/65
7522	2/28	8/62	7567	9/28	10/60	7612	10/28	12/66	7657	3/29	10/63
7523	2/28	11/60	7568	10/28	11/60	7613	10/28	12/40	7658	3/29	10/66
7524	3/28	9/64	7569	10/28	11/60	7614	11/28	7/65	7659	3/29	11/66
7525	3/28	3/60	7570	10/28	9/61	7615	11/28	10/66	7660	3/29	12/65
7526	3/28	11/62	7571	10/28	5/61	7616	11/28	1/65	7661	3/29	10/66
7527	3/28	3/60	7572	10/28	5/62	7617	11/28	12/40	7662	3/29	1/66
7528	3/28	3/60	7573	10/28	12/60	7618	11/28	9/63	7663	3/29	12/40
7529	3/28	10/61	7574	10/28	12/62	7619	11/28	3/61	7664	4/29	1/65
7530	3/28	10/66	7575	10/28	3/60	7620	11/28	8/61	7665	4/29	7/65
7531	3/28	2/67	7576	10/28	9/60	7621	11/28	5/62	7666	4/29	9/65
7532	4/28	3/63	7577	10/28	3/65	7622	11/28	7/64	7667	4/31	11/66
7533	4/28	11/66	7578	10/28	3/65	7623	11/28	4/64	7668	5/31	10/66
7534	4/28	3/67	7579	11/28	7/64	7624	11/28	8/61	7669	5/31	2/65
7535	4/28	1/66	7580	11/28	9/61	7625	11/28	5/61	7670	5/31	10/60
7536	4/28	6/62	7581	11/28	8/63	7626	11/28	4/61	7671	6/31	11/66
7537	4/28	8/60	7582	11/28	8/63	7627	11/28	4/66	7672	6/31	3/60
7538	4/28	6/59	7583	11/28	3/63	7628	12/28	7/64	7673	7/31	11/66
7539	4/28	2/63	7584	12/28	7/64	7629	12/28	10/67	7674	7/31	12/66
7540	4/28	4/61	7585	12/28	3/60	7630	12/28	8/62	7675	8/31	11/66
7541	4/28	6/60	7586	12/28	3/60	7631	12/28	5/66	7676	8/31	8/65
7542	11/27	5/62	7587	1/29	11/64	7632	12/28	9/61	7677	8/31	11/65
7543	12/27	10/65	7588	1/29	10/62	7633	12/28	9/62	7678	9/31	1/62
7544	12/27	12/65	7589	1/29	12/63	7634	12/28	9/61	7679	9/31	8/63
7545	12/27	8/62	7590	2/29	11/66	7635	12/28	11/60	7680	10/31	7/65
7546	12/27	7/62	7591	2/29	3/60	7636	12/28	3/60	7681	10/31	8/65
7547	12/27	12/63	7592	8/28	3/66	7637	12/28	4/61			

Nos 47289 and 47383 were first withdrawn in 12/66 and reinstated in 2/67.
The following were fitted with vacuum control gear for motor trains:-
7477 4/34; 7478 4/34; 7479 4/34; 7480 5/34; 7481 4/34.
The following were transferred to the War Department in 3/40 and subsequently written off in 12/40:-
7589, 7607/11/3/7/59/60/3 (became WD Nos 14, 10, 9, 8, 15, 12, 11, 13);
five returned and were restored to British Railways stock as follows:-
47589 10/48; 47607 11/48; 47611 10/48; 47659 11/48; 47660 9/48.
In addition Nos 7620/4/9/31/8/43 were prepared as WD Nos 23, 24, 22, 20,
19 and 21 but were not taken).
Nos 7456 and 7553 were regauged to 5ft 3in gauge and transferred to the
Northern Counties Committee in 8/44.

2-6-6-2 Garratt

3 locomotives numbered 4967-99 and renumbered 7967-99 in 1938-9.

No	New	Wdn	No	New	Wdn	No	New	Wdn	No	New	Wdn
7967	8/30	11/57	7968	8/30	9/57	7969	8/30	7/57	4970	8/30	6/55

No	New	Wdn	No	New	Wdn	No	New	Wdn	No	New	Wdn
7971	8/30	11/56	7979	9/30	1/57	7986	11/30	7/57	7993	11/30	12/55
7972	9/30	4/57	7980	10/30	2/57	7987	10/30	5/57	7994	11/30	3/58
7973	9/30	4/57	7981	10/30	10/56	7988	10/30	8/56	7995	11/30	7/57
7974	9/30	5/56	7982	10/30	12/57	7989	10/30	11/55	7996	12/30	6/56
7975	9/30	6/55	7983	10/30	1/56	7990	11/30	5/55	7997	4/27	2/56
7976	9/30	4/56	7984	10/30	2/56	7991	11/30	12/55	7998	4/27	8/56
7977	9/30	6/56	7985	10/30	6/55	7992	11/30	3/56	7999	4/27	1/56
7978	9/30	3/57									

No 7986 was built with a 9 tons capacity rotating bunker which was replaced by a 10 tons bunker in 1/32 (the displaced bunker was fitted to
No 7997 in 12/32). 10 tons bunkers were fitted to others as follows:-

10/31   7971
11/31   7968/9/70/2/87/9/90/2
12/31   7967/73/5/6/9/82/4/8/91/3
 1/32   7974/7/8/80/5/95/6
 2/32   7981/3/94

2-8-0 Class 8F

852 locomotives built to the following requirements:-

LMS	331
Ministry of Supply	208
Railway Executive Committee	245
LNER	68

(a) 331 locomotives built to LMS orders

No	New	Wdn	No	New	Wdn	No	New	Wdn	No	New	Wdn
8000	6/35	3/67	8036	8/36	3/68	8072	12/36	12/44	8108	2/39	9/67
8001	6/35	1/65	8037	9/36	12/65	8073	12/36	4/67	8109	2/39	1/66
8002	7/35	9/66	8038	9/36	12/44	8074	12/36	11/67	8110	2/39	7/67
8003	6/35	3/66	8039	9/36	7/65	8075	12/36	4/67	8111	3/39	3/68
8004	6/35	11/65	8040	9/36	12/44	8076	12/36	11/67	8112	3/39	11/65
8005	6/35	3/66	8041	9/36	12/44	8077	12/36	3/68	8113	3/39	10/67
8006	9/35	1/65	8042	9/36	12/44	8078	12/36	8/65	8114	3/39	3/67
8007	9/35	1/65	8043	9/36	12/44	8079	12/36	12/66	8115	4/39	7/68
8008	10/35	4/64	8044	9/36	12/44	8080	12/36	10/66	8116	4/39	9/65
8009	10/35	12/62	8045	9/36	5/68	8081	1/37	3/68	8117	4/39	3/68
8010	10/35	1/68	8046	9/36	1/68	8082	1/37	4/67	8118	4/39	6/66
8011	10/35	5/67	8047	9/36	12/44	8083	1/37	11/66	8119	5/39	12/67
8012	12/36	3/68	8048	10/36	12/44	8084	1/37	11/67	8120	5/39	1/66
8013	12/36	12/44	8049	10/36	12/44	8085	1/37	8/67	8121	5/39	4/67
8014	12/36	12/44	8050	10/36	3/66	8086	1/37	12/44	8122	5/39	2/67
8015	1/37	12/44	8051	10/36	12/44	8087	1/37	6/42	8123	6/39	3/67
8016	1/37	11/65	8052	10/36	12/44	8088	1/37	12/66	8124	6/39	5/68
8017	1/37	11/67	8053	10/36	3/67	8089	1/37	2/66	8125	6/39	10/67
8018	2/37	10/67	8054	10/36	9/67	8090	1/37	4/68	8126	1/41	4/67
8019	2/37	12/44	8055	10/36	11/67	8091	2/37	12/44	8127	1/41	10/66
8020	2/37	8/65	8056	10/36	5/68	8092	2/37	4/66	8128	1/41	5/67
8021	3/37	12/44	8057	10/36	5/67	8093	2/37	11/67	8129	1/41	3/66
8022	3/37	12/44	8058	10/36	12/44	8094	2/37	9/65	8130	2/41	2/67
8023	3/37	12/44	8059	10/36	12/44	8095	2/37	2/65	8131	3/41	5/67
8024	3/37	11/67	8060	10/36	4/68	8096	12/38	10/65	8132	3/41	6/68
8025	4/37	12/44	8061	11/36	9/67	8097	12/38	7/65	8133	4/41	12/66
8026	4/37	6/68	8062	11/36	7/68	8098	1/39	3/67	8134	4/41	1/66
8027	7/36	3/65	8063	11/36	3/68	8099	1/39	7/65	8135	5/41	9/65
8028	7/36	12/44	8064	11/36	5/66	8100	1/39	9/67	8136	8/41	3/67
8029	8/36	2/67	8065	11/36	2/66	8101	1/39	8/66	8137	9/41	10/66
8030	8/36	12/44	8066	11/36	6/42	8102	1/39	8/65	8138	9/41	10/65
8031	8/36	12/44	8067	11/36	10/67	8103	2/39	10/66	8139	12/41	11/66
8032	8/36	12/44	8068	11/36	6/42	8104	2/39	7/67	8140	1/42	4/64
8033	8/36	6/68	8069	11/36	11/64	8105	2/39	3/67	8141	1/42	5/67
8034	8/36	12/44	8070	11/36	11/67	8106	2/39	6/67	8142	2/42	11/66
8035	8/36	3/67	8071	12/36	6/42	8107	2/39	4/68	8143	3/42	11/66

No	New	Wdn	No	New	Wdn	No	New	Wdn	No	New	Wdn
8144	4/42	1/64	8191	5/42	7/68	8313	12/43	9/67	8360	7/44	6/65
8145	4/42	5/65	8192	5/42	3/68	8314	12/43	12/65	8361	8/44	10/66
8146	7/42	1/67	8193	5/42	1/68	8315	12/43	8/67	8362	8/44	12/67
8147	7/42	7/66	8194	6/42	8/67	8316	12/43	4/67	8363	8/44	11/67
8148	7/42	6/65	8195	6/42	4/66	8317	1/44	3/68	8364	8/44	9/67
8149	8/42	1/67	8196	6/42	10/68	8318	1/44	11/68	8365	9/44	5/68
8150	8/42	1/64	8197	6/42	4/68	8319	1/44	6/68	8366	9/44	10/65
8151	9/42	1/68	8198	6/42	9/65	8320	2/44	3/67	8367	9/44	8/66
8152	9/42	3/67	8199	6/42	2/67	8321	2/44	6/68	8368	9/44	6/68
8153	9/42	3/68	8200	6/42	1/68	8322	2/44	5/68	8369	10/44	6/68
8154	10/42	7/67	8201	6/42	3/68	8323	2/44	6/68	8370	10/44	11/66
8155	10/42	9/66	8202	7/42	6/67	8324	2/44	6/67	8371	10/44	10/67
8156	11/42	8/65	8203	7/42	4/66	8325	3/44	5/68	8372	10/44	12/66
8157	12/42	5/67	8204	7/42	8/67	8326	3/44	7/66	8373	11/44	6/68
8158	1/43	9/67	8205	7/42	12/67	8327	3/44	6/68	8374	11/44	6/68
8159	1/43	3/67	8206	7/42	5/68	8328	4/44	9/65	8375	11/44	9/67
8160	2/43	7/67	8207	7/42	1/66	8329	4/44	5/68	8376	11/44	7/67
8161	2/43	9/67	8208	8/42	9/67	8330	5/44	9/65	8377	12/44	10/67
8162	2/43	6/67	8209	8/42	4/64	8331	9/43	2/66	8378	12/44	8/65
8163	3/43	6/67	8210	8/42	4/64	8332	10/43	10/67	8379	12/44	3/67
8164	3/43	10/67	8211	8/42	11/67	8333	11/43	6/65	8380	12/44	5/68
8165	3/43	3/67	8212	8/42	6/68	8334	11/43	1/68	8381	12/44	11/67
8166	4/43	10/67	8213	8/42	7/66	8335	11/43	3/68	8382	1/45	10/67
8167	4/43	8/68	8214	8/42	11/67	8336	12/43	12/67	8383	1/45	1/66
8168	4/43	6/68	8215	8/42	7/66	8337	12/43	9/67	8384	1/45	5/68
8169	4/43	11/67	8216	8/42	1/64	8338	1/44	6/68	8385	2/45	11/66
8170	5/43	6/68	8217	9/42	2/65	8339	1/44	10/66	8386	2/45	8/67
8171	5/43	9/67	8218	9/42	9/67	8340	1/44	8/68	8387	3/45	1/65
8172	6/43	5/64	8219	9/42	12/66	8341	2/44	4/64	8388	3/45	10/66
8173	6/43	7/65	8220	9/42	8/67	8342	2/44	8/66	8389	3/45	8/65
8174	7/43	4/67	8221	9/42	2/67	8343	2/44	2/67	8390	3/45	5/68
8175	8/43	2/66	8222	9/42	11/67	8344	3/44	3/68	8391	4/45	12/65
8176	3/42	8/67	8223	9/42	11/66	8345	3/44	2/68	8392	4/45	6/68
8177	3/42	3/67	8224	9/42	3/68	8346	3/44	7/66	8393	4/45	8/68
8178	3/42	11/66	8225	9/42	10/66	8347	3/44	7/67	8394	5/45	6/67
8179	3/42	1/64	8301	9/43	3/67	8348	4/44	7/68	8395	5/45	9/67
8180	3/42	3/67	8302	10/43	1/66	8349	4/44	10/66	8396	5/45	1/64
8181	4/42	2/66	8303	10/43	7/66	8350	4/44	9/67	8397	6/45	10/66
8182	4/42	5/68	8304	10/43	2/68	8351	5/44	1/68	8398	6/45	3/66
8183	4/42	7/65	8305	11/43	1/68	8352	5/44	11/67	8399	6/45	9/67
8184	4/42	7/65	8306	11/43	7/64	8353	6/44	9/66	8490	6/45	9/65
8185	4/42	2/67	8307	11/43	2/68	8354	6/44	11/66	8491	7/45	6/68
8186	4/42	10/66	8308	11/43	4/68	8355	6/44	9/65	8492	7/45	2/68
8187	4/42	1/67	8309	11/43	3/66	8356	6/44	6/68	8493	8/45	2/68
8188	4/42	5/66	8310	12/43	12/67	8357	6/44	9/66	8494	8/45	3/67
8189	5/42	7/65	8311	12/43	9/66	8358	7/44	9/66	8495	8/45	10/67
8190	5/42	12/67	8312	12/43	2/65	8359	7/44	9/67			

No 8003 was fitted with a sloping throatplate boiler in place of the original vertical throatplate type in 5/38.

Locomotives requisitioned for military service 1941; 51 were prepared as follows:-

1/41: Nos 8012-6/8-23/5/8/30-2/8-41/3/5/7/8/86/91/4
2/41: Nos 8024/34/42/4/6/9/51/2/8/9/61/6/8/9/71/2/7-80/5/7/8/93

The following returned to LMS and British Railways service, regaining the original numbers:-

6/43: Nos 8024/69/78-80/5/8/93
7/49: No 48045
8/49: No 48046
9/49: No 48061
0/49: Nos 48016/39
2/49: Nos 48012/8/20/77/94

No 8025 was purchased by British Railways in 7/57 and renumbered 48775.
Nos 8024/69/78-80/5/8/93 were not written off LMS stock; Nos 8066/8/71/
87 were deleted in 6/42, No 8077 in 12/43 and remainder in 12/44).

(b) 53 locomotives built for military use used by the LMS and GWR in 1940-1. During this period they ran with LMS numbers.

No	New	Wdn	No	New	Wdn	No	New	Wdn	No	New	Wdn
8226	9/40	9/41	8240	10/40	9/41	8253	12/40	1/41	8288	8/40	9/41
8227	10/40	7/41	8241	10/40	1/41	8254	12/40	7/41	8289	8/40	7/41
8228	10/40	2/41	8242	10/40	1/41	8255	11/40	2/41	8290	9/40	9/41
8229	10/40	7/41	8243	10/40	1/41	8256	11/40	7/41	8291	9/40	9/41
8230	10/40	2/41	8244	10/40	9/41	8257	11/40	7/41	8292	10/40	9/41
8231	10/40	7/41	8245	11/40	1/41	8258	11/40	7/41	8293	10/40	10/41
8232	12/40	7/41	8246	11/40	7/41	8259	11/40	2/41	8294	10/40	9/41
8233	12/40	7/41	8247	11/40	7/41	8260	11/40	9/41	8295	10/40	9/41
8234	12/40	7/41	8248	11/40	2/41	8261	11/40	7/41	8296	10/40	9/41
8235	11/40	1/41	8249	11/40	3/41	8262	12/40	7/41	8297	11/40	2/41
8236	11/40	1/41	8250	11/40	1/41	8263	12/40	7/41	8298	11/40	7/41
8237	9/40	9/41	8251	11/40	2/41	8286	8/40	9/41	8299	11/40	7/41
8238	10/40	1/41	8252	11/40	1/41	8287	8/40	7/41	8300	11/40	9/41
8239	10/40	7/41									

The WD numbers of these locomotives were 300-37 and 400-14 in the above order. New is the date of loan and Wdn is the date of return. Several worked for a short while on the LMS for a second time in 1941, Nos 312/6/7/24/6/7 and 405, joined by WD Nos 423/6/7. No 8293 (WD No 407) did not go overseas and returned to LMS service (see below).

(c) 23 locomotives built for military use used by the LMS in 1942-3 and subsequently taken into stock in 1943.

No	New	Wdn	No	New	Wdn	No	New	Wdn	No	New	Wdn
8264	5/42	7/66	8270	6/42	12/66	8276	7/42	11/67	8282	8/42	6/68
8265	5/42	6/67	8271	6/42	8/67	8277	7/42	4/66	8283	8/42	9/67
8266	5/42	6/67	8272	6/42	3/68	8278	7/42	8/68	8284	8/42	7/66
8267	5/42	5/68	8273	6/42	8/65	8279	8/42	10/67	8285	9/42	9/65
8268	5/42	10/67	8274	6/42	9/66	8280	8/42	5/66	8293	-	6/68
8269	5/42	7/67	8275	6/42	6/67	8281	8/42	9/67			

Apart from No 8293 (see above) which returned to LMS service in 2/42 the New date is the start of the loan and Wdn is final condemnation by British Railways. Nos 8264-85 ran as WD Nos 549-51/3/5-71 and 623 until recalled by the WD in the summer of 1943 and then became LMS stock in 11/43 (Nos 8265/7/79/80/2/5) and 12/43 (Nos 8264/6/8-78/81/3/4); in addition WD Nos 552/4 (both 5/42) had been on loan with this batch. No 8293 was finally taken into LMS stock in 6/43.

(d) 245 locomotives built to Railway Executive Committee order.

No	New	Wdn	No	New	Wdn	No	New	Wdn	No	New	Wdn
8400	6/43	8/68	8421	12/43	2/68	8442	6/44	2/68	8463	1/45	6/64
8401	7/43	9/65	8422	12/43	3/66	8443	6/44	10/66	8464	1/45	8/67
8402	7/43	12/67	8423	12/43	7/68	8444	6/44	2/66	8465	2/45	3/68
8403	7/43	7/65	8424	12/43	2/68	8445	7/44	5/68	8466	2/45	5/67
8404	7/43	8/66	8425	12/43	11/67	8446	7/44	7/65	8467	3/45	6/68
8405	8/43	7/66	8426	12/43	6/66	8447	7/44	1/66	8468	3/45	2/68
8406	8/43	9/65	8427	1/44	8/65	8448	7/44	7/68	8469	3/45	12/67
8407	8/43	12/64	8428	1/44	8/66	8449	8/44	5/67	8470	4/45	11/67
8408	9/43	11/67	8429	1/44	9/65	8450	8/44	9/67	8471	4/45	4/68
8409	9/43	3/65	8430	3/44	4/65	8451	9/44	5/68	8472	5/45	5/66
8410	9/43	7/68	8431	3/44	5/64	8452	9/44	1/66	8473	5/45	11/67
8411	9/43	7/67	8432	3/44	10/66	8453	9/44	4/68	8474	5/45	9/67
8412	10/43	12/66	8433	3/44	4/68	8454	9/44	7/67	8475	6/45	10/66
8413	10/43	10/65	8434	3/44	12/65	8455	10/44	11/64	8476	6/45	8/68
8414	10/43	10/66	8435	4/44	5/67	8456	10/44	9/67	8477	6/45	9/66
8415	10/43	7/66	8436	4/44	12/67	8457	10/44	9/67	8478	6/45	6/65
8416	11/43	6/65	8437	5/44	3/68	8458	11/44	4/67	8479	7/45	2/66
8417	11/43	4/67	8438	5/44	11/67	8459	11/44	3/67	8500	2/44	12/65
8418	11/43	8/66	8439	5/44	11/67	8460	12/44	9/67	8501	6/44	7/67
8419	11/43	5/65	8440	6/44	2/67	8461	12/44	1/65	8502	8/44	1/66
8420	11/43	4/64	8441	6/44	4/68	8462	12/44	11/66	8503	9/44	2/68

No	New	Wdn	No	New	Wdn	No	New	Wdn	No	New	Wdn
8504	9/44	6/68	8545	2/45	2/67	8625	4/43	6/66	8665	3/44	8/68
8505	9/44	10/67	8546	2/45	7/68	8626	5/43	1/68	8666	4/44	7/68
8506	10/44	9/67	8547	3/45	3/67	8627	5/43	3/66	8667	4/44	3/66
8507	10/44	3/68	8548	3/45	5/68	8628	5/43	9/66	8668	5/44	12/66
8508	10/44	1/64	8549	3/45	5/68	8629	6/43	8/66	8669	5/44	11/67
8509	11/44	5/67	8550	4/45	9/67	8630	6/43	7/65	8670	7/44	9/66
8510	6/43	1/68	8551	4/45	5/68	8631	6/43	2/68	8671	12/43	8/67
8511	3/44	6/66	8552	5/45	4/67	8632	6/43	2/68	8672	1/44	11/66
8512	4/44	9/66	8553	5/45	3/68	8633	7/43	3/66	8673	5/44	11/67
8513	4/44	3/67	8554	6/45	8/66	8634	8/43	8/65	8674	3/44	12/67
8514	5/44	10/66	8555	6/45	1/66	8635	8/43	10/66	8675	3/44	9/67
8515	6/44	1/66	8556	7/45	8/67	8636	8/43	8/67	8676	4/44	10/67
8516	7/44	12/66	8557	7/45	7/67	8637	9/43	9/67	8677	5/44	1/68
8517	7/44	11/67	8558	8/45	10/65	8638	9/43	1/66	8678	6/44	6/68
8518	8/44	7/65	8559	8/45	1/68	8639	9/43	1/68	8679	12/43	10/66
8519	9/44	7/68	8600	2/43	11/66	8640	10/43	5/67	8680	12/43	9/66
8520	10/44	9/66	8601	2/43	6/65	8641	10/43	11/66	8681	1/44	7/67
8521	10/44	5/66	8602	4/43	7/67	8642	10/43	4/64	8682	1/44	9/65
8522	11/44	8/67	8603	5/43	6/67	8643	11/43	6/67	8683	1/44	2/68
8523	11/44	2/66	8604	6/43	4/67	8644	11/43	1/66	8684	1/44	4/68
8524	12/44	4/64	8605	7/43	8/66	8645	11/43	5/67	8685	2/44	4/67
8525	12/44	10/65	8606	9/43	8/66	8646	11/43	5/68	8686	2/44	11/66
8526	12/44	8/66	8607	9/43	8/65	8647	12/43	4/66	8687	2/44	5/68
8527	12/44	10/66	8608	10/43	2/66	8648	12/43	7/67	8688	2/44	7/65
8528	2/45	8/67	8609	10/43	1/68	8649	12/43	2/65	8689	2/44	7/65
8529	4/45	6/68	8610	4/43	8/65	8650	10/43	8/67	8690	3/44	3/67
8530	4/45	3/66	8611	5/43	12/64	8651	11/43	11/66	8691	3/44	3/66
8531	4/45	9/67	8612	7/43	6/68	8652	11/43	6/68	8692	3/44	6/68
8532	4/45	3/68	8613	7/43	7/67	8653	11/43	8/65	8693	3/44	4/67
8533	5/45	5/68	8614	8/43	4/68	8654	11/43	9/64	8694	4/44	3/66
8534	5/45	10/67	8615	9/43	2/66	8655	11/43	8/67	8695	4/44	8/67
8535	6/45	8/67	8616	10/43	10/66	8656	11/43	8/65	8696	4/44	12/67
8536	6/45	1/67	8617	11/43	2/68	8657	11/43	10/64	8697	4/44	12/67
8537	7/45	10/67	8618	9/43	9/67	8658	11/43	7/65	8698	5/44	3/66
8538	8/45	3/67	8619	10/43	3/66	8659	11/43	5/66	8699	5/44	9/67
8539	8/45	1/66	8620	11/43	6/68	8660	11/43	6/65	8700	5/44	3/68
8540	12/44	11/67	8621	11/43	1/66	8661	7/44	9/65	8701	5/44	3/67
8541	12/44	6/66	8622	11/43	11/67	8662	7/44	11/66	8702	5/44	5/68
8542	12/44	6/67	8623	12/43	10/66	8663	2/44	11/66	8703	6/44	9/67
8543	1/45	2/66	8624	12/43	7/65	8664	2/44	11/67	8704	6/44	9/65
8544	1/45	2/68									

(e) 68 locomotives built to LNER order built as LNER Nos 7651-75 (renumbered 3100-24 in 1946 and then 3500-24 in 1947) and Nos 3125-67 (renumbered 3525-67 in 1947). All transferred on loan to LMS in 1947, except No 3554 transferred to London Midland Region in 1/48) and further renumbered 8705-72.

No	New	Wdn	No	New	Wdn	No	New	Wdn	No	New	Wdn
8705	6/44	3/67	8721	8/44	9/67	8737	11/45	5/65	8753	10/45	3/67
8706	6/44	3/66	8722	8/44	5/68	8738	12/45	12/66	8754	10/45	5/67
8707	6/44	4/67	8723	8/44	8/68	8739	12/45	1/67	8755	10/45	9/66
8708	6/44	4/67	8724	9/44	10/67	8740	1/46	3/68	8756	11/45	1/67
8709	6/44	7/67	8725	9/44	8/67	8741	2/46	10/67	8757	11/45	12/67
8710	7/44	9/67	8726	9/44	9/66	8742	3/46	3/67	8758	12/45	12/67
8711	7/44	1/67	8727	9/44	3/67	8743	3/46	3/67	8759	12/45	11/65
8712	7/44	6/67	8728	9/44	3/67	8744	5/46	3/68	8760	12/45	3/66
8713	7/44	3/66	8729	9/44	12/67	8745	4/46	5/68	8761	1/46	1/65
8714	7/44	11/67	8730	9/45	8/68	8746	5/46	5/68	8762	1/46	2/66
8715	7/44	7/68	8731	9/45	8/67	8747	5/46	8/66	8763	2/46	4/68
8716	7/44	8/65	8732	10/45	11/66	8748	6/46	4/66	8764	2/46	12/67
8717	7/44	3/67	8733	10/45	5/65	8749	8/46	3/68	8765	3/46	8/68
8718	8/44	4/66	8734	10/45	9/64	8750	8/46	1/68	8766	3/46	9/67
8719	8/44	8/65	8735	11/45	10/67	8751	9/46	2/67	8767	3/46	8/67
8720	8/44	6/68	8736	11/45	8/66	8752	10/46	8/68	8768	3/46	9/67

No	New	Wdn	No	New	Wdn	No	New	Wdn	No	New	Wdn
8769	4/46	8/65	8770	5/46	4/67	8771	5/46	12/65	8772	6/46	1/64

(f) 29 locomotives purchased by British Railways which had not been LMS stock.

No	New	Wdn	No	New	Wdn	No	New	Wdn	No	New	Wdn
8246	5/40	1/66	8254	7/41	8/66	8261	2/42	8/67	8290	6/41	8/65
8247	6/40	7/68	8255	8/41	12/66	8262	6/41	11/65	8291	7/41	7/66
8248	7/40	12/65	8256	9/41	4/67	8263	10/41	8/66	8292	8/41	4/68
8249	7/40	12/66	8257	8/40	7/68	8286	7/40	9/66	8294	11/41	8/68
8250	8/40	4/66	8258	10/41	8/67	8287	7/40	6/67	8295	12/41	9/65
8251	9/40	11/66	8259	10/41	6/65	8288	8/40	2/67	8296	12/41	9/66
8252	12/41	5/68	8260	11/41	11/65	8289	10/40	10/66	8297	1/42	7/65
8253	7/41	8/68									

The WD numbers had been 70300/1/11/4/8/32/63/76/8/84/94/5/8, 70504/18/44/76/84 for Nos 48246-63 (WD Nos 70395, 70576/84 were built as Nos 321, 373 and 506 respectively) and 70401-3/13/38/40/2/3/6/7/9 for Nos 8286-92/4-7. They entered traffic as follows:-
8/49: No 48288
9/49: Nos 48247/57/8/62/3/87/90/2
10/49: Nos 48250/3/6/60/96
11/49: Nos 48248/9/52/89/94/5/7
12/49: Nos 48246/51/4/5/9/61/86/91
(These were the second series of locomotives to carry these numbers; it should be noted that Nos 48246-51/6/86-9 had previous run with LMS numbers in 1940-1, none of which were restored).

(g) 3 locomotives purchased in 7/57 by British Railways.

No	New	Wdn	No	New	Wdn	No	New	Wdn
48773	6/40	8/68	48774	8/40	7/65	48775	4/37	8/68

The WD numbers 70307/20 and 70583 (renumbered 500/1/12 in 1952) and all three had run on the LMS before as 8233/46 and 8025 respectively (initially BR Nos 90733-5 were allotted and the second locomotive appeared briefly as No 90743!). All three were withdrawn in 12/62 and reinstated in 9/63.

0-8-0 Class 7F

175 locomotives.

No	New	Wdn	No	New	Wdn	No	New	Wdn	No	New	Wdn
9500	3/29	6/50	9522	6/29	5/49	9544	8/29	2/60	9566	10/29	8/57
9501	3/29	3/50	9523	6/29	2/51	9545	8/29	7/57	9567	10/29	2/50
9502	4/29	6/51	9524	6/29	12/53	9546	8/29	10/49	9568	10/29	5/51
9503	4/29	8/54	9525	6/29	3/49	9547	8/29	5/57	9569	10/29	1/50
9504	4/29	4/49	9526	6/29	8/49	9548	8/29	1/52	9570	10/29	8/55
9505	4/29	10/60	9527	6/29	5/49	9549	8/29	4/49	9571	10/29	5/51
9506	4/29	10/52	9528	6/29	8/49	9550	9/29	8/49	9572	11/29	9/49
9507	4/29	4/49	9529	6/29	1/50	9551	9/29	3/49	9573	11/29	12/49
9508	5/29	1/62	9530	7/29	6/49	9552	9/29	8/56	9574	11/29	8/50
9509	5/29	5/59	9531	7/29	10/50	9553	9/29	2/50	9575	11/29	5/50
9510	5/29	9/51	9532	7/29	5/56	9554	9/29	8/55	9576	11/29	10/49
9511	5/29	5/59	9533	7/29	7/49	9555	9/29	4/57	9577	11/29	3/49
9512	5/29	5/49	9534	7/29	9/49	9556	9/29	4/50	9578	11/29	5/59
9513	5/29	10/49	9535	7/29	11/50	9557	9/29	11/55	9579	11/29	6/50
9514	5/29	8/50	9536	7/29	10/57	9558	9/29	4/51	9580	11/29	3/51
9515	5/29	11/59	9537	7/29	5/50	9559	9/29	4/49	9581	11/29	6/49
9516	5/29	8/50	9538	7/29	8/57	9560	9/29	12/57	9582	11/29	5/59
9517	5/29	3/49	9539	8/29	10/49	9561	9/29	6/50	9583	11/29	8/50
9518	6/29	3/49	9540	8/29	5/51	9562	9/29	4/49	9584	11/29	8/49
9519	6/29	3/50	9541	8/29	7/50	9563	10/29	5/52	9585	11/29	2/51
9520	6/29	5/50	9542	8/29	3/49	9564	10/29	9/49	9686	11/29	7/59
9521	6/29	4/49	9543	8/29	8/50	9565	10/29	3/49	9587	11/29	6/51

No	New	Wdn	No	New	Wdn	No	New	Wdn	No	New	Wdn
9588	12/29	12/49	9610	2/31	5/51	9632	12/31	3/49	9654	3/32	12/49
9589	12/29	6/51	9611	2/31	8/49	9633	1/32	3/49	9655	4/32	3/50
9590	12/29	5/51	9612	2/31	9/53	9634	12/31	6/50	9656	4/32	9/49
9591	12/29	12/52	9613	3/31	7/49	9635	12/31	11/50	9657	4/32	2/57
9592	12/29	5/59	9614	3/31	6/49	9636	1/32	8/50	9658	4/32	8/49
9593	12/29	5/51	9615	3/31	4/50	9637	1/32	6/61	9659	4/32	2/57
9594	12/29	9/51	9616	3/31	3/49	9638	1/32	6/56	9660	4/32	3/51
9595	12/29	12/51	9617	4/31	6/51	9639	1/32	8/49	9661	4/32	1/52
9596	12/29	4/50	9618	4/31	10/61	9640	1/32	5/59	9662	5/32	5/59
9597	12/29	5/49	9619	4/31	8/50	9641	1/32	12/50	9663	5/32	4/51
9598	12/29	1/59	9620	10/31	1/56	9642	2/32	7/49	9664	5/32	2/57
9599	12/29	8/49	9621	11/31	1/50	9643	2/32	12/49	9665	6/32	8/50
9600	12/30	8/53	9622	11/31	6/49	9644	2/32	5/49	9666	6/32	4/56
9601	12/30	4/49	9623	11/31	1/51	9645	2/32	12/49	9667	6/32	5/59
9602	12/30	2/54	9624	11/31	2/60	9646	2/32	3/49	9668	6/32	11/61
9603	1/31	2/56	9625	11/31	1/51	9647	2/32	7/49	9669	6/32	4/49
9604	1/31	6/49	9626	12/31	5/49	9648	2/32	9/57	9670	6/32	7/49
9605	1/31	2/50	9627	12/31	10/61	9649	2/32	12/50	9671	6/32	3/52
9606	1/31	6/49	9628	12/31	6/50	9650	3/32	5/51	9672	6/32	3/57
9607	1/31	7/49	9629	12/31	5/49	9651	3/32	12/50	9673	7/32	2/51
9608	2/31	7/53	9630	12/31	3/49	9652	3/32	8/49	9674	7/32	2/60
9609	2/31	10/50	9631	12/31	4/51	9653	3/32	8/50			

RAILCARS

Sentinel Steam Railcars

15 steam railcars built as Nos 2233, 4143-54, 4349 and 44; all except
No 44 became Nos 29900-13 in 1933.

No	New	Wdn	No	New	Wdn	No	New	Wdn	No	New	Wdn
29900	-/25	7/35	29904	6/27	8/35	29908	6/27	7/35	29912	6/27	5/35
29901	6/27	9/35	29905	6/27	5/35	29909	6/27	7/35	29913	7/29	12/39
29902	6/27	6/35	29906	6/27	6/35	29910	6/27	9/37	44	2/29	11/33
29903	6/27	6/35	29907	6/27	5/35	29911	6/27	6/35			

No 44 was jointly owned with the LNER; in 11/33 it became solely LNER
property as No 51915 and was withdrawn in 7/44. In the 1933 carriage
renumbering scheme of the LMS this vehicle had been allotted No 29988.

The LMS also had an interest (as joint owners) in the four Sentinel
Steam cars of the Cheshire Lines Committee, Nos 600-3, new in -/29 and
withdrawn in 10/44.

Leyland diesel mechanical railcars

3 railcars.

Numbered 29950-2 they entered service in 2/34 and were withdrawn in
4/51.

Diesel hydraulic articulated train

1 train of three vehicles.

Numbered 80000-2 the train entered service in --/38 and ran trials until the latter part of 1939. The train was withdrawn in 2/45 (the two
power cars were later converted into self-propelled overhead line maintenance train for the Manchester South Junction & Altrincham line).

DIESEL LOCOMOTIVES

0-6-0 diesel hydraulic

1 locomotive (converted from 0-6-0T steam locomotive).

No	New	Wdn
1831	5/34	9/39 (on trial from 11/32)

0-4-0 diesel mechanical

1 locomotive (allotted No 7400 but entered traffic as No 7050)

No	New	Wdn
7050	11/34	3/43 (became WD No 224)

0-6-0 diesel mechanical

7 locomotives ordered as Nos 7401-7; Nos 7401-3 became Nos 7051-3 in 1934 and remainder commenced work as Nos 7054-7.

No	New	Wdn	No	New	Wdn	No	New	Wdn	No	New	Wdn
7051	5/33	12/45	7053	11/34	12/42	7055	12/34	4/39	7057	2/35	1/44
7052	1/34	12/43	7054	11/34	5/43	7056	10/35	5/39			

No 7054 later became WD No 26.
No 7057 was returned to the makers and in 1/45 started work as NCC No 22, taken into UTA stock 10/49 and withdrawn 4/65.

0-6-0 diesel electric

```
  1 locomotive   new 1934 (jackshaft drive 250 hp);      No  7058
 10 locomotives  new 1936 (jackshaft drive 350 hp);      Nos 7059-68
 10 locomotives  new 1936 (twin-motor drive 350 hp);     Nos 7069-78
  1 locomotive   taken into stock 1936 (as Nos 7069-78); No  7079
 40 locomotives  new 1939-42 (jackshaft drive 350 hp);   Nos 7080-7119
106 locomotives  new 1945-53 (twin-motor drive 350 hp);  Nos 7125-31 and
                                                     BR Nos 12045-12138
```
(No 7058 was supplied as No 7408 but was renumbered 7058 in 1934).
British Railways allotted No 13000 to No 7058 but it was not renumbered.
Nos 7074/6/9-99, 7110-31 were renumbered 12000-44 in 1948-52.

No	New	Wdn	No	New	Wdn	No	New	Wdn	No	New	Wdn
7058	2/34	11/49	7077	-/36	12/40	7096	5/40	10/67	7115	3/42	6/67
7059	5/36	11/44	7078	-/36	12/40	7097	6/40	11/67	7116	3/42	5/66
7060	-/36	12/42	7079	4/34	6/56	7098	7/40	10/67	7117	3/42	8/64
7061	-/36	11/44	7080	5/39	11/67	7099	7/40	11/66	7118	5/42	12/67
7062	-/36	11/44	7081	5/39	12/67	7100	10/41	12/42	7119	6/42	12/67
7063	-/36	11/44	7082	5/39	9/67	7101	10/41	12/42	7120	5/45	1/69
7064	-/36	11/44	7083	5/39	10/67	7102	11/41	12/42	7121	6/45	10/68
7065	-/36	12/42	7084	5/39	7/67	7103	11/41	12/42	7122	6/45	10/68
7066	-/36	12/42	7085	9/39	7/67	7104	11/41	12/42	7123	8/45	10/68
7067	10/36	11/44	7086	11/39	9/67	7105	11/41	12/42	7124	10/45	10/68
7068	10/36	12/42	7087	12/39	9/67	7106	12/41	12/42	7125	12/45	1/69
7069	1/36	12/40	7088	12/39	3/66	7107	12/41	12/42	7126	8/47	10/68
7070	-/36	12/40	7089	12/39	12/67	7108	12/41	12/42	7127	9/47	10/68
7071	-/36	12/40	7090	1/40	11/67	7109	12/41	12/42	7128	10/47	10/68
7072	-/36	12/40	7091	3/40	10/67	7110	1/42	12/67	7129	11/47	10/68
7073	-/36	12/40	7092	3/40	10/67	7111	1/42	12/67	7130	2/48	10/68
7074	4/36	5/61	7093	4/40	9/67	7112	2/42	11/67	7131	3/48	10/68
7075	-/36	12/40	7094	4/40	10/67	7113	2/42	10/67	12045	4/48	1/69
7076	8/36	2/62	7095	5/40	10/67	7114	2/42	11/67	12046	6/48	1/69

No	New	Wdn	No	New	Wdn	No	New	Wdn	No	New	Wdn
12047	9/48	1/69	12070	8/50	10/69	12093	8/51	5/71	12116	8/52	8/69
12048	12/48	1/69	12071	8/50	10/71	12094	9/51	10/71	12117	8/52	1/69
12049	12/48	10/71	12072	8/50	12/68	12095	12/51	3/69	12118	9/52	4/71
12050	2/49	7/70	12073	9/50	11/71	12096	12/51	1/69	12119	9/52	11/68
12051	3/49	10/71	12074	9/50	1/72	12097	12/51	2/71	12120	9/52	12/68
12052	4/49	6/71	12075	9/50	11/71	12098	2/52	1/71	12121	9/52	6/71
12053	4/49	6/71	12076	10/50	12/71	12099	2/52	6/71	12122	9/52	6/71
12054	5/49	7/70	12077	10/50	10/71	12100	3/52	2/69	12123	10/52	6/67
12055	7/49	6/71	12078	10/50	1/71	12101	4/52	8/70	12124	10/52	11/68
12056	8/49	10/71	12079	11/50	8/71	12102	6/52	1/71	12125	10/52	6/69
12057	9/49	1/69	12080	11/50	4/71	12103	3/52	5/72	12126	10/52	11/68
12058	10/49	4/71	12081	11/50	6/70	12104	4/52	5/67	12127	10/52	10/72
12059	11/49	1/69	12082	11/50	10/71	12105	4/52	1/71	12128	10/52	7/70
12060	11/49	2/71	12083	11/50	10/71	12106	4/52	7/70	12129	11/52	9/67
12061	11/49	10/71	12084	12/50	5/71	12107	5/52	12/67	12130	11/52	8/72
12062	12/49	4/70	12085	12/50	5/71	12108	5/52	1/71	12131	11/52	3/69
12063	12/49	1/72	12086	12/50	7/69	12109	6/52	11/72	12132	11/52	5/72
12064	12/49	3/69	12087	12/50	6/71	12110	6/52	11/72	12133	12/52	1/69
12065	12/49	5/71	12088	6/51	5/71	12111	7/52	12/71	12134	12/52	11/72
12066	12/49	3/69	12089	6/51	9/70	12112	7/52	10/69	12135	12/52	6/69
12067	2/50	1/69	12090	6/51	6/71	12113	7/52	2/71	12136	12/52	12/71
12068	3/50	12/67	12091	7/51	6/70	12114	7/52	10/70	12137	1/53	11/68
12069	7/50	3/71	12092	8/51	3/69	12115	8/52	10/70	12138	1/53	11/68

Nos 7059-68 became WD Nos 213, 19, 214-7, 20/1, 218, 22 respectively.
Nos 7069-73/5/7/8 became WD Nos 18, 3, 16/7, 4, 5, 6, 7 respectively.
Nos 7100-9 became WD Nos 49-58 (Nos 7110-5 ran for a while as WD Nos 59-64 until put to work on the LMS).
(Nos 7120-5 were ordered as WD Nos 274-9 but were put directly into LMS service).

Co-Co diesel electric

2 locomotives.

No	New	Wdn	No	New	Wdn
10000	12/47	12/63	10001	7/48	3/66

(Numbers were not altered by British Railways).

Bo-Bo diesel electric

1 locomotive.

No	New	Wdn
10800	6/50	8/59

(later used by Hawker Siddely for the experimental locomotive Hawk).

NORTHERN COUNTIES COMMITTEE:

In addition to LMS No 7057 mentioned above the NCC made use of three diesel locomotives, also built by Harland & Wolff of Belfast:-

17 0-6-0DH (X Class), new 10/36, on loan from 12/37 and purchased 8/41; withdrawn in 1970.

28 Bo-BoDE, new 5/37, on loan from 7/45 (later purchased by UTA).

20 0-4-0DH, new -/38, on loan from 1/45 to 4/46 (later purchased by UTA).

4-4-0   U1 Class

4 locomotives.

No	New	Wdn	No	New	Wdn	No	New	Wdn	No	New	Wdn
1	5/24	4/47	2	7/24	4/47	3	11/26	10/46	4	1/31	4/49

These were partial reconstructions of old locomotives Nos 59 (4-4-0),
62 (4-4-0), 33 (2-4-0) and 52 (2-4-0) respectively.
No 4 became No 4A in 5/47.

2-6-4T WT Class

18 locomotives.

No	New	Wdn	No	New	Wdn	No	New	Wdn	No	New	Wdn
1	4/47	6/68	6	8/46	9/70	50	4/49	10/70	54	7/50	2/70
2	5/47	6/68	7	9/46	6/68	51	5/49	2/71	55	7/50	10/70
3	5/47	6/70	8	9/46	6/68	52	5/49	6/68	56	8/50	10/70
4	5/47	6/71	9	6/47	6/68	53	6/49	6/71	57	8/50	5/68
5	8/46	10/70	10	6/47	6/70						

0-6-0   V Class

3 locomotives built as Nos 71-3 and immediatley renumbered 13-5.

No	New	Wdn	No	New	Wdn	No	New	Wdn
13	2/23	8/64	14	2/23	5/61	15	3/23	12/61

Rebuilt to V1 Class in 2/53, 9/51 and 12/53 respectively.

4-4-0   U2 Class

14 locomotives.

No	New	Wdn	No	New	Wdn	No	New	Wdn	No	New	Wdn
74	7/24	4/63	78	7/24	3/60	82	5/25	1/56	85	5/34	3/60
75	7/24	6/56	79	8/25	1/56	83	5/25	1/56	86	1/35	3/60
76	7/24	9/59	80	11/25	12/61	84	12/29	12/61	87	5/36	8/57
77	7/24	1/56	81	12/25	8/57						

In addition U Class 4-4-0 Nos 70-3 (new 1914-22) were altered to U2 Class
in 11/24, 3/27, 2/37 and 12/37 respectively.
Nos 84-7 were renewals of older 4-4-0 Nos 20, 67, 59 (ex No 5 in 1925)
and 63 respectively.

2-6-0   W Class

15 locomotives.

No	New	Wdn	No	New	Wdn	No	New	Wdn	No	New	Wdn
90	7/33	6/56	94	6/34	5/65	98	2/37	8/64	102	4/40	6/56
91	7/33	5/65	95	10/34	8/64	99	5/38	5/65	103	3/42	12/59
92	7/33	10/57	96	5/35	12/61	100	1/39	12/59	104	10/42	5/65
93	8/33	5/65	97	7/35	12/65	101	6/39	6/56			

Sentinels No 91 (locomotive) and 401 (railcar) were new 5/25 and 4/25
respectively; both were withdrawn in 1932.

0-6-0T Y Class, ex-LMS Nos 7456 and 7553, became NCC Nos 18 and 19, being withdrawn 6/56 and 7/63 respectively.

ALPHABETICAL INDEX TO NAMED LOCOMOTIVES

Some names were carried by more than one locomotive, having been exchanged. Many locomotives were not initially named, but names removed before the end of 1947 are marked *.

This list does not detail names of pre-LMS locomotives.

Name	No.	Name	No.
Aboukir	5681	City of Bradford	6236
Achilles	5697	City of Bristol	6237
Aden	5633	City of Carlisle	6238
Agamemnon	5693	City of Chester	6239
Ajax	6139*	City of Coventry	6240
Ajax	5689	City of Edinburgh	6241
Alberta	5562	City of Glasgow	6242
Anson	5672	City of Hereford	6255
Arethusa	5696	City of Lancaster	6243
Argyll and Sutherland		City of Leeds	6244*
Highlander	6107	City of Leeds	6248
Armada	5679	City of Leicester	6252
Assam	5583	City of Lichfield	6250
Atlas	6134*	City of Liverpool	6247
Atlas	5737	City of London	6245
Australia	5563	City of Manchester	6246
Ayrshire Yeomanry	5156	City of Nottingham	6251
		City of St. Albans	6253
Bahamas	5596	City of Sheffield	6249
Bangor	5523	City of Stoke-on-Trent	6254
Barbados	5597	Civil Service Rifleman	6163
Barfleur	5685	Cochrane	5656
Barham	5653	Codrington	5676
Baroda	5587	Coldstream Guardsman	6114
Basutoland	5598	Collingwood	5645
Beatty	5677	Colossus	5702
Bechuanaland	5599	Colwyn Bay	5525
Bellerophon	5694	Comet	6129*
Bengal	5577	Comet	5735
Bermuda	5600	Condor	6145*
Bhopal	5594	Connaught	5742
Bihar and Orissa	5581	Conqueror	5701
Black Watch	6102	Cornwallis	5666
Blackpool	5524	Coronation	6220
Blake	5650	Courageous	5711
Bombay	5576	Courier	6147*
Boscawen	5642	Croxteth	5500*
Bradshaw	5518	Cyclops	5692
British Columbia	5559	Cyprus	5605
British Guiana	5601		
British Honduras	5602	Dauntless	5717
British Legion	6170	De Robeck	5678
Britannia	5700	Defence	5722
Bunsen	5512	Defiance	5728
Burma	5580	Drake	5659
		Dreadnought	5718
Caernarvon	5515	Duchess of Abercorn	6234
Caledonian	6141*	Duchess of Atholl	6231
Cameron Highlander	6105	Duchess of Buccleuch	6230
Cameronian	6113	Duchess of Devonshire	6227
Camperdown	5680	Duchess of Gloucester	6225
Canada	5553	Duchess of Hamilton	6229
Central Provinces	5582	Duchess of Kent	6212
Ceylon	5604	Duchess of Montrose	6232
City of Birmingham	6235	Duchess of Norfolk	6226

157

Alphabetical Index to Named Locomotives (continued):

Alphabetical Index to Named Locomotives: (continued):